# Path of the Seeker

## Book One

# Path of the Seeker

## Book One

The Way of Return
At the Gate of Discipleship
Between the Desert and the Sown

Nargis Jessie Dowland

Sulūk Press
New Lebanon New York

Published by Sulūk Press
an imprint of Omega Publications, Inc.
New Lebanon NY
www.omegapub.com



Reprinted by kind permission of the Sufi Movement.

Cover image from Shutterstock.com
Cover design by Sandra Lillydahl

This edition is printed on acid-free paper
that meets ANSI standard X39–48.

Nargis Jessie Dowland (1866–1953)
Path of the Seeker: Book One
The Way of Return, At the Gates of Discipleship,
Between the Desert and the Sown
1.Sufism 2. Mysticism 3. Spirituality
I. Dowland, Nargis Jessie II. Title

Library of Congress Control Number: 2015953251

Printed and bound in the United States of America
ISBN 978–1–941810–13–2

## Contents


Foreword vii

Acknowledgments ix

The Way of Return 3
The Song of Return 5
From the Silence 126

At the Gate of Discipleship
Foreword 131
At the Gate of Discipleship 133
Words of the Master Heard in the Silence 240

Between the Desert and the Sown
Foreword 245
Part One 247
Part Two 293
Part Three 360
Words of the Master Heard in the Silence 361

Index 365

Nargis Jessie Dowland
1866–1953

# Foreword

THE works of Nargis Jessie Dowland have long been out of print, with only a few copies preserved in public and private collections. A new generation of readers is now invited to read and be inspired by these classics of spirituality, and to follow the author on a journey progressing through the stages of seeking, discovering guidance, and continuing on the pilgrimage toward the ultimate goal of unity with the source of all life.

Nargis Dowland was an early editor and publisher of the works of her Sufi teacher, Hazrat Inayat Khan. She used phrases from his writings and those of other spiritual teachers as seed thoughts to inspire her own deep reflections on the stages of the path of return. On this journey each seeker travels on a unique but shared passage through life, passing through desire and purpose, illusion and truth, suffering and pleasure, through the self-created landscapes of one's own thoughts, always in search of balance and harmony, and guided by the voice and presence of the Beloved that are found within one's own heart.

This volume, titled *Path of the Seeker: Book One,* combines three separate shorter works: *The Way of Return* (1952), *At the Gate of Discipleship* (1924), and *Between the Desert and the Sown* (1923). A subsequent volume, *Path of the Seeker: Book Two,* will contain three additional works: *The Lifted Veil, Wine From the Tavern* and *Thoughts are Things*, along with a biographical portrait of the author.

In keeping with the conventions of her time, Nargis Dowland used masculine pronouns for indeterminate gender and for

God. Because this practice is today considered to be biased, every effort has been made to neutralize gender throughout this volume, with the goal of making *Path of the Seeker* more accessible to a contemporary readership. Exception has been made for quoted passages and for poetry in order to preserve the accuracy of the quotes and poetic cadence. Other exceptions include instances where the word *man* is referenced in relation to other related terms such as *hu-man* and *manas* (mind). References to God as Father involve a particular familial concept of the author and were also preserved as originally written, along with traditional religious terms like *Prince of Peace* and *Son of Man*. The term *Christ* is sometimes used to refer to the historical Jesus, and at other times appears in a more universal perspective as referring to the Spirit of Guidance. Because of the fluidity and uncertainty of the author's intention regarding these different identifications, the masculine gender of Christ is also preserved.

Sandra Lillydahl

# Acknowledgments

*Path of the Seeker* is the result of the persistent and dedicated efforts of Nancy Barta-Norton, who used her professional librarian skills to locate and obtain copies of the writings of Nargis Dowland and her correspondence with Hazrat Inayat Khan. Nancy also provided the author's biography for *Path of the Seeker: Book Two*, which is based on the results of her extensive, in-depth research on the life and work of Nargis Dowland. Without Nancy's devoted work, *Path of the Seeker* would not have been brought into existence.

Many thanks are also due to those who have with kindness and generosity provided the materials, permissions, and advice that have made it possible to make Nargis Dowland and her works known once again to today's readers.

Qahira Wirgman and the Nekbkaht Foundation in Suresnes, France, have provided invaluable assistance with advice, photographs, copies of Nargis Dowland's writings and personal documents. Murshid Ameen Carp and Murshid Karimbaksh Witteveen generously gave the International Sufi Movement's permission to publish *At the Gate of Discipleship*, *Between the Desert and the Sown*, and *The Lifted Veil*. Hamida Verlinden from the International Sufi Headquarters in The Hague, The Netherlands, provided copies of correspondence between Nargis Dowland and her teacher, Hazrat Inayat Khan. The International Institute of Social History in Amsterdam, The Netherlands, provided a copy of *Thoughts are Things*. And invaluable editorial advice and assistance was provided by Cannon Labrie.

# The Way of Return

A Collection of Mystical Thoughts and Essays

*From the cowardice that shrinks from new truth,*
*From the laziness that is content with half-truths,*
*From the arrogance that thinks it knows all truth,*
*O! God of truth deliver us.*

*—An Ancient Prayer*

*"Watchman what of the night?"*
*The watchman said, "The morning cometh, and also the night: if ye will inquire, inquire ye; return, come'."*

*—Isaiah 21:11–12*

*They shall be My people and I will be their God;*
*for they shall return unto Me with their whole heart.*

*—Jeremiah 24:7*

# The Song of Return

*There is no 'two' unless you are a worshiper of form;*
*Before Him who is without form, all becomes one.*[1]
—*Jalal ad-Din Rumi*

SOULS in form bound; souls so earthbound,
Back in time ere worlds their birth found,
Ere the universe had risen
Ere the spirit knew its prison,
Ere the rise of day and night
In the uncreated light,
Steeped in early morning glory,
There began your life's true story.

Ye of My life were a part,
E'en before Creation's start;
Sparks within one central flame,
Whose ye are and whence ye came.
But to gain the truth essential,
That ye all are gods potential;
Ye in earth life must involve ye
Through its stages to evolve Me;
When you see but as I see,
You'll know that you are one with Me.

When ye see but Me in devil,
When ye feel but Me in evil,
Know but Me in ocean's swell,
Find but Me in deepest hell,
Hear but Me when earthquake's shock
Frees the life fast bound in rock;
All the world's but part of My life,
And for all time knit to thy life;
You will see but as I see,
I in you and ye in Me.

---

1 Jalal al-Din Rumi, *Selected Poems from the Divani Shamsi Tabriz*, trans. Reynolds Alleyne Nicholson (Abingdon: Routledge, 1898).

Highest spirit, lowest matter,
I, who binding forms do shatter,
I am dreaming in the root,
I am waking in the brute
Rising in the life of man,
To the limits of My span.
When ye know all beings Me,
When as self ye cease to be;
Seeing then but as I see,
All as one, not thee and Me.

# 1

WOULD-BE travelers upon the way of return do not always remember that before they can begin the returning, any obligations that may have been incurred or duties undertaken in the everyday life must first be fulfilled.

The road leading to the entrance of the way cannot be strewn with broken promises nor unfulfilled duties, which, if allowed to accumulate, would not only be a hindrance to the aspirant but may also obstruct others traveling the same path. Otherwise they may find themselves, sooner or later, on the path of illusion, which lies parallel and very close to the way of return. It must be recognized for what it is by all seekers of the way before they can proceed in safety.

It is true that there are guides to assist and show light upon the way, but there are false as well as true guides. After having had experience of both, each aspirant must endeavor to see for themselves, by the light of intuition developed by prayer and meditation, the true from the false guides.

Because self-deception is so easy, Jesus gave the warning: "For there shall arise false Christs and false prophets, and shall shew great signs and wonders; insomuch that, if it were possible, they shall deceive the very elect."[1]

> *And many false prophets shall arise, and shall deceive many.*
> *—Matthew 24:11*

1 Matthew 24:24.

## 2

THE path of return has many bypaths that attract and allure; all good and interesting paths, but woe to the one who tarries! For each time one does so, one is farther from the journey's end.

Whoever would be swift must keep the eyes fixed, head held up, never falter, turning neither to right nor left. Even though the gifts offered on the way seem rare and wonderful, they all are but shadows of the real, shadows of the bliss that awaits at the end.

Keen sight and steady aim must be the watchword of the pilgrim. Very close to the end of the return path, many great things are offered. All the virtues wait there, the most beautiful and shining ones; and many are detained from taking the final necessary steps by the beauty of the gifts and the attraction of their presence. But the travelers who are single-minded, one-pointed, never taking their gaze from the goal they are trying to reach, need have no fear. They will not see where their feet are treading, will not even be conscious of those standing by the wayside nor the beauty of their proffered gifts. They will only see the light and be drawn by invisible cords of love, which are ever around them, until they reach their journey's end and enter into that "peace which passeth all understanding."[1]

1 Philippians 4:7.

# 3

*Until the heart is empty, it cannot receive the knowledge of God.* [1]
—*Inayat Khan*

THE way of return really means a returning to God from self, and from all the things hitherto thought so important for the self.

Needless to say, this turning is, and always must be, entirely spontaneous. Unless a person wants, more than anything else in life, to realize God, it is useless even to try to seek the way of return; one would never find it. So in order that travelers may be quite sure of the real object of their search, every kind of substitute is offered to try to lure them from reality by the guardians of the path. This is for their own safety, to enable them to know, without any shadow of doubt, what it is they really want.

Although the way of return seems perfectly straight and simple, and all that a traveler has to do is to turn round and keep right on to the end, when the traveler starts to tread the way so many interesting and fascinating things are found, and people who offer every kind of knowledge and the fruits of occult science—most difficult to resist, because they all appear part of the reality the traveler is seeking. So, of course, they are; but to experience them at the beginning of returning, before the end is in sight, means delay. The whole journey may then take very many lives and millions of years to

1 Inayat Khan, *The Bowl of Saki* (Southampton: Book Depot for Sufi Literature, 1921).

accomplish instead of ending by the swift way of singleness of purpose.

"Seek ye first the kingdom of God and His righteousness, and all these things shall be added unto you."[2] That is the secret of the quick return. In God there is everything, and whosoever finds God has every need fulfilled, for they will then hear with understanding the threefold chord of wisdom, power and love, and find completion.

2 Matthew 6:33.

# 4

THERE is one God, one gateway to which we must all find the latch; but many paths lead to it. Only souls unencumbered can enter the straight gate and contact the master. Those who desire to follow the shining ones must renounce all earthly desires. Having passed through the gate and started to climb the path, the dross of earthly things drops away. The soul, in a sense, discards its luggage.

It is most important that this renunciation should be thorough, for one single thought of longing for earthly pleasures will delay the progress of many years. Only by complete renunciation is it possible to reach even the footstool of the higher ones. Earthly loves there may be, and earthly work must be attended to, but nothing must hold the soul when it has begun the upward climb.

This experience does not come to everyone. Only those who have several times passed the gate of rebirth will feel the urge to try the path of return. But the joy and rewards are great, for whoever tries and works to the desired end, there is no weariness in the journey.

Nothing but intense desire can lead a person upon this path, and then it would be no more a sacrifice than it would be for a child to leave a game when it hears the voice of a loved father calling it. It just turns round and runs as quickly as it can to find him; the game is forgotten, the child is only conscious of its father.

A soul upon the return journey receives many tests and even temptations. Many shadows beset the path as a mirage, but the aspirant must step on bravely. There are many years of sitting at the feet of the master, many stumbling blocks, many bitter tears, before the latch of the door of entry to the path is found. It is a steep and winding path, and on it are some who have failed and are waiting there until they can try again; for no one who has entered can ever turn back. They may sink down for a time, but those who have tried ever so little, they will have their reward.

The would-be accepted disciples must hold on, keeping always implicit faith in the power of the masters. All they ask is to hold fast when everything seems dark. Few there be who can stand this test. Complete control of all emotion is essential, but those who fail can start again. No one can succeed at once, the pull of the earth is so strong; but many souls gain the top of the mountain and receive illumination.

The children of the earth must keep steadily on, heads up, eyes in front. The goal is eternal peace. Love and faith are everything. The soul that unselfishly loves is at the beginning of its pilgrimage, for to give of oneself brings great gain on the spiritual side. To love's awakened vision, sacrifice is not sacrifice, but love's thank offering and thanksgiving.

Hold your faith whatever may beset you and always, always put God first.

## 5

*Search thyself, O seeker of God,*
*And thou shalt find His secret abode.*

THE various accounts in myth and story of journeys taken by pilgrims in search of the Holy Grail, to secret places difficult of access, and the tales told of the arduous labors, the difficulties and tests placed in the path of the seeker, are all reflections in the material world of the light behind them. The mere journeying, however arduous the journey, or even the finding of a master of wisdom and receiving the master's instructions and aid, is not sufficient to take one very far upon the search for God, although the fact of having undertaken such a task is an outward demonstration that the soul is awakening to the vision of truth. The real journey taken by the true mystic, who lives in the constant practice of the presence of God, is quite other. It is possible the mystic may take such a physical journey through forests and deserts, and almost inaccessible places, but as said before, that is but the outer cover: the real journey is taken within. The path that the traveler must take to reach the shrine where dwells the living God is entirely within the self. And the experience of the outer journey is used for the purpose of opening the eyes to the inner truth of each obstacle overcome and each difficulty solved, and therefore may be for some, although not all, a necessary experience; because inner truths must be seen and realized, they cannot be told.

According to the mystic teaching, there are seven meanings underlying every symbol or expression of a truth. For this reason the great masters of wisdom taught their disciples in parables, for only those may see who have eyes to see. And even they may not at first see all that underlies the spoken or written word, for only one who has conquered the self can endure the vision of light.

The reason the search for God is called a *journey* is because the seeker is continually passing things, both familiar and unfamiliar, and meeting experiences unfamiliar and strange, which must also be passed. Not for one moment must the seeker remain in any experience, however beautiful or pleasant, after learning the lesson it is destined to teach; and in this sense it is a journey. What the traveler seeks is the Holy Grail, or secret altar. And the farther one travels in the inner life, the further one is away from the outer self, or false ego, and the closer to the God within Whose dwelling place is the human heart.

# 6

*Thus saith the Lord: Seek ye me and ye shall live.*
*—Amos 5:4*

HOW long will you look for God in temples made of stone, or seek to draw nigh to God through sacraments, rites or priestly interventions?

All systems of religious thought or practice are designed to teach the value of goodness and remind of the suffering and penalties that await those who disregard nature's laws. These teachings, if followed, produce those who are good, moral, upright; and it is most necessary that they should be observed by all civilized peoples, for without these observances, civilization would relapse into savagery and barbarism. But such beliefs and practices, although inculcating goodness and morality, do not of themselves necessarily advance any person one step upon the path in the search for God—Who rides upon the whirlwind,[1] but Whose dwelling place is in the human heart, the "temples not made with hands."[2]

1 Psalm 104:3.

2 Acts 7:48.

# 7

*If a man loves me, he will keep my words; and my Father will love him; and we will come unto him, and make our abode with him.* —*John 14:23*

SEEK, seek! O man, and you shall find.
The ways of search are long and wide;
How far the seeking ere we find
The God for whom we search?
No guiding star save that within the soul,
No guiding voice, save one,
Which in the stillness says:
"Not until thou seekest Me in all there is
Can I be found of thee.
In darkness and in light,
In evil and in good,
In ways of sin, as well as temple, church, or mosque,
In paths too foul for Me to tread
In ways where evil men in cruelty have fought,
Even there may I be sought.
"I am the Lord, there is none else,
I form the light and create darkness;
I make peace and create evil;
I, the Lord, do all these things."[1]
There is no height too high, nor any depth too low,
Where I may not be found,
For I am all that is.

1 Isaiah 45:7

But never can a seeker find
Awhile he seeks with eyes so blind,
That he can see Me in one place alone.
I, the all-pervading Love, am equally at home
In wayside inn, in temple, or on throne.
But if thou wilt that I shall dwell with thee,
A place within thy heart thou must prepare for Me.
The inner chamber of the heart of man
Must be swept clear of envious thoughts,
Of things unclean;
Naught selfish, cruel nor mean may stay,
Although by eyes of other men, perchance unseen.
Then if thou bidst Me
I will enter in and sup with thee,
And in the mystery of at-one-ment
When thou shalt know that
"I am in my Father and He in me and I in you,"[2]
Then also shalt thou surely know
That evermore upon the upward path until the end
There is within thine inner room,
When thou shalt seek Him there—a Friend.

> *God's meeting place with man is in the heart. And in a still small voice He speaks, and he who hears is still.*[3]
>
> —*Levi H. Dowling*

> *The truth is independent of outward form. It shines as brightly in the tavern as in the mosque or the church. Moreover, the religion of the heart, which alone has value, is not the monopoly of any particular creed.*[4]
>
> —Jalal ad-Din Rumi

---

2 John 14.20.

3 Dowling, Levi H. *The Aquarian Gospel of Jesus the Christ: The Philosophic and Practical Basis of the Religion of the Aquarian Age of the World and of the Church Universal.* (London: L.N. Fowler, 1908).

4 Jalal ad-Din Rumi, *Selected Poems from the Divani Shamsi Tabriz.*

# 8

*I am the way, the truth and the life. No man cometh unto the Father but by me.*

*—John 14:6*

JESUS, when he was on earth, did not say: "Ask someone to show how to find God." He said, "Seek and ye shall find; knock and it shall be opened to you";[1] and "Say not lo here, and lo there, for the kingdom of God is within you."[2]

There is only one God, and although many roads lead to God, there is only one gate, which one must oneself unlatch if one would find the God Within.

The gate or door through which all must go through is the Christ. By whatever name He may be called in different lands by different peoples, Christ is the same giver of life. The name is not important, because the name is that given to the form in which the universal cosmic Christ chooses to manifest God's all-pervading love to humanity.

1 Matthew 7:7.

2 Luke 17:21.

# 9

*He gave them angel's food from heaven, but they had to go out and gather the manna daily for themselves. None are dispensed from taking trouble.*[1]

—*Evelyn Underhill*

ALL the greatest things, the great and glorious things—God, truth and beauty—must be continually sought.

Never cease your seeking. For it is the search itself that creates the glory and the wonder, which passes as a vision and like a vision, cannot be held, but is for the moment only. If this were not so, the joy of seeking and finding could not be lasting. If the things of the spirit were as those of the material world, they would soon fade, absorbed into the familiar life of every day's common task.

But no one need feel discouraged. If once the great things have been glimpsed by wondering eyes, they can always be rediscovered; for hidden in the heart of time lies the mystery of eternal youth, which has been sought down the ages and which some even sold their birthrights to possess.

When a true seeker has realized the inner meaning of "Nothing can be found until it is lost," a new heaven and a new earth will unfold before the wondering gaze; and the teachings of the seers and sages since the world began become illuminated. The seeker will know that whoever would hold must love; that every day is a fresh beginning wherein all things whatsoever are possible of attainment. That joy

1 Underhill, Evelyn, *Abba; Meditations Based on the Lord's Prayer.* (London: Longmans Green Co., 1940).

of discovery always awaits a real seeker, as does the dawn of each newborn day, fresh from the hands of God.

In this life of perpetual youth—for where wonder reigns, age has no dwelling place—"the first fine careless rapture"[2] is every day recaptured. Past and future are extinguished in the light of eternal now.

No need to store of today's manna for tomorrow.

No burden of past to weigh upon the spirit.

No fear of future to stand as a specter in the path.

Nothing can grow old or stale that is remade at each day's dawn by this divine alchemy of God.

2 Browning, Robert, "Home Thoughts From Abroad." 1845.

# 10

THE perfection of beauty can only be known by those who are able to pass through the gateway of wonder: "Wondering, ye shall find the kingdom." To understand the spirit of beauty, one must become one with it; then for all eternity it is one's possession, and no thing, nor person, can take it away. Thereafter one is king of one's own domain.

No one can ever see beauty unless they are capable of wonder; it is the greatest gift given to humanity. Every child brings this with it when it comes to earth "trailing clouds of glory,"[1] but in a world whose ideal is material success, this priceless gift has little opportunity of growth.

Only through the eyes of wonder can the beauty that is God be seen. While they are closed, God can never be found; but when they are wide open, then in every place will one see beauty, and one's whole world be changed from darkness to light. No one in whom the wonder spirit sleeps can know the world of fairies, the perfect beauty of trees, flowers and of all growing things.

Verily, wonder may be called a magic wand that can turn every common thing into a beauty, filling the soul with ecstasy; for it beholds a vision of God. And this is the heritage of every man and woman, not belonging only to the artist soul.

1 Wordsworth, William, "Ode: Intimations of Immortality from Recollections of Early Childhood." 1804.

# 11

IT is recorded in the Christian scriptures that Pilate asked Jesus, "What is truth?" but received no answer.[1]

Many people in all ages and climes since Pilate's day have asked the same question, and some are bewildered because their questioning is unanswered. They say, "Tell us the truth about God, that we may believe." The reason why these questions are not answered is because they cannot be. No person can tell another the truth about God; each must seek and find for themselves. One can never be told, and even if one could, the mere telling would not satisfy.

If God is everywhere, God must be sought everywhere. What makes the search so difficult for many people is that when they have found something that they think is the truth and afterwards find it unsatisfying, they discard it and look elsewhere. This may happen several times, but, as all aspects of truth are necessary before it can be seen as a whole, not one should be discarded as being useless or outlived. Every one will be needed before the search is ended.

To try to resolve spiritual realities into material facts is not possible, and words are not very helpful; suggestions only can be offered. An analogy is sometimes of use if not taken too literally. Most people are fond of solving puzzles; there is one called a jigsaw puzzle. A picture is painted on a board that is afterwards cut out by a saw into numerous small pieces, all of different sizes and shapes. Some are very odd looking, and some appear to have no part of a pictures on them; but every one is necessary to complete the puzzle, even the ugly

1 John 18:38.

dark pieces, and also those that only form the background. When each piece has been fitted into its right place—and it can fit into no other—then once again the picture can be seen as a whole "as it was in the beginning,"[2] and the subject of it understood. The solver who has put each piece into its rightful place has had the joy of a completed work. This is a very crude illustration. It is also paradoxical, because truth must first be seen within before it can be recognized without. But anything that will urge people to think for themselves may be useful if they are sincerely seeking God as a spiritual reality.

> *The truth cannot be spoken, and the spoken word is not necessarily true.*[3]
>
> —*Inayat Khan*

2 "Gloria Patri."

3 Inayat Khan, *The Bowl of Saki*. (Southampton: Book Depot for Sufi Literature, 1921).

# 12

*Truth cannot be put into words; it must be seen by the light of our own intuition.*[1] —*Inayat Khan*

## The Pilgrim

A pilgrim stood at heaven's gate,
Hoping to enter in,
Freed from earth's ugliness, pain and sin,
To live in the joy of his Lord in the light
Where no vileness could stain his robe of white
He had kept unspotted and clean.

"Come in," said the man who stood at the gate,
"You've a long way yet to go,
This is but one of the heavenly gates;
There are seven you know.
You cannot enter the seventh gate
Until you have walked through hell
To conquer evil and death through strife.
It is the only way.
The road on earth the Master trod,
Through deepest hell, to the throne of God
And everlasting life."[2]

The pilgrim passed through; but naught could see
As he looked around, no shining light;
No angel voices he thought to hear.
All was silent, dark and drear.
Bewildered he sank on the barren ground.

1 Inayat Khan, *Aphorisms*. (Geneva: Sufi Publishing Association, 1929).
2 "Eli, Eli, lama sabachthani." Matthew 27:46.

"I've journeyed long on this path," he sighed,
"So sure I knew the way!
Oh! Thou man at the gate, why have I failed?
Tell me, I pray."

"Man cannot walk the earthly ways
In robes kept free from stain.
'Tis the inner garb, unseen by men,
The wedding robe must be unspotted and clean.
Thou hast been searching outside thyself
For what there can never be found.
Seek within, in the depths of your heart.
You'll find heaven and hell—and the gates as well
Are but symbols for guides on man's way of return
To God, from whence he came.
When the last, the seventh gate, is reached
Life's great paradox is revealed:
Man loses himself as man, to find himself
As part of the Mighty Whole
And one with all that is.
The way is long, the promise sure[3]
To all who overcometh:
Life for evermore."

3 "He that overcometh shall inherit all things; and I will be his God, he shall be my son." Revelations 21:7.

# 13

*To faith, or one who has faith, all things are possible.*

*—Mark 9:23*

THE teaching of Jesus, nearly two thousand years ago, that "If ye have faith, nothing shall be impossible to you,"[1] is as true today as when it was given; but how many of us really believe it? Some people think the only meaning of faith is a particular form of religious belief, such as the Catholic Church or the Protestant faith. Few understand faith as a creative power that cannot fail to create whatever is desired. The words of the master when he was on earth were not idle words nor meaningless words, but the inner truth is difficult to realize. It is also difficult to put into words.

The power of creative faith is so great that, if used for any gratification of the personal self, the result is disastrous.

Living force, if evoked by faith, can be used for good or evil creation. There is only one force. It is the motive that causes it to give birth to constructive or destructive work.

1 Matthew 17:20.

# 14

*Out of the shell of the broken heart arises the new born soul.*[1]

*—Inayat Khan*

IF people could have a true conception of the meaning of pain and suffering, it would give a great sense of peace to their souls. In the truest sense, suffering is not the punishment for misdeeds.

The immortal soul sleeps in a person until it is awakened to the knowledge of its true being, its source and origin; and the awakening is by means of emotion. But the heart must feel deeply, otherwise the emotion only touches the surface; and the soul still slumbers although it may turn in its sleep.

Joy and sorrow both are necessary, because a deep and lasting joy can never be experienced without sorrow or anguish. They are two sides of one and the same thing. If this teaching were fully realized, human beings would understand the difficulties with which life surrounds them and would strive to learn the lessons emotion is meant to teach.

Only strong souls are capable of experiencing either a great joy or a great sorrow. The more awake a soul, the more intensely it feels and responds to emotion of any kind. The small person lives in little pleasures and little joys, neither of which is capable of giving freedom to the imprisoned soul. It is the broken heart that can be transmuted into wings, not one who, afraid of greatness, lives in the false safety of life's petty things. Great souls have always realized this truth.

1 Inayat Khan, *The Gayan*.

*Lord, Thy most poignant arrow take*
*And stab my spirit broad awake.*[2]
*—Robert Louis Stevenson*

*Break me, Oh! God, disgrace me,*
*Torment me if You will—*
*But save me from self-complacency,*
*from little interests and little successes,*
*and the life that passes like the shadow of a dream.*[3]
*—H.G. Wells*

2 Stevenson, Robert Louis, "*The Celestial Surgeon.*"
3 Wells, Herbert George, *The New Machiavelli.* (London: *The English Review*, 1911).

# 15

*Keep God in remembrance till self is forgotten.*[1]

*—Jalal ad-Din Rumi*

IF you can look deeply enough, you will see that there is only one spirit behind all forms of manifestation.

It is the forms, or masks, that make so-called good or evil beings. By the action and reaction of spirit and form, or spirit and matter—matter being solidified spirit—a soul of a person, of a nation or of a planet is born.

A soul is individual only so long as it retains a form, which becomes either good or evil according the creative thought generated. But it is immortal when it has merged into, or returned to, the One Spirit from which it emerged, as ice returns to water that could not be manifest as a form unless it became ice.

These words are quite inadequate to explain the reality—no words can do that. They are only suggestions for thought.

"So God made man in His own image."[2] God manifested as a human being. The unmanifested is beyond and above all thought by the human mind.

*It is difficult for our feeble minds to grasp the simple Truth:*
*The Incomprehensible cannot be comprehended.*[3]

*—J.D. Beresford*

1 Jalal ad-Din Rumi, *Selected Poems from the Divani Shamsi Tabriz.*

2 Genesis 1:27.

3 Beresford, John Davys, "What I Believe."

## 16

*And whatever is the seed of all beings, that am I…nor is there aught, moving or unmoving, that may exist bereft of Me.*[1]

*—Bhagavad Gita*

THE sun, the moon, and the planets of night,
The stars in the heaven all glowing with light,
Are giving forth life,
God's Life.

The churches, the people, their prayers, their belief,
The bodies who're buried in earth beneath,
Are upheld by one life,
God's Life.

The waters, the fish, the ships as they ride,
The pebbles, the sand and the incoming tide,
Teem with one life,
God's Life

The forests, the fields, the leaves of the trees,
The uplands, the lowlands, the valleys and leas,
Are filled with one life,
God's Life

Mountains shaken by earthquake shocks,
Gold and crystals, stones and rocks,
Have potential life,
God's Life.

1 *Bhagavad Gita: the Lord's Song*, trans. Annie Besant (London: Theosophical Publishing Society, 1896).

The soft summer rains and the hurricane wild,
The northeast gale and the south wind mild,
Are showing forth life,
God's Life.

The clouds, the storms and the ether of space,
The death of a nation, the birth of a race
Are determined by life,
God's Life.

*The earth is the Lord's and the fullness thereof; The world and they that dwell therein.*

*—Psalm 24:1*

## 17

*Raise a stone, and there thou shalt find Me; cleave the wood and there am I.*

*—Henry Van Dyke, after* The Gospel of Thomas.

PEOPLE must cease thinking of God as something apart from themselves, sitting away above the earth on a throne surrounded by angels and archangels. It is because truth cannot be put into words that symbols are used, but the only thing that will help this suffering world today is not vague ideas so high and aloof as to be beyond human reach, but thinking and trying to realize that, in very truth, "Nearer is God than breathing, closer than hands and feet."[1] God can be met anywhere and in any place that people frequent: in their own homes, in their business, their workshops and factories; in all places where people are fighting, on land, on sea, or under the sea and in the air; in churches, temples and mosques; in places of entertainment or in public houses. Everywhere people go, either singly or in groups, God is there too, even in what are called *the haunts of sin*. It must be so because the innermost being of a person is God, however deeply covered by ignorance or buried in personal ego. So long as a person is a human being, God is in the midst of that person, however blinded eyes may be to behold this truth.

If in these days of darkness, a human cry for aid and deliverance is wholly sincere, and a person is ready to accept the consequences of the answer to that cry, it will never be in vain. One's eyes, "the eyes to see," and ears, "the ears to hear,"[2]

1 Tennyson, Alfred, "The Higher Pantheism."

2 Proverbs 20:12.

will be opened and one will know, without any shadow of doubt, that in all difficulties, dangers, and sorrows that may await, there walks beside one, through them all, a Friend who will never fail. "There is a friend that sticketh closer than a brother."[3]

> *Who comforteth us in all our tribulations, that we may be able to comfort them which are in any trouble, by the comfort wherewith we ourselves are comforted of God.*
>
> *—2 Corinthians 1:4*

---

3 Proverbs 18:24.

# 18

THE manifested universe is the embodied thought of God the Creator, sustained and nourished by God's life, of which every living and breathing thing contained therein, from planet to atom, partakes; for all "live and move and have their being"[1] in God Who is the Only Being.

If the divine sustenance of the thought of God were withdrawn for one moment, the whole universe would be reduced to elementary essence.

A human being, made in the image of God, is a reflection in miniature, a microcosm of the macrocosm; therefore there is latent within, the power of creative thought.

Meditation upon this truth is profitable, and one aspect of the inner meaning of sacrifice can be seen by those who have insight. For if an embodied thought can only be sustained by the life of its creator, an ideal, in order to be realized, demands sustained concentration of thought, which necessitates a controlled or master mind. And in some cases, if the ideal be greater than the person, may demand the life of the material body to make an ideal a living thing, as at times, to bring to birth a living child, the life of the mother must be given.

Although this entails suffering, as must all breaking of form, nevertheless, to the real self this action is no sacrifice as the world counts sacrifice. Rather is it a great opportunity, for by such an act the bonds of self are broken, and one is free to claim the Father's promise.

> *He that overcometh shall inherit all things; and I will be his God, and he shall be my son.* —*Revelations 21:7*

1 Acts 17:28.

# 19

ONE of the most essential lessons, as also perhaps one of the most difficult, which must be learned by all who tread the return path, is that of the control by the aspirants of their emotions.

This does not mean that one should not feel emotion nor become indifferent to the suffering of others—quite the reverse. A person must develop the emotional nature to the utmost, must feel and try to alleviate pain and sorrow wherever one meets it; but must strive when doing so, to keep complete control of one's own feelings, because emotion controlled can become power to help and to heal. The greater the emotion felt, and the more it is controlled, the greater the power that may, by this means, be used to help suffering humanity.

Sympathy, if expressed by sorrowing with those in sorrow or weeping with those who weep, does not give the help and healing that it may appear to do. It rather increases the sorrow by addition of another's own emotion, who will, by being impressed with another's depression, have taken within the germs of that depression, thus limiting the power to give comfort or consolation.

Those who wish to console the suffering and have mastered the lesson of control of their own emotion, can do so by thought and prayer to a far greater extent than by any spoken words. Controlled emotion remains deep and lasting, but emotion expressed or given out will often increase rather than decrease the trouble they are trying to cure.

# 20

*But there is a spirit in man; and the inspiration of the Almighty giveth them understanding.*

*—Job 32:8*

WORDS are totally inadequate to express the real meaning of *the God Within.* It is almost impossible to form a clear thought, as the brain automatically pictures something—whatever the idea of God means to a person—as shut inside, dwelling within either the body or the heart. But if the God Within can be thought of as light, which is able to illumine whatever problem is perplexing, it gives a different, although still most inadequate, idea of this mystery.

We can think of a ray of light from without, penetrating through to within, having no definite form, as rays of the sun can shine through anything that is open to receive them. Light may be thought of as being impersonal and universal, and at the same time individual, so long as it is held in one place, losing nothing, neither gaining anything; but always illuminating and making dark places light, so that it becomes possible for one to see with open and clear vision the answer to any problem.

*In him was life; and the life was the light of men.*

*—John 1:4*

# 21

*The hidden God becometh known and general to mankind in the created world of things, which He hath fashioned and designed.*

—*Angelus Silesius*

THE secret of a person's power lies in identification with the true self, or the God Within. When one can identify oneself with the ensouling force instead of with the thing ensouled, then a human personality may become a vehicle for divine force. But in order to be of real use, a person must keep complete control of all the bodies used to contact life in the world and make sure that they are in tune with each other, so that, as one instrument, they may be ready for the master's use.

A person's body must be under control of the mind, and mind must be subject to the heart; for according to the teaching of the mystics, the heart is the abode of God.

When this identification has been attained, one can live in complete faith and can prove for oneself the truth of the teaching of Jesus that "Faith is the substance of things hoped for"[1] and that all thing are possible to one who has faith.

Humanity stays a long time in the wilderness of self, trying to satisfy itself with restless wanderings in pursuit of happiness, while, if we knew how to "be still and know that I am God,"[2] life would become easy instead of difficult and full of sorrow.

1 Hebrews 11:1.
2 Psalm 46:10.

# 22

FORM is a vehicle or garment used by the soul of a person, either singly or collectively, in order to gain experience in a material world.

The experience needed is for a purpose, and when that purpose is attained the form is no longer necessary; but before the purpose is achieved many forms may be used and eventually cast aside. From each there is some lesson to be learned, but no form should be retained after that particular lesson has been absorbed.

Breaking of a form always means that the life within the form needs expansion for its growth. It is broken from within, as a bird breaks its shell when it can no longer contain the growing life.

If you can take a very, very long view, you will see that this is so, whether it be a physical form, a race, a group, an organization, a country or a planet.

The secret of a successful balanced life lies in the breaking of form, not only the garments a person wears as a human being, but of every form used for a purpose in the world of form.

The unenlightened are apt to confuse the form with the purpose for which it was formed, until the spirit becomes stifled by the organization, by refusing to acknowledge that any particular form, however beautiful, used to protect a growing life must in time be broken, so that the life within may have freedom to rise on the wings of its own aspiration.

# 23

*Except the shell break in the nest,*
*how can we hear the lark's song?*

MOST of the pain and sorrow of life is caused by the breaking of form; and yet—strange paradox!—the human spirit progresses by, and only by, the breaking of form. It is the only way to find happiness, for while held in bondage to form of any kind, "caged, cabined and confined,"[1] it cannot rise to seek the freedom that is the breath of spiritual life: freedom to seek the return path leading to the Father's house, from which it is exiled; freedom to forget or to remember; freedom to drop the burdens the mind has accumulated through countless ages of the outward journey; freedom to seek and to find eternal youth, the spirit's own prerogative, for age has no part nor lot in the life of the spirit; freedom to find its native land, the land of joy and wonder where past mistakes are erased, and only the essence of the experience of joys and sorrows remains to fuse into one and become that which is neither but the result of both. And with the fusing comes the knowledge that only experience can fashion the wings the spirit uses to soar above all that imprisons it in form.

Breaking the cords of bondage does not mean that in order to be free the human spirit must leave the physical body nor neglect ordinary work in the world—for without these one could not progress—but that when free, "free from the yoke of bondage,"[2] one can, while in a physical body, living an

---

1 Rowland-Skemp, Thomas, "The D'eyncourts of Fairleigh."

2 Galatians 5:1.

ordinary life in the world, control conditions instead of being controlled by them; can rise above them until they are under the feet and one is able to walk upon the waters of emotion instead of being drowned in them, and so gain mastery over mind and matter. This can only be achieved when one is using a physical body: highest spirit and lowest matter united by the mind. Thus, when the cords of bondage are broken, are we "born of the spirit."[3]

> *And ye shall know the truth, and the truth shall make you free.*
>
> —*John 8:32*

3 John 3:5.

# 24

*Verily, the form breaketh, but the spirit liveth for evermore.*

REGRET not the breaking of form of any kind. All forms must break because they are transitory and but covers for the growing life they protect. This is the law throughout nature: the growing life, or idea, must have, in the beginning, the protection of a form; but directly it has outgrown that form, it will of itself break the form from within in order to find one more suitable for its expression.

Life in manifestation must have form of some sort. There is no life apart from form on this planet, also there is no life without movement. Growing life gathers around it form after form, which constantly breaks according to the need of the life force using it. But when a form breaks, it does not mean that the life within is dead; rather is the breaking a sign of expansion.

The purpose is not in the form, although the form is used for the purpose. The purpose is in the mind that conceived and fashioned the form. Therefore never regret the breaking of any form. Form after form may be used and cast aside for the evolution of a particular purpose, but even so, there need be no regret for those who have eyes to see and understand the working of nature, which is the same through the universe. Even in a broken form there is no loss, for every atom of which it was composed has its own ensouling life and is used over and over again in various ways and formation.

Every created thing must necessarily, in time, be destroyed. Creation and destruction are the two aspects of a duality.

One cannot exist without the other, so where there is no destruction of form, there is no creative life or movement.

The wise will not try to hold a breaking form, realizing it but breaks to release the spirit, ever seeking fresh forms for a fuller expression until the fulfillment of the original purpose has been achieved.

# 25

PRAYERS of petition are often answered by the breaking of form, although seldom recognized as such because this may be accompanied by pain and sorrow. If, for instance, a prayer is a sincere desire for knowledge of truth, or to know love in its fullness, the Angel of Pain visits the heart of the seeker and breaks down the barriers that are preventing the seeker's eyes from beholding "the things pertaining unto his peace."[1]

Breaking of form is always painful, but if a seeking soul has demanded and prayed for the open vision, forms must be broken to enable the light imprisoned within the heart to shine forth.

Forms must be recognized for what they are: covers of truth made for its protection from the hand of those who, unprepared and ignorant of reality, would use it as a destroying instead of a constructive force. So knowledge of the purpose of the forms covering truth is essential before they can be removed with safety.

Until these forms are broken there can be no experience of "the peace which passeth all understanding,"[2] although the necessity for the breaking of form is not understood until after the pain and sorrow have been endured and the lesson learned.

---

1 Luke 19:42.

2 Philippians 4:7.

## 26

*Shiva is the Destroyer as Vishnu is the Preserver, and both are the regenerators of spiritual as well as of physical nature. To live as a plant the seed must die...*
*That to live is to die has been too little understood in the West. Shiva the Destroyer is the Creator and Saviour of spiritual man as He is the good gardener of nature—He weeds out the plants, human and cosmic, and kills the passions of the physical to call to life the perceptions of the Spiritual man.*[1]

—*Helena Blavatsky*

THE seed must die that the plant may live. It is in the darkness of earth, exposed to the elements, that the covering or outer shell of every seed gradually decays in order that the living germ it contains may expand and come to fruition as a living plant, able to give forth the flowers and fruit, each of its own kind.

The atoms forming the protective shell, although too few to cover a growing plant, are still living their own life in many and various forms. So weep not for the covers, life is of more value than form.

1 Blavatsky, Helena Petrovna, *The Secret Doctrine* (London: Theosophical Society, 1895).

# 27

*Man proposes but God disposes; therefore free will is absence of self-will.*[1]

*—Jalal ad-Din Rumi*

A HUMAN being has free will, but within limits; the limitation we have ourselves created by our thoughts and actions in the past. We must reap what we have sown. "Be not deceived; God is not mocked; for whatsoever a man soweth, that shall he also reap."[2] But by altering thoughts, which a person is always free to do, we can sow for a better reaping. If this were not so, all people would be puppets instead of actors in life's drama.

Complete freedom of will is attained only when we have voluntarily given up personal will and are ready to do the will of God, at all times and in all circumstances.

When this can be done, then at the time of reaping there are no debts to be paid off; and we can reap the full reward of a later sowing: the ability to be of further service and "stand fast in the liberty wherewith Christ hath made us free."[3]

*And be not conformed to this world; but be ye transformed by the renewing of your mind, that ye may prove what is that good, and acceptable, and perfect, will of God.*

*—Romans 12:2*

*For as he thinketh in his heart, so is he.*

*—Proverbs 23:7*

---

1 Jalal ad-Din Rumi, *Selected Poems from the Divani Shamsi Tabriz.*
2 Galatians 6:7.
3 Galatians 5:1.

# 28

*If man knew what is behind his free will, he would never call it "my will" but "Thy will."*[1]

—*Inayat Khan*

PRAYER should be an endeavor to get in touch with God, the God Within, to know God's will for us and for humankind; not merely asking that pain, evil and suffering may be taken away from us or from the world, but rather to show us how we ourselves can alter conditions by using the gifts of God of free will and creative thought, by asking for courage to endure and strength to do the will of God.

Such prayers, if sincere, will always be answered. That is inevitable: the answer arises in the prayer itself. To accept and act upon the answer may not be easy, but to do so is the only way to find peace in one's heart and in the world.

It is useless to sit still and expect or think that God is going to do everything for us. In the one sense, of course, God does, inasmuch as we live and breathe and have our being in, and are part of God. But a human being, as a part, must work for the whole, as the hands must work for the physical body of which they are a part.

The prayer, "Thy will be done,"[2] should not be interpreted as simply resignation to the will of God: that no more is necessary in the difficult situations that everyone has to meet than to sit with folded hands, in resignation to whatever befalls as being the will of God.

1 Inayat Khan, *The Gayan*.

2 Matthew 6:10.

If the inner meaning of the prayer, "Thy will be done on earth," is understood, then it will be clear to all who have insight that if God's will can be done on earth, we must do it. We must listen to the voice of God Within to learn the will of our Father in heaven and do it on earth. How else can it be done except by humanity?

It is just this acceptance of divine guidance, and the ordering of our daily lives and actions in accordance with that guidance, which gives the strength we need to overcome all difficulties. And by that overcoming, to gain an inner peace that will sustain us through every trial, no matter how hard it may be, which we have to meet in the journey through life.

## 29

EVERY soul receives exactly what it demands, and the real demand of every soul is answered; it cannot be otherwise, humanity having free will. The guide can only show the way but can compel no one. Even the guide cannot be found until a soul has demanded it.

Until people themselves ask for guidance, it cannot be given. There is one thing very necessary for travelers in search of truth to understand, and that is the advice or instructions given by a guide. Whenever any definite direction is suggested, or instruction given by a spiritual teacher to the pupils, either by words or only by presence, it is never an instruction suggested or given by the teacher alone. The teacher is only the interpreter. The real speaker is the inner selves of the pupils. And if the pupils will meditate upon the words spoken or transmitted in silence by the teacher, the pupils will realize it is what they, in their inmost being, know. It is true that the personality may not know, because one has been unable to still the mind sufficiently to hear the voice of the God Within. It is for this reason that a guide able to hear the voice of God everywhere, in another's as well as in the guide's own heart, is demanded by an earnest seeker.

# 30

*And God said, let us make man in our own image.*
*—Genesis 1:26*

BY that divine utterance, humankind inherited, among other attributes, the God-like gifts of creative thought and free will with which to start the long pilgrimage in a world of duality, conditioned by the pairs of opposites; a world in which humanity is given the opportunity of attaining God-realization, or that perfection of which Christ spoke when he said: "Be ye therefore perfect as your Father in heaven is perfect."[1] In other words, of returning to the Father's house.

When a person realizes that by using the gift of free will one is able to control one's own destiny, that person can, by the power of thought, create the environment necessary for the evolution of self-consciousness to God-consciousness, which is the end of the long journey.

When this stage is reached, the traveler no more sees "as through a glass darkly,"[2] but all things are clear. Having found the secret of the pairs of opposites, one knows that whoever loses their life shall find it, and that what is held is lost.

All the pairs of opposites must be united or balanced; that is the secret. The union of both results in perfection, but unless the balance is complete and can be so held in equilibrium, destruction instead of perfection would ensue.

The method of neutralization, uniting the pair of opposites or, in Sufi terms, resolving *jelal* and *jemal* to *kemal*, cannot be learned from books, neither can it be communicated

1 Matthew 5:48.

2 1 Corinthians 13:12.

from one person to another, but only realized by the inner consciousness. Responsibility rests with a person alone as to whether, when neutralized, kemal becomes a power of constructive or destructive force, since it can be either. And if, for one moment, the balance is upset, it may be a deadly weapon in the hands of those who still desire glorification for the personal self, bringing untold harm to themselves and others. Hence the absolute necessity of turning God-ward and renouncing, by voluntary surrender, any desires keeping the soul earthbound, and untying all ties which hold it to earth, before making any attempt to tread the return path leading to perfection. "Among thousands of men, scarce one striveth for perfection, and of those who attain, scarce one knoweth Me in essence."[3]

Those treading the path of return must have complete knowledge, realization and experience—knowledge alone is not enough—of the laws of balance, and the steadfastness necessary to hold and to keep the scales in equilibrium. It is also necessary to understand that to untie does not mean to break. The return path cannot be strewn with broken promises nor half-finished tasks. These must be fulfilled, but whatever ties hold the soul must be gently untied by the hand which tied them. Then will the traveler understand, having clear and open vision, that reality must be reached through knowledge of the unreal.

The way to heaven is through the gates of hell, and only through the darkness of desolation and loneliness is found the joy that no one can take away, and the love which passes all understanding, for "Love is God and God is love."[4] The two utterances of Jesus on the cross, "My God! My God! Why hast Thou forsaken me?"[5] and "Father, forgive them; they know not what they do",[6] illustrate this teaching.

3 Bhagavad Gita.

4 1 John 4:16.

5 Matthew 7:46.

6 Luke 23:34.

# 31

*I believe in the resurrection of the body*
*and in the life everlasting.*
*—Nicene Creed*

HOW often are these words spoken by those whose lips repeat the words, but whose hearts understand them not at all. And yet they contain teaching which leads to eternal life, if one will endeavor to search and understand. Jesus said, "Ye must be born again,"[1] and "Unless a man be born again he cannot see the kingdom of God."[2] It is the second birth, or spiritual rebirth, which creates this body of resurrection, not the earthly or physical body born from the mother's womb, which disintegrates at the death of the body. It is the spiritual body that conquers death, and in which the soul lives the life everlasting.

This body must be made by one's own self while inhabiting an earthly body, by refining all the vehicles, physical, emotional and mental; by pure thought; control of emotion; and constant effort to learn and practice, in deed and in truth, the teaching of the Christ, who was from the beginning and who is accessible to all, whatever their race or religion. The formation of a resurrection body is not a miracle performed instantaneously, but a long process of constant endeavor and many failures. Just as birth of a physical body is through pain and suffering, so also is the second birth in the human heart.

1 John 3:7.
2 John 3:3.

# 32

*Grant us to know that it is not the beginning, but the continuing of the same, until it be thoroughly finished, which yieldeth the true glory.*

*– Sir Francis Drake's Prayer*

IF the lesson of each failure and sorrow is learned and left behind, and the pilgrims have courage to persevere to the end, the reward is great: a joy that can never be taken away; for they can now live in a body that knows no death, and may work and live for humanity on this planet or any other. They are no more "under the yoke of bondage"[1] but have the freedom of the Father's house. They can now work and rest, know beauty, harmony, companionship, true happiness and laughter, and that "perfect love which casteth out fear."[2] Things will be known as they are and not as they appear, for the pilgrims will now be free from "the delusion of the pairs of opposites"[3] and find completion.

*Be not deceived; God is not mocked; for whatsoever a man soweth, that shall he also reap. For he that soweth to the flesh shall of the flesh reap corruption; but he that soweth to the spirit shall of the spirit reap life everlasting.*

*—Galatians 6:7-8*

1 Galatians 5:1.

2 1 John 4:18.

3 Bhagavad Gita.

# 33

*There are many facts, but one truth. Facts can be put into words, truth cannot.*

*—Inayat Khan*

THE birth of Christ in the human heart is also the birth of his resurrection body. It is this birth that conquers death, and when it is fully formed, then the words of Jesus: "I am the resurrection and the life,"[1] are understood.

This explanation is most inadequate and is only given as a clue, which every seeker must work out individually. It is just as impossible to explain spiritual truth in words today as it was when Jesus was on earth and taught the multitudes in parables. Even to his disciples, who were to continue his teaching after his own passing, there were many things he would have told them if they had been able to understand; but he said: "I have yet many things to say unto you, but ye cannot hear them now."[2]

1 John 11:25.

2 John 16:12.

# 34

*Truth is within ourselves; it takes no rise from outward thing, whate'er you many believe. There is an inmost Centre in us all, where truth abides in fullness.*[1]

*—Robert Browning*

THE wave of spiritualism is in answer to the great demand. Collective demand has a great cumulative force, but what should be understood is that the only thing that really matters is to find God, and that human beings have free will and will always receive what they demand.

Those who demand materialized forms will see materialized forms; and those who demand God will find God. But they must demand; a person can only receive, in reply to that demand, whatever is desired. Only those with a strong will can be helped. Those who never know what they want are tossed about by every wind that blows; no one can help them until they learn to help themselves.

Denizens of the lower levels of the astral plane often try to sap the strength of whoever they can touch. Also, many undesirable thought forms seek re-embodiment wherever they can find an entry into the minds of people on earth.

A few words of warning should be given wherever possible, for the danger is grave and may cause harm to those who are quite unaware of such danger. The warning is to all who frequent séances or receive so-called spirit messages by any other method.

There are people who believe anything, and will act upon advice given that they think comes from one who has left the earth,

1 Browning, Robert, "Paracelsus."

without any proof whatever of the identity—frequently assumed—of the one who gives it and who is probably no more able to give such advice than any casual stranger met in the street. It is possible, however, sometimes to read the thoughts in the minds of enquirers, and answers acceptable to them are given. In this way the contact is encouraged to continue.

The danger against which this warning is given, besides weakening self-reliance and lessening the desire to seek within one's own heart for answers to life's problems, is that entities who have suddenly lost the earthly bodies to which they were attached can, and do, drain the life force from those who contact them in this way. And very subtle methods are used to induce unsuspecting people to listen. It is during this time of a negative attitude on their part, that undesirable thought forms can gain force for themselves by depleting the vitality of living people.

It is understandable that those who have lost companions dear to them should try by any means to obtain assurance, if they have it not, of the continuity of life after death of the body. But any wishing to use this method of reassurance should first possess control, complete and absolute, of their emotions; also a measure of mind control, to enable them to distinguish between the truth or falsity of messages received from the world of illusion. Otherwise, the effect of such methods of communication, if continued, may be disastrous, and result in the devitalizing of mind and body.

# 35

*Mysticism is an experience. It cannot be studied, put into words, explained or talked about. Those who write explanations of it, or talk about colors, spirits, vision, experiences, etc., are not true mystics.*

*—Inayat Khan*

KEEP the feet steadily upon the spiritual path; turn neither to the right nor to the left; look not before nor after, but up and straight ahead. Walk in sure faith, keeping your thoughts ever upon God, and you shall surely find God.

Only a master can safely tread the path of psychism. It is the illusion of illusions, a path leading to a world full of dangers, deceptions and delusion, false conceptions and false ideas.

The veil has been lifted between the two worlds; the demand was made and must be met. To all but the strong who are firmly established in the knowledge of God, it is a grave menace. Do not desire psychic development nor occult power; desire only God and the knowledge of God. Those who would know of the doctrine must live the life. "Seek ye first the kingdom of God and His righteousness, and all these things shall be added unto you"[1] for use in the service of humanity. This is the only safe way of progress.

The study of the doctrine of reincarnation is not always helpful to a seeker for God, because by fixing the mind upon and occupying yourself with past existences, you cannot lose yourself in God, which is the goal of the mystic. You would always be looking backward instead of going forward.

1 Matthew 6:33.

The aim of the mystic is to withdraw to the inner center of being, which really means that the mind is only occupied with the personality while something has to be decided upon or planned. And when a course of action is settled and started, the mind can then withdraw to occupy itself with the life of the soul. The activities of the personality may, in time, become almost mechanical to the real self, which, when not occupied, becomes practically oblivious of them, just as the ordinary functions of the body are carried on although the mind is quite unconscious of the way in which they work.

It is difficult even to try to describe this curious double life. Only those who have had any experience can understand. Strangely enough, it does not follow that the personal life or activities of the personality are of less interest. In some odd way, every act of daily life seems more important and more interesting; only everything appears to be done without effort instead of with difficulty, almost as though one were watching instead of doing and, all the while, intensely interested.

*When we try too much, we miss the joy in the agony of doing.*
*—Inayat Khan*

# 36

> *By the delusion of the pairs of opposites, sprung from attraction and repulsion, O Bharata, all beings walk this Universe wholly deluded.*
>
> —*Bhagavad Gita*

THE secret of existence is to be found in the knowledge and realization of the pairs of opposites. We cannot examine or analyze motion, but were it inactive, it would cease to exist.

People in the material world are, if anything, that which they reflect, either God or devil; for they are capable of both. The ideal is that the reflection should be neither one nor the other, but perfection: the result, or essence, of the action and reaction of both. But only the perfect can know perfection, for they must be that which they aspire to understand. Until this stage has been reached, people can only know in part by watching reflections of God and devil, which are constantly before view, reflecting one and ignoring the other; reflecting what they call good, striving to become like unto it; and then reflecting evil, which, as it is the opposite of good, they strive to cast away.

Not until a person can accept both, has mastered in the self the mystery of divine alchemy and has the courage to put both good and evil into the crucible, can one know that perfection which is the essence of all things, the Only Being.

# 37

*Be ye therefore perfect, even as your Father which is in heaven is perfect.*
*—Matthew 5:48*

THE balance of good and evil, as of all the pairs of opposites, is perfection. None can tread the path of return until they have passed through the gates of heaven and hell, where the way of return begins.

This path is not for every person in this cycle of evolution, but those who enter it and continue until the end become masters of the path, masters of wisdom and guides of evolving souls. Having balanced the pairs of opposites, their task is finished.

The completion of a task well done gives a great joy. The divine ecstasy, which comes through much tribulation, is worth all the pain and sorrow, and cannot be had without it.

No one can experience divine illumination who has not experienced the darkness of hell.

The pattern and example of the perfect human being is Jesus Christ. He descended into hell, he ascended into heaven. Having mastered both, he lives and reigns for evermore; and having been lifted up, has power to draw all unto him, until they also, through him, may find God and the kingdom of God.

People sometimes think that this is a process that is done for them; that by the suffering and death of Jesus they can receive salvation and forgiveness of sins; that they of themselves have nothing to do but believe.

"Believe on the Lord Jesus Christ and thou shalt be saved."[1] The real interpretation of this teaching is not always understood. It is true that through him people can reach God, the Father of all, because he is one with the Father; but all who aspire to be drawn up to Christ, to attain, and to understand the at-one-ment, to participate in the wonder and the glory, must also tread the path of sorrow and suffering. To follow the steps of the master, they must descend into hell.

Jesus endured the cross to show "The way, the truth and the life"[2]; not to remove all sorrow and suffering, nor even sin, from their lives, but to help them, by the examples of his own life and death, to overcome all things[3] and receive the crown of life; to understand the meaning of "Whoever loseth his life shall save it"[4]; and that only through the death can man reach the glorious resurrection. For only by one's own efforts can the necessary strength be generated for the second birth, by which one is born of the spirit; a necessity for all who would tread the path of return to the Father's house.

> *To him that overcometh will I grant to sit with me on my throne; even as I also overcame and am set down with my Father on His throne.*
>
> —*Revelations 3:21*

1 Acts 16:31.
2 John 14:6.
3 John 16:33.
4 Matthew 6:25.

# 38

LOVE is the greatest thing a human being can ever know, but really to know love means a long pilgrimage and much suffering. It cannot be felt or experienced, except through a cover or form. Humanity, knowing so little of reality, associates love with the form it uses for its expression; so when the form breaks and a loved companion is lost, it is difficult to understand that only the form has disappeared, not the love. Also, what is perhaps more difficult to realize, is that the same love can use another form.

It is like electricity transmitted from a power plant to places prepared to receive it. A bulb is put into a lamp, the current turned on, and you have light. If in time the bulb breaks, there is apparently no light; but if another bulb is put into the lamp, there is again light, the same light—the light that has always been available. It is the same with love.

If you can accept this teaching and endeavor to understand that there is only one love, which can reach you through many forms, you will not feel all is lost when the form breaks. The same manifestation of love may return, using another form for its expression, as the electric current uses another bulb to give light. You must believe this, or it cannot happen. Unless you believed you could get light from the same electric current by replacing a broken bulb with a fresh one, you would not do it and, consequently, would remain in darkness. Faith is needed to realize that the physical form, however dearly loved, is but a cover for love given and received.

Yes, it is a difficult teaching but a true one, nevertheless.

*Many waters cannot quench love, neither can the floods drown it.*

*—Song of Solomon 8:7*

# 39

*No man hath seen God at any time.*
*If we love one another, God dwelleth in us,*
*and His love is perfected in us.*

*—1 John 4:12.*

THE personalities we love are in reality but the masks through which God speaks to the human soul. God is love, and only through love can one approach God. Therefore, to all those to whom we give our love, however great, however devoted that love may be, however apparently individual we may think it, we are really giving it to God.

The essential thing is that we must love human beings or we cannot love God. "He that loveth not, knoweth not God; for God is love."[1] This teaching can only be grasped intuitively and very gradually. Do not try to understand it with the mind. "We are even as shadows, He is all who seek. Lo, by Him is spoken every word we speak."[2]

Behind all the physical masks, be they men, women, children or animals, there is but the One, the Only Being, love alone who, without the veiling by the masks, we as human beings could never approach. As the physical sun would blind physical eyes without a shade, so our spiritual eyes would be blinded by the glory of His sun, which may only be looked upon "through a glass darkly."[3]

1 1 John 4:8.

2 Jalal ad-Din Rumi, *Selected Poems from the Divani Shamsi Tabriz.*

3 1 Corinthians 13:12.

*Then of the Thee in me who works behind*
*The veil, I lifted up my hands to find*
*A lamp amid the darkness; and I heard*
*As from without—the me within Thee blind!*[4]

*—Omar Khayyam*

4 Khayyam, Omar, *The Rubaiyat*, trans. Edward Fitzgerald. (London: Quaritch, 1986).

# 40

*There is no truer truth obtainable by man than comes of music.*[1]

*—Robert Browning*

*In the beginning was the Word, and the Word was with God, and the Word was God.*

*—John 1:3.*

BY the utterance of God the heavens and the earth were called into being; to every embodiment its own note and tuning. "Then God said: "Let us make man in Our image."[2]

Human beings and their bodies are fashioned by the great artificer, the Divine Harmonist. God voices a note, and as the sound thereof whirls into space, the atoms of matter responsive to its tuning gather around in rhythmic formation, until its embodiment is complete and the uttered note becomes human.

The created sound is of God, and from God, and in God. It was God, it is God, and will be God when, as humanity, it shall cease to be.

These embodied, or materialized, sounds vibrate according to the pitch of their tuning when the keynote or Christ note is played by the master player; for every variety of tone, overtone and undertone, in countless numbers, is needed to form the discordant harmonies and harmonious discords necessary to complete the earth symphony, for which they were called into being and made flesh.

---

1 Browning, Robert, "Charles Avison."

2 Genesis 1:26.

*So shall my word be that goeth forth out of my mouth; it shall not return unto me void, but it shall accomplish that which I please...For ye shall go forth with joy, and be led forth with peace; the mountains and the hills shall break forth before you into singing.*

*—Isaiah 55:11-12*

# 41

THE cause of what is called *sin* is the turning away of the human soul from the vision of its true self and identifying itself with the garments it wears, thus making a false self, separate and apart from God, the origin and source of its being.

In order to return to the state of sinlessness typified by the Garden of Eden, this false ego that has been created must be destroyed by its creator. One by one, the covers with which the soul is wrapped must be dropped, until it stands face to face with God in the state of original purity, "naked and unashamed."[1]

This experience cannot be described. Who can describe the merging of a river into the ocean, of losing its identify as river and becoming sea? Or tell the story of the return of the elements to their original condition, to the ether from which they came forth as earth, water, fire and air? Neither can the return of humankind to God be spoken of.

Whosoever would learn the mystery of the path of return must put off their shoes of material understanding and walk with naked feet to meet their Lord.

1 Genesis 2:25.

# 42

EVIL must eventually be passed through the crucible of fire until it is transmuted when the pairs of opposites merge once again into One, and there is neither good nor evil but perfection, the Only Being. Spirit can solidify until it becomes matter, as vapor can solidify into ice and, unless the temperature be altered, remain ice. But when heat is applied, it becomes again as it was in the beginning.

## 43

How long must the pilgrim tread the earthly way?
*Until his night be past, and he can see the day.*

Why must he walk so oft in darkness black
  as night?
*Because he stands in his own shadow,*
  *which obscures the light.*
*When he can turn and face the sun without a fear,*
*Then will the shadow fall behind, and the way be clear.*

Why does he linger in the dark so long, if light
  is always there?
*He needs must learn in deepest night the strength*
  *and will to dare,*
*The truth that will all doubts and fears dispel:*
*That he, to find reality, must pass through hell.*

# 44

THE mysteries of the kingdom of God are hidden in the human heart, the only place where they can be found and where also lies the solution of all problems.

The way of the heart is really the way of return, and is usually cluttered up with so much rubbish, accumulated by the personality through ages of wrong thinking, that the process of its removal is extremely difficult and generally painful. The task of removal is not one that everyone is prepared to attempt, much less to carry through to the end; although until they do so, they can never know the mysteries nor find their own place in the Father's home, from which humanity has been exiled since the beginning of its pilgrimage as humankind: the pilgrimage undertaken for the purpose of becoming, through free will, *hu-man*: balanced, self-controlled, steadfast, reliable, willing and able to take part in the Father's work.

By altering thoughts, those who have cleared the path leading to the heart will find an open door through which they may pass if they are willing to leave behind everything once thought necessary. The door is so narrow that, unless they did so, they could not get through. However, strange paradox, having left all, they find inside the door all that had been left outside, and are free to keep what they wish to keep. But as they can now see everything as it is and not what it was once believed to be, they realize that, having learned the lessons taught, the forms may be left behind.

Only the result of experience—the essence of the teaching—is necessary to fit someone to work for humanity, in the course of which one will be able to become a selfless worker; thus fulfilling the high destiny of humanity to work out the purpose of God's will upon earth.

# 45

*The light shineth in the darkness and the darkness comprehended it not.* —*John 1:5*

THE Prince of Darkness watched the Lord of Light
Walk through the "Cities of the Dreadful Night,"[1]
And as he watched, he laughed with glee,
Saying: "There are no dwellings left here for Thee."
"'Tis true," said the Lord, "you have burnt my churches,
Laid waste the temples made with hands;
Yet, still I find My dwelling place
Amid these ruined lands.
You have but destroyed the symbols, where weary minds take rest
As they climb the steps of reality in their age-long quest.
The real place of My abode, over that you have no control;
You may leave a nation in ruins, but you cannot touch her Soul
Though temples made with hands may fall,
According to your vile plan.
The dwelling place of God remains, within the heart of man."

*Know ye that ye are the temple of God, and the spirit of God dwelleth in you.*

—*1 Corinthians 3:16*

1 See Rudyard Kipling's, *The City of the Dreadful Night.*(New York: Alex. Grosset and Co., 1899)

# 46

*The man filled with the knowledge of names and forms has no capacity for the knowledge of truth.*[1]

*—Inayat Khan*

THE message of God, which from time's beginning has been brought to the world by God's messengers in every age, in order to bring to human beings—made in the image of God—the knowledge of their kinship as children of the Father.

The messengers have taught this in various ways, according to their perception of the truth to which they were attuned.

As the message is an answer to the cry, conscious or unconscious, of humanity for freedom from bondage of self, it must be given to every person in that person's own tongue.

During the lives of the messengers, the message they bring is alive; for the messengers' words are living and life-giving, and in them each soul can find the answer to individual problems.

Although truth is one, its interpretations are as many as are the souls of humankind; and everyone can reach freedom by following one's own path to God.

After the passing from earth of the messenger of the time, there is always a tendency to crystallize the message into a definite form. And as the years pass, it becomes more and more imprisoned and made four-square and exact, with the disastrous effect that, instead of being a living truth responding to the cry of humanity, it becomes fixed and bound, set into one form to which all must conform or remain outside until the life-giving power is entirely lost.

1 Inayat Khan *The Bowl of Saki.*

Form-makers say there is only one way to God and all must walk therein or perish. Their eyes being fixed upon the form, it is perhaps natural they cannot see the life; for those who contemplate form become, in time, incapable of seeing the ever-moving living truth, which can never become solid or fixed in any one place but is everywhere in the universe, the same yesterday, today and forever.

> *The path man takes from every side is Mine, O Partha.*
> *—Bhagavad Gita*

# 47

THE veils that cover the messengers are not primarily to test the insight of the seeker, although some such testing is necessary, but for the safety of the community and the protection of the prophets who, in the physical body, are limited by time. For although they are always ready to give with both hands to a sincere seeker, and to no one who asks can they refuse the blessing, as they become known among people there must be some means of keeping away the merely curious who would waste precious time, and also those who seek only to enrich themselves at the expense of others by obtaining an increase of power through occult means. All who come within the master's aura receive a quickening that stimulates to action whatever is hidden in the heart, whether it be good or whether it be evil.

The person who is willing to learn is taught the method by which undesirable growths can be uprooted; but it is a paramount importance that those who, if thus quickened would become a power for evil in the world, should not come within one's aura; for no one having been in the presence of the master with seeing eyes can remain the same.

Messengers of God are, therefore, hidden under many and various veils that only those who seek may find; and the messengers' teaching is given in parable that only those who have ears may hear. For the messengers need no proclamation; they neither seek nor desire recognition from the world. The work they achieve and the words they speak are the heralds of their greatness. They will ring out through the ages a true note, bringing life to all those who hearts can respond to the vibrations of truth. And the souls who are turning in sleep will hear and become restless until they awake to behold, with open vision, the beauty of God.

# 48

INITIATION is a word about which there is much misunderstanding. One who has been admitted by initiation to any cult, society, order, brotherhood or any other activity, means quite simply a beginner and does not, as many people imagine, denote a high stage of spiritual development.

If an initiation is given on earth by a master, it is for the purpose of opening a door through which initiates may see themselves in the light of truth, and thus be given the opportunity of understanding their many failings so that they may, if they will, begin to correct them.

Initiations on the inner planes are of the spirit, known only to the spirit. Such an experience would of itself seal the lips of the recipients, who would probably, in some cases certainly, be unaware of such initiation in waking consciousness.

# 49

TEACHING received from the inner planes must not be confused with what is heard in séances and spiritualistic circles, which is only the shadow side of truth and as different from the real teaching as light is from darkness. Very great discrimination is needed by one to whom this teaching is given, and the intuition must be developed before one can distinguish the real from the unreal. Many are the tests that must be encountered that are subtle and not easily recognized, so let the pupils examine every teaching by the guiding light within their own hearts before acting upon advice given.

Inner teaching cannot often be given because of the ignorance of the people. In olden days this was not so when humankind had faith in the unseen, but now the majority are so encased in materialism they think everything of this kind either supernatural or of the devil. They have forgotten, or perhaps have never read, the many instances in their own scriptures of the teachings and warnings given by the great ones on the inner planes to the people on earth, for their guidance and help; and great indeed is their loss.

Whoever is striving to tread the spiritual path must, sooner or later, receive false teaching; this is for one's own safety. Intuition and discrimination are the two qualities most necessary for an aspirant to develop. For every step taken, guided by a teacher, there is a corresponding pull back from the shadow side; but if a step is taken by the aspirant without any help save that of one's own intuition, then the aspirant will have the strength to stand and the opportunity to discriminate between the true and false teachings.

In reality, both true and false are from the same source, sometimes even from the same teacher. Always there must be tests, for no spiritual teacher would encourage a pupil to walk upon the path unaided, until the teacher was sure that pupil had developed sufficient intuition at least to hesitate before acting upon advice given from the inner planes.

> *Satan comes in most beautiful garbs to hide from man's eyes his highest ideal.*[1]
>
> —*Inayat Khan*

1 Inayat Khan, *The Gayan*.

## 50

*Ye shall know them by their fruits.*
*—Matthew 7:16.*

WHOEVER has received spiritual initiation will show, in the initiate's ordinary daily life, the fruit of the spirit, not because of being conscious of having received an initiation—the initiate would not, except perhaps in very rare cases, be aware of any such happening in the waking consciousness—but because it is as natural as it is natural for an apple tree to bear apples. The fruit may feed many people, but the tree remains unconscious and indifferent as to whom it feeds. Its purpose is to produce fruit and, in so doing, fulfills its life's purpose. The true purpose of a life's fulfillment is known only to God.

# 51

*Words are good but they are not the best.*
*The best is not to be explained in words.*
*The spirit in which we think and act is the great matter.*
*—Johann von Goethe*

WHEN seekers for God have traveled as far as the intellect can take them upon the path of seeking—and it is most necessary that both reason and intellect should be satisfied—they become restless, because the truth they are seeking seems to have eluded them. This is a stage that all seekers for God must eventually reach. It is here that the path of knowledge ends and the path of turning begins.

Travelers who have courage and from whose heart the cry of "O! that I knew where I could find God," is sincere, will now find themselves upon the path of unknowing, which to an earnest seeker is most bewildering. Everything so carefully learned and assimilated must be laid aside. The traveler's ideal of God and all cherished ideas fall away one by one, as things for which the traveler has no further use, until at last one is able to realize that everything met upon the outer journey was illusion, and that only by turning inward to one's own innermost being can one find God enthroned in the human heart, God's only dwelling place.

Strange though it may appear, no travelers can find the inner path until they have trodden and mastered the outer; it is the only way. It does require courage, great courage, to drop everything the intellect has gathered on the path of seeking and to stand alone, without any of the clothing the mind has woven for their protection. But if they have courage to go forward, they will soon realize that such coverings, although necessary on the outward journey, would, if retained, obscure the light that now begins to flood one's whole being, showing without any shadow of doubt that the path to God begins and ends in humankind itself, about which no explanation can be written. Each individual must realize and interpret this teaching by the light that has been found within one's own heart.

# 52

*I will go before thee, and make the crooked places straight; I will break in pieces the gates of brass, and cut in sunder the bars of iron.* —*Isaiah 45:2*

TO aspirants for discipleship who have courage and strength to know that adversity accepted and faced can become a friend, "as a thief in the night,"[1] come the great spiritual experiences, so quietly, and sometimes so naturally that those to whom they come do not realize at the time that an experience has really happened.

There is nothing dramatic, no outer or conscious preparation, save the preparation of life, the great initiator itself. They may not even know they have been tested before each experience, until perhaps long afterwards, when the eyes to see have been opened and it is possible to look back along the road that has been traveled. Then may they wonder at the distance their feet have journeyed, the many milestones passed upon the way, the apparently overwhelming difficulties resolved, things which at one time it seemed impossible to overcome. They are not now even conscious of things which used to hold them back. Verily, have the bars of iron been broken and the crooked places made straight.

Always is the promise sure to "him that overcometh."[2]

*Cast not away therefore your confidence, which hath recompense of reward. For ye have need of patience, that, after ye have done the will of God, ye might receive the promise.*

—*Hebrews 10:35-36*

---

1 1 Thessalonians 5:2.

2 Revelations 3:12.

# 53

THE importance of self-development through study, prayer and meditation cannot be overestimated. They are most helpful and, at a particular state in human evolution, a necessity. But it should be realized as a stage of the journey and not an end in itself.

"Be ye perfect as your Father which is in Heaven is perfect,"[1] is the goal; but this goal cannot be reached unless one understands the reason for self-development and finding God within one's own heart. It is not only that a person may find the life everlasting, but also that one may be able to serve humanity; for without such service, freedom from bondage cannot be attained.

All the great ones, the elders of the race who have themselves become perfected, have demonstrated this by their sacrifice and service to humanity, to hasten the process of their redemption.

The mystery hidden behind this is that because humanity is one, there can be no final liberation for any until all are free; because all, from the highest to the lowest, constitute the One Whole. Therefore, the separate parts must each be perfected before the cosmic Christ, still crucified in matter, can arise in his resurrection embodiment of redeemed humanity.

---

1 Matthew 5:48.

# 54

*The loaf holds many grains of corn, and myriad drops the sea; so is God's oneness multitude, and that great multitude are we.*

*—Angelus Silesius*

CAN human beings have any knowledge of God apart from God's manifestation?

As a human being is a manifestation of God, it is obviously impossible that the part can know the whole. To understand, to analyze anything, it is necessary to be outside and apart from it. Humanity being in God and of God cannot, therefore, have any knowledge of God apart from God's manifestation, through any mental process. And even of that, only an infini tesimal part can be understood, and the whole but postulated as a necessary hypothesis.

Mystics have claimed knowledge of God by a process of God-identification: "Losing himself outright he finds himself in the eternal light"[1]; but such knowledge cannot be communicated. In answer to the questing spirit of humanity as to what is God, one word only may be given: love.

If, therefore, one would have knowledge of God, one must understand and experience for oneself the love that annihilates self. In this freedom of surrender there can be no consciousness of separateness, for beyond the limitations of self-love, the "middle wall of partition"[2] having been broken, the soul knows itself one with limitless love.

1 Inayat Khan, *Hindustani Lyrics* (London: Sufi Pub. Society, 1919).

2 Ephesians 2:14.

What is one apart from one's vehicle? Again the answer is obvious. How can the part know itself while deluded by the illusion of separateness? People see each other as individual and separate because they identify themselves with the vehicles that make a human body; and as no two vehicles are alike, it is natural that the individuality and immortality of a person, as a human being, should be assumed. But the soul, or the God Within, is human only so long as a person inhabits these vehicles. When, through them, one has experienced what one wills to experience, that person is no longer bound by the limitation of a separate individuality.

The point may be illustrated by taking an analogy, although no analogy is really adequate. Some air balloons whose colored films or envelopes, when expanded, each surround and enclose a particular or individualized portion of, shall we say for want of a true definition, colorless space. But such enclosures or individualization do not remove from space the parts enclosed; they are still of it and in it, and upheld by it. Neither is there any alteration in composition. The difference of size, shape and color is in the envelope, which merely creates an appearance of separateness for a limited time; the time being dependent upon the texture and workmanship of the enclosing envelope, which, for the purpose of this illustration, we will call a human being—physical, emotional and mental. Yet the God Within is above and beyond the vehicles that God inhabits.

When they break or disintegrate the life, hitherto isolated within the covering matter, automatically becomes one with its source, the separated individuality being but an illusion, a limitation in time.

What is all this for? Why the manifestation?

According to the ancient mystery teaching, manifestation is the divine play of God, a game of hide-and-seek wherein God, hiding from the Divine Self as humanity, experiences the supreme joy of seeking the Divine Self as God.

Everyone, therefore, made in God's image, if they would experience the joy of life, must seek to discover or uncover the God Within for themselves.

> *An answer in words is delusive; it is really no answer to the questions you ask....*
> *The soul answers never by words but by the thing itself that is inquired after.*[3]
>
> *—Ralph Waldo Emerson*

3 Emerson, Ralph Waldo, "The Over-Soul."

# 55

*Then ye shall call upon me and ye shall go and pray unto me and I will hearken unto you.*
*Jeremiah 29:12*

IN times of trial and danger it is natural people to call upon God for help, whatever their creed or religion; and if God's help is asked for in the sure and certain faith that prayer will be answered, it will be. Help will always be given to do the difficult task. Strength will always be sent to bear the heavy burden, although it may not be that the difficult work is done for us, as is sometimes expected; nor the heavy weight we are carrying removed, even though, at times, it may seem more than we can bear. What God sends in answer to a sincere prayer for help, in any difficult situation, is strength to bear and courage to endure. Such help will never fail.

If we were relieved of all our difficulties, how could we grow in strength?

Life is full of difficulties, and the purpose of human life on earth is to overcome them, until they lie under our feet and we become masters of our destiny instead of being mastered by it. Only by facing, with courage and endurance, whatever life brings to us, can we become "more than conqueror through Him that loved us,"[1] until we come unto the measure of the stature of the fullness of Christ.

*We may, if we please, avoid all the great pains of life, but at the cost of its deepest joys.*

*—Catherine Dodd*

1 Romans 8:37.

# 56

*Failure in life does not matter: misfortune is standing still.*[1]

—*Inayat Khan*

TO show repentance for past mistakes or shortcomings does not mean only to be sorry for one's failures. The real meaning of repentance is newness of life as the result of being sorry: a new beginning, after having shed the burdens of past faults, having seen them in their true perspective, and to start afresh.

The fresh start would not, this time, be made in ignorance of the result of wandering from the straight path; for by our mistakes and failures we should have learned what only those things could teach: the pain and sorrow for ourselves and others, the debts that must be paid and the realization that all the time we were seeking happiness in places where it is never found. All valuable lessons are only learned through repeated failures, until the need for repentance is so insistent that we are ready to pay all debts in full and turn round. With that turning comes the realization that all the time we had been chasing shadows—shadows of the real, shadows of happiness thrown upon our path—causing confusion and clouds, hiding the truth that happiness can never be found afar off but has its dwelling place always within the human heart, where is the kingdom of God.

1 Inayat Khan, *The Gayan*.

# 57

*Wherefore the law was our schoolmaster to bring us unto Christ, that we might be justified by faith. But after that faith is come, we are no longer under a schoolmaster.*
—*Galatians 3:24-25*

SIN and virtue, goodness and badness, pleasure, pain, sadness, happiness: all these are just names necessary for use while bound by time and space.

While a child is at school, the rules of the school are most important, and the breaking of them brings punishment; so the child must either observe them or suffer, but this is only to train it to obey and recognize those who are in authority over it. The rules themselves are meaningless, and when the child has passed out of the school it knows that this is so.

In the same way, all a person's experiences in the world are to teach the true meaning of life. Whether the experiences are pleasurable or painful is not the important thing. What is important is that one should understand the meaning of every experience and learn the lesson it is meant to teach.

# 58

THE importance of balance on every plane of one's being must be realized by aspirants to discipleship; balance in things physical, mental and spiritual, for without it there can be no progress, either in the outer or in the inner life.

It is a universal need, for the balanced person stands upright and can never be overthrown by the winds of fate nor depressed nor downtrodden by any of the difficulties that beset every person in daily life. Still more is balance necessary to one who aspires to tread the spiritual path, and the further one goes upon the way, the greater will be one's need.

God holds the scales, humanity provides the material to balance them.

From the cradle to the grave, balance will bring achievement. Achievement brings victory, and victory leads to the gates of heaven.

Beyond the gates of heaven is the sevenfold path where the seven tests await the aspirant, and, in passing through each gate, a test is experienced. One essential thing is required: absolute calm and poise. Although heavy rocks may vibrate down the hill to crush one, one must not turn back but resolutely keep on.

Another test in the modern world is the test of financial security. If one has not much money and places faith in the higher powers, one will meet obligations, one will be able to live; but the trust and the faith must be perfect, no doubt of any kind must be allowed to enter the mind.

# 59

THIS planet, the Earth planet, is ruled by the pairs of opposites. And when this law is understood, many problems now so difficult to solve will become simple; although, without a knowledge of the working of this law, they appear quite insoluble.

The first and most important step for a person is the understanding and mastery of one's self and of the law of neutralization. Nothing in this world can exist without its opposite. Spirit creates matter by solidifying part of itself, creating duality; thus light manifests its own shadow by which, and only by which, light can be known to humanity. Darkness, or shadow, has no existence apart from light. When the pairs of opposites are balanced there is equilibrium, or perfection; but this cannot be until the law governing them is realized and acted upon.

The method cannot be told in words, but must be sought and found by each individual, in one's own inner consciousness, by developed intuition. A few words only many be given as suggestions. Jesus said, "Resist not evil"[1] and "Be ye perfect as your Father in Heaven is perfect,"[2] which is the end of humanity's long pilgrimage.

The perfect person is the balanced person. Having positive and negative qualities in equal proportions, one, therefore, is neither positive nor negative but the result of the union of both, which is neither. One has learned how to tread the path

1 Matthew 5:39.

2 Matthew 5:48.

of nonresistance and to neutralize, in oneself, hatred by love, sorrow by joy, destructive thought by creative thought, vice by virtue, uncleanness by purity, and desire by renunciation.

All the shadow side, or what is called *evil*, is negative; and light or love is positive. So when one has obtained mastery over the self, one has the power to utilize that law of neutralization, when all darkness and the powers of darkness are absorbed into and become one with light, as darkness is negative to light.

On the plane of morality, this works out as absorption in God and entire forgetfulness of the individual ego; but this teaching is not safe for anyone to pursue unless, and until, they have obtained complete mastery of all their bodies: physical, emotional and mental.

## 60

IF you want to do anything, never see any difficulty about it. So many people fall short of achieving their purpose because they think: "How can I deal with the many difficulties surrounding me?" which is fatal to success. Whatever you want to do, whether it be a great thing or only something comparatively unimportant, whatever it may be, do not see any difficulty.

Difficulties will disappear if you do not look at them. If you see only the thing you wish to do and hold it steadily and firmly in your mind, refusing to admit any thought that could hinder your purpose and, especially, an idea of failure, the success is sure.

## 61

EVERYONE has a purpose to fulfill in life, which no other can do for them; neither can they fulfill another's purpose.

To ensure harmonious living, each in their own place should work with hands or brain or both, for the good of the whole, of which all are a part.

However great or small the purpose of each life may be, it is equally important to the life of the planet, as each atom in the physical body is important—in its own place—to the physical well-being of that body.

None is higher nor lower than another, though all are different and necessary. Unity is the keynote, not uniformity—which would be meaningless and monotonous—but unity, which creates harmony.

Only thus can there be peace in a world of infinite variety, or physical health in the human body.

## 62

*Whom God teaches not, man cannot.*
*—Gaelic saying*

A teacher everyone can be in some class of life's school,
All who are content to lead and not aspire to rule.
But if each would be what he would teach,
Is there any need to preach?

Walk thyself along the path, if thou would show the way
To those behind who follow, words not for thee to say.
Let thine own life be pure if sin thou wouldn't cure;
Thine acts and thoughts be true if thou wouldst
wrong undo.

Let thine own heart be calm if thou wouldst offer balm.
This is the better way—
To *be*; and let thy silence teach what words can never say.

"Beware, beware; good can choke up a soul as much as evil."

"But if someone does not do it, how can good be done?"

"Live so, live so that, by the sanctity of thy life,
good will be performed involuntarily."[1]

1 "My Brother's Face." (Author unknown)

# 63

*All the world's a stage, and all the men and women merely players.*[1]

*—William Shakespeare*

IF we could behold with God-like vision the end from the beginning, which in reality are not two but one—one in essence, but in manifestation appearing as two—we would know that the great illusion we call *physical existence* is but a drama played upon the stage of life. All important to the players, intensely interesting during the hour of its presentment; but at the end of the play, they all return to the life of reality that was theirs before the play was enacted.

*But maybe someday when the last curtains fall,*
*Perhaps we'll find that life was not the play*
*But just a dress rehearsal after all.*

1 Shakespeare, William, "As You Like It."

# 64

THE ideal of perfection of everything exists in the divine mind of God. The pattern is in the world of ideas. Knowledge of it can be known if this reservoir of mental matter can be contacted, but it will be shaped and colored by the brain of the individual. In that sense only is it original

A mind able to contact this world can bring away as much as it can see, can carry, so to speak; only it must give the form that makes it what is known on earth as original thought.

## 65

IF you take a lump of wax, warm it until it is soft, mold it into various forms, then put these forms into a cool place until they are cold and set, they will retain their form and will remain separate just so long as they can be kept cold. However close they may be to each other, they will retain their separateness and their own particular form. One may be a flower, another a candle, another an image, all having different names and each a different purpose; but all are of the same substance, and the original design or purpose was in the mind of the hand that molded the form.

If you now were to apply warmth to all these separated objects, they would first of all begin to lost their form, and then gradually would all melt and become again the one substance from which they were originally made.

# 66

ALL meditation, occult practice, or striving for self-development are quite useless to help seekers upon the spiritual path in their search for God, unless they can bring down to physical plane activities the teaching they receive in this way upon the inner planes, and live it simply and unobtrusively in ordinary daily life. That is the way, the only way, that is allowable or desirable for anyone upon the path of return to bring, to those within one's circle of influence, a knowledge of the light that is within the self.

More than this would not only be undesirable but would, in some cases, be positively harmful. Teaching, when thus uttered or expressed, may be said to have been learned; but stored up within solely for the benefit of the inner life of a person, it would, instead of helping one forward, become a drag upon one's feet, heavy with the weight of a false ego.

# 67

*In quietness and confidence shall be your strength.*
*—Isaiah 30:15*

THE stillness demanded by the injunction, "Be still and know that I am God,"[1] does not necessarily imply the cessation of outer activities nor any interruption of the ordinary life's work, but an inner stillness, which, once having been attained, cannot be entirely broken; although a short time alone each day, if only for a few minutes, is a necessity in order to maintain that quietness and confidence wherein lies our strength, unshaken amid all the noise and tumult by which we are surrounded.

1 Psalm 46:10.

# 68

*Calm Soul of all things make it mine*
*To feel amid the city's jar;*
*That there exists a peace of Thine*
*Man did not make nor cannot mar.*[1]
*—Matthew Arnold*

WHAT means "The peace of God which passeth understanding?"[2]
How can man know and where doth lie the way?
O traveler who hath found! Wilt thou not say?
The way to peace which passeth knowledge,
The peace you seek to know,
Through mind alone can ne'er be known.
It lieth not in quiet paths, through soft green sward,
Nor far from all life's toil and strife.
He who was called "The Prince of Peace" the secret knew,
He brought a sword![3] And his peace he gave,
"Not as the world giveth"[4]
To those who trod with him the stony way,
And in themselves fought and overcame the enemies to their peace.
Still is the promise sure, to "him who overcometh,"[5]
To him is given the Crown of Life.
'Tis thus, O man, within thyself the way, the only way.
To find the peace of God which passeth understanding.

1 Arnold, Matthew, "Lines Written in Kensington Gardens."
2 Philippians 4:5.
3 Matthew 10:34.
4 John 14:27,
5 Revelations 3:21.

## 69

ONE of the greatest difficulties in the spiritual life is to attain, with complete understanding, the method of continual adjustment of everything life brings to people in their everyday lives.

Whoever has attained poise has also the power to achieve. A person can never be shaken by whatever comes of joy or sorrow but will stand as a rock, against which the waves of confusion and unrest beat in vain. But poise is not a gift; it must be worked for and won by continual effort, by constant watching and readjustment of the life forces within one, that the whole may be kept steady and balanced. Thus can disciples be ready and willing to serve as the master needs their service.

People with poise are dependable servants and can be trusted to carry out faithfully any task given to them until it is finished, without being diverted from that task by any diversion they may meet, nor even by calls for assistance from those around them. All these distractions can be, and often are, used by the shadow side to prevent or delay the master's work, which can only be done efficiently by those who are, at any rate for the time being, one-pointed, determined to carry out the purpose entrusted to them.

People whose great desire is to serve their fellow humans and help raise those who have fallen, should understand that if and when they are chosen for a particular work, it is because they are able to carry out that work, which can only be successfully done if they let nothing interfere with its accomplishment. The more humane and sympathetic they are, the more ready will they be to listen to any cry for aid, even when they are about their master's business. But if they realize that the work given them is their real work, given perhaps, because however unworthy, they are the only available instruments for something that must be done, they will then also realize that whatever and from whatever place other demands are made upon them, they are, for the moment, not for them to consider. The master will send aid to those others in need when the servants are doing their master's work.

# 70

*In the adoration and benediction of righteous men*
*The praises of all the prophets are kneaded together,*
*All their praises are mingled into one stream,*
*All the vessels are emptied into one ewer.*
*Because He that is praised is, in fact, only One.*
*In this respect all religions are only one religion.*
*Because all religions are directed towards God's light,*
*These various forms and figures are borrowed from it.*[1]

—*Jalal al-Din Rumi*

NO religion is an end in itself. All are preparatory, or elementary, systems and necessary means of instruction that everyone needs before they are able to understand the higher teaching enabling them to find the kingdom of heaven within. Not all religions teach in the same way, but all are designed to prepare humanity for the knowledge of truth. And as there is only One Truth, it is not important how nor in what way the lessons are learned, so long as they are learned.

It is, of course, possible for truth to be found without going through the preparatory courses, but this is very rare. Some form of religion is still necessary for the majority and should be established in every country; for where people are gathered together for worship, help and comfort can be found.

1 Jalal al-Din Rumi, *The Masnavi,* trans. E.H. Whinfield (London: Trubner, 1898).

# 71

*And before him shall be gathered all nations; and he shall separate them one from another, as a shepherd divideth sheep from the goats...Then shall he say unto them on the left hand 'Depart from me, ye cursed, into everlasting fire, prepared for the devil and his angels'...And these shall go away into everlasting punishment, but the righteous unto life eternal.*

*—Matthew 25:21, 32, 46*

WHAT is the real meaning of this teaching? It is a symbolic description of a happening in the human soul or the soul of a nation, where evil has been allowed to enter in and take possession there.

Thoughts are living entities, and undesirable thoughts must be destroyed by those who created them. The creators of the evil rife in the world today—authors of the lust for power, cruelty, and other foul things filling the world with horrors unspeakable and more deadly than anything since the beginning of humankind—must reap as they have sown; and will, when brought before the bar of justice, be judged and condemned by their own thoughts, to remain in the prison of their own creating until they have learned how to undo the suffering they have caused to their fellow humans before being allowed to try again to become decent members of the human race. They must learn, in other classes of the school of life, the lesson they have refused to learn or apply to daily life, particularly the lesson that everyone must, sooner or later, learn: that of the family in God, the Father of all. This must be learned and practiced before these unhappy ones can begin to tread the long path of the soul's return and realize, in the oneness of all life, that the human being is one with God.

"Woe unto the world because of offenses! For it must need be that offenses come, but woe unto that man by whom the offenses cometh!"[1]

When the human bodies, or garments worn by the soul, are so defiled and filthy that they cannot be cleansed, they must be destroyed or disintegrated; but the souls and minds will live in the world of their own making until they undo all the evil they have created.

> *God is not mocked; For whatsoever a man soweth that shall he also reap.*
>
> *—Galatians 6:7*

1 Matthew 18:7.

# 72

*I am come that they may have life*
*and have it more abundantly.*
*—John 10:10*

THIS life-giving power, which Jesus came to give, is for all the bodies that constitute a human being, particularly the mental body where thoughts are generated.

Thoughts can be so weak as to be stillborn, and therefore useless, or can be full of vitality and become living things. People themselves are thought into being by God and, being made in God's image, have also the potential power of creative thought.

Our thoughts, if reinforced by the love of Christ, can become powerful and mighty to heal and to help suffering humanity. There is, however, the other side of thought-power, which can produce evil and, if allowed to grow uncontrolled, may become a great force of destruction and chaos.

Both good and evil thoughts multiple quickly and, as like seeks like, they soon become great armies of good and of evil beings in the unseen world made of human thoughts, and reinforced and upheld there by them. Take heed, therefore, what thoughts you create and allow by reinforcement to become powerful.

# 73

*The passport to the life of the spirit is the completed earthly task.*

THE great ones who are serving humanity on the inner planes and guiding human evolution need the help and cooperation—the willing cooperation—of human beings; for God speaks to us on the physical plane through the lips of human beings.

Truly the harvest is great, but the laborers are few. Many offer themselves for the master's work, and indeed believe they are doing it, and yet they do not progress very far. The harvest is still waiting to be reaped and garnered, and made into food for which the people are hungering.

God has prepared the harvest, but people must do this part in preparing the food. Help is sent from God to those in need through God's messengers, and by them through the dwellers upon earth who are willing to be tuned to receive and transmit their messages. But they must be available, ready when needed to answer and transmit the call without delay; otherwise they would be useless for such work, which requires instant response to a demand. Much of the transmitting is done during sleep, "He giveth His beloved during their sleep,"[1] but the ready response and immediate carrying out of any given task must be learned in the everyday life of the world.

Many people today are impatient of training of any sort, and yet, without life's elementary training, how can they be trusted with work on the inner planes needing absolute accuracy, sustained patience, and single-mindedness? The first

1 Psalm 127:2 as translated by Martin Luther.

essential lessons that must be learned by all who aspire to work in the fields of God, are those which must be learned in the school of life—not only learned, but mastered, before there can be any progress in the inner life or any real use made of those who aspire and whose great desire is to heal and to help suffering humanity.

It may be thought that meditation, concentration and self-development are more important. These things are undoubtedly necessary and most helpful in assisting one to attain self-control and self-mastery, but the lessons must be learned first. And before one can be trusted with the master's work, an aspirant must be tested by them, not for the sake of the testing but for the aspirant's own safety.

First, there must be singleness of heart. Any work undertaken must be put first, and nothing allowed to interfere with its accomplishment. Unless a person is willing and able, while carrying out a particular task, to be thus one-pointed, it is useless to proceed. The master must have dependable workers who can be trusted to carry out any given instructions; and how can the reliability and dependability of anyone be tested other than by the little ordinary things life teaches, such as patience, fortitude, fidelity, carrying out until finished whatever is undertaken, however insignificant. It is not the importance, or otherwise, of the work that matters, but its achievement.

These essential lesson, which must be mastered before anyone can be trusted with work on the inner planes, are not in compliance with an arbitrary rule, but for the protection of the workers when brought into contact with spiritual forces of which they have no knowledge.

*He that is faithful in that which is least, is faithful also in much.*
*—Luke 16:10*

# 74

*The profit of the earth is for all; the king himself is served by the field.*

*—Ecclesiastes 5:9*

IN the new age, which is even now emerging from the old, the plan to be tried is that of a community of nations intended, eventually, to include all nations.

The passing age has failed lamentably in cooperation in every phase of human life, even in the workshop of God, and instead has taken for its watchword, "everyone for themselves," disregarding the claim of others and of their weaker neighbors' inability to defend themselves from aggressions or to obtain a fair share of the earth's produce. This has, unfortunately, been the ruling motive among nations, groups of people and individuals, although there have always been, and still are, many selfless people and groups who have endeavored to serve humanity without thought of self-interest. But these have been in the minority, too few to balance the selfishness of the great majority and adjust the balance of justice between right and wrong.

The result of this has been a vast accumulation of evil thoughts, which have been added to through centuries by all sorts and conditions of people in every part of the world, until it has become concentrated into a force powerful enough entirely to destroy it.

However, at last it has been recognized, even by those who have so long been blinded by self-interest, that in order to live in security and freedom themselves, others must also be made secure; also that the evil force must be fought where it has been centralized at any expense, even of life itself, in order that civilization may be saved. Many are beginning to see that this evil must be fought within themselves, as well as against the enemies of freedom on the battlefields. To those in whom spiritual insight is awakening, the earth's travail may be seen as a dire necessity. For, as in a physical body pain is a warning of danger to the health or even the life of that body, so the pain and suffering by which humanity is now almost overwhelmed is needed to awaken the world to behold its own danger before it is too late to avoid entire annihilation, which, unless it is fought and overcome, would certainly be brought about.

To all who are fighting for the good of humanity, either in the inner or in the outer sphere of conflict, the message is given: Be of good courage; "Fear none of those things which thou shalt suffer...be thou faithful unto death and I will give thee a crown of life."[1]

---

1 Revelations 2:10.

# 75

WE must work for peace on earth and goodwill toward all, without ceasing, however long it may take to achieve. The time may seem unending to us who are limited by time, but looked at from the viewpoint of eternity, it may appear different. "For a thousand years in Thy sight are but as yesterday when it is past, and as a watch in the night."[1] So from that angle, it is perhaps not so surprising that the teaching given by Jesus nearly two thousand years ago, for peace upon earth and goodwill toward all, should not even yet be practiced. We shall probably never know the result of any effort for peace we may make, any more than the tools used by a master hand for work can know or see the result of that work, although without the tools it could not have been accomplished.

Master workers in the realm of the mind, as in mechanized workshops, need tools to enable them to work according to plans that cannot be executed without them. And although the tools must be well and truly made, strong as tried steel, they are of no special importance when the work for which they were made is finished. It is the work that matters, not the tools used to create it. So although all our efforts and thoughts for world peace may seem to us to achieve nothing, sometime, long after our day, they may be used by a master builder to form part of a structure necessary to complete a plan and, in that sense, are of great importance.

1 Psalm 90:4.

# 76

*For as the body is one, and hath many members, and all the members of that one body, being many, are one body; so also is Christ.*

*—1 Corinthians 12:12*

AT this time of world travail, the testing time of nations and also of every person, nothing matters so much as one's service to one's fellow human. And now is the opportunity given, as never before, to those on the path of discipleship and of aspirants on that path, to give out wherever and to whomsoever possible, the result of the teaching they have received.

This will mean that their own progress will be entirely forgotten in the all-absorbing work of service in ordinary everyday life, which once may have seemed so uninteresting but can now be recognized, by all who have eyes to see, as the place and the way in which the master's work can and must be done. They will, when completely awakened, realize the great privilege of following, however far behind, the way trodden by the Master of masters, and know it as the real path of discipleship leading to God, wherein they can praise "the God of all comfort; who comforteth us in all our tribulation, that we may be able to comfort them which are in any trouble, by the comfort wherewith we ourselves are comforted of God."[1]

1 2 Corinthians 1:3-4.

# 77

A PARTIAL explanation of the reason for so much suffering is that the Earth planet is in travail because a new age is being born; and every living being partakes in some degree of its suffering. As all are part of the One Whole, it is inevitable, but the end is near, hence the increased pain. Deliverance will surely come.

The plan is that the new age shall be one of unity and fellowship for all humanity; but to ensure this, much, very much evil and corruption in the hearts and minds of the people must be entirely eliminated. This is being done wherever people cooperate with the will of God and open their hearts to the all-pervading love of Christ, the teacher of angels and humans.

As in a physical birth of a person, a new age is born an infant, not fully grown; therefore it must be guided until its maturity, which takes time.

The help of all men and women of goodwill on earth is, and will be, needed for this work, as also on the inner plane.

Today the opportunity is offered to all would-be servers, known or unknown (unknown of people, but known to the master), to join the fellowship of service to humanity.

# 78

A MODEL of the plans for world government in the new age has long been on the mental plane. Many people have sensed them and written books on the subject, some known and some unknown.

Such plans are always prepared during the last century of an age, so that they may be received on earth before the birth of a new age.

The plans, when received, are all colored and molded by the brains of the various recipients; thus they are different in form and words, although the ideas are the same.

When the time is ripe, all the various forms, from many sources all over the world, will be received and sorted by a master mind on the physical plane who will give a complete system of world government in the master mind's own way, either by writing or speaking. The others have been, and still are, collecting the material from which the master mind can select the most useful to work into the world plan as a whole, which must have humanity's cooperation.

This work will necessarily take some time to materialize and to overcome the opposition and prejudice, as it must be overcome, from people who dislike change of any kind. Without movement there is no life.

The new age will be an age of light and life for all people, eventually.

# 79

*Behold, the Lord's hand is not shortened, that it cannot save; neither his ear heavy, that it cannot hear; but your iniquities have separated between you and your God, and your sins have hid his face from you, that he will not hear.*

*—Isaiah 59:1*

THERE are already signs of the dawn of a new age. It is a red dawn, for before the beginning of any age there is always a time of great desolation, bloodshed and the breaking of every kind of form. This is inevitable. If an edifice is rotten, it must be pulled down and destroyed before another and better one can be built to take its place.

It is the same with nations and continents. This has happened many times in the world's history and is what is taking place now. There is so much that must be destroyed before the sun of the coming age can rise, breaking through the clouds of night.

The teaching given by Jesus the Christ nearly two thousand years ago has not yet made the world realize that humanity—all people, not only the followers of Jesus—is one fellowship in the family of God, because, as a whole, it has not practiced it. Many temples and churches have been built in every land to commemorate and spread Christ's gospel of love, and gold without stint has been laid upon their altars; but still people have not understood, except the few whose words were not heeded. Instead, humans have fought grievous wars against each other in the name of religion, and have tortured and burnt alive many who refused to accept the Christian creed of one particular church as the only way of salvation, thinking and truly believing that in that way they were doing the work that the master left his followers to carry out. This seems strange when one remembers his teaching, which is entirely opposed to such methods. Cruelty and coercion could never win people to worship God, Who is love.

Gradually, century by century, a god of force, created by evil and twisted thoughts, has usurped the throne of love, until today the god of force is demanding greater and greater sacrifices to be laid upon its altar. And rivers of blood are flowing around its throne, into which are being cast men, women and little children to feed an unholy lust for cruelty, oppression and torture.

But now, at the coming of dawn, people are stirring in their sleep. The eyes of those closed so long are beginning to open. Their ears, deaf for centuries, are listening to the cries for aid of their fellow humans. Their hearts, stifled by the accumulation of ages of wrong thinking, gathered by the mind and blocking the entrance, are beginning to feel, although perhaps in some cases unconsciously, the love of God that Jesus came to teach, as a light shining in the darkness. They are arising in thousands, throwing off their cloaks of selfishness and sloth, and as one vast army from all corners of the earth, are going forth to war, as the knights of tradition went forth, to slay the dragon of evil seeking to destroy their souls and lay waste the lands of their ancestors.

Theirs is a hard and bitter task and a great fight, for arrayed against them is the whole army of the forces of evil, and no quarter can be given to those fighting under that banner. It must be, it will be, a fight to the death, but the hands of those fighting for the right against might will be strengthened by the will to conquer, inasmuch as they try to "loose the bands of wickedness to undo the heavy burden and let the opposed go free," "to deal their bread to the hungry and bring the poor that are cast out to their home." "Then shall they call and the

Lord will answer,"[1] and "When the enemy shall come in like a flood, the Spirit of the Lord shall lift up a standard against him."[2]

Those who endure to the end shall have great reward. "They shall build the old waste places; shall raise up the foundations of many generations, and shall be called the repairers of the breach, the restorers of paths to dwell in."[3]

> *Thus saith the Lord God; "In the day that I shall have cleansed you from all your iniquities, I will also cause you to dwell in the cities, and the wastes shall be builded."*
>
> *—Ezekiel 36:33*

1 Isaiah 58: 6-7,9.
2 Isaiah 59:19.
3 Isaiah 58:12.

# 80

*Hatred stirreth up strife; but love covereth all sins.*
*—Proverbs 10:12*

WHATEVER a person sends forth from the heart returns as a boomerang to the sender, if not immediately, still none the less surely, either soon or late. Hate cannot be overcome by hate. This is a truth that can never be violated without, in some way, hurting the one who hates. And yet because of the evil things in the world today, how can this deadly thing be overcome, as it must be by some means, or the whole earth will become poisoned.

Jesus said, "I say unto you, love your enemies, bless them that curse you, do good to them that hate you,"[1] but except in a few cases, this seems an impossibility to the millions of people who have been, and still are, suffering every kind of persecution and oppression: loss of country, of families and homes, who have been made into slaves and worse than slaves. But if the whole world is filled with clouds of hatred, how can there be peace for anyone anywhere, living in such an atmosphere?

There is only one way to overcome hatred: by its opposite, love. This does not mean that the oppressed peoples must love their oppressors—this, at their present stage of evolution, they cannot do—but that the clouds of hate must be neutralized by clouds of love. Some way must be found to generate enough love to neutralize the terrible thought forms now in the world. These can, of course, in a short time be

1 Matthew 5:44.

disintegrated and rendered harmless to humanity; but the forms made by evil thoughts of hatred and revenge, and worse things than these, live long after their creators have left the earth. To find the means to destroy the poison they have been, and still are, generating is a task for all who are working for the good of humanity, on the earth and also on the inner plane. Love is the only antidote for this poison, which must be given by human beings. The elders of the race are pouring it out incessantly, but without the help and cooperation of men and women on the earth, it is not enough.

The power of love is able to balance all the evil let loose in the world today, and will do so if enough people believe in it sufficiently to practice it and to pray without ceasing, which can be done by anyone anywhere. No special place is necessary. It does not matter where nor when we pray, but how. Prayer with faith is a mighty force from hearts where love is, and can be used to balance the evil of hate, which is in danger of poisoning the world.

All people of goodwill who have understanding of the power of thought can give valuable help if they will build up thoughts of sympathy for all who are suffering and thoughts of healing for the sick and wounded, which can be done by strong and steady thought. Vague or sentimental thought will achieve very little, if anything.

Sympathy must be shown by deeds as well as thought. The hungry must be fed, the naked must be clothed, the homeless and the orphans cared for and the sick nursed back to health. This can be done by those who have the understanding heart and, therefore, know that all humankind, however grievous their faults and shortcoming, are nevertheless all children of one God; and if any are left to starve and suffer without succor, all the world will suffer with them.

Whenever there is danger of evil becoming strong enough to overpower good, as at the present time of the world's upheaval, help is sent from the inner planes to those who will accept it, to vitalize the seeds of love that are latent in every human being. But they must cooperate willingly with the all-pervading love of Christ and ask for the help, or they cannot receive it. A person is free to choose, but if enough people respond to the love force, which can be reinforced by the elders, the terrible power of hate now rife in the world can be neutralized, and civilization go forward into the new age more quickly than would otherwise be possible.

As light is more powerful than darkness, that even a candle can dispel it, so is love more powerful than evil. And if a comparatively small number of selfless people are responsive to the light, they can radiate enough to dispel the darkness that is covering the earth.

## 81

THE past is but a sad or happy dream,
The future unreal as pictures shown upon a screen;
The present only, can be lived in, known and seen.
Yet, from the past our present hath took shape,
As from the present we our future make.
And from both past and present must be won
Time's secret knowledge that these three are one.

*Forget the past, think not of the future, mind the now.*
*—Inayat Khan*

# 82

LIFE goes on and on like a wheel, from birth to death and from death to birth. The things we feel so serious are as nothing to the great ones. When you have the outer crust of your soul broken, the fine things can reach the center of your heart; then life becomes joyous and all life is beautiful. But the path is an upward path until the gate is found, and then many moons ere the latch is lifted. Having entered the path, you begin the way of return. Many troubles and tribulations beset, but courage will be your watchword. Hold the head high, you will find your teacher—called *master*, *murshid*, *guru*, what you will—waiting at every difficult corner. The teacher will give you to drink of the waters of life, and ambrosia fruits to ease your hunger.

The journey will not weary you, because you will have found your nirvana in the all-seeing light, in the all-protecting arms. Verily, the reward is great for those who care enough to press on. Love finds the way always, true spiritual love in a world of cares and darkened by war clouds. The voice shall say, "Fear not." It will sound as a silver trumpet. Press on and do your work and give a cheering word to your neighbors. Happiness and true fellowship are coming for the nations of the world; all that has been written will be fulfilled, and people shall work peacefully as it is said in the scriptures, "Dwell safely every man under his vine and under his fig tree,"[1] and we shall see it fulfilled. There can be work for all according to ability. More land cultivation will give work to many; and in

1 Micah 4:4.

time, places to train the unemployable will be arranged, for joy and love must be brought to all, whatever their condition.

Life is a strange game; how to play it with a smile? Each day a new beginning; an open and kindly heart, and willing service must be brought.

Lift your eyes up to the hills. You will find spiritual things and answer to your questions. There also the "peace of the flowing air, the peace of the running wave,"[2] and the deep peace that passeth all understanding.

2 Gaelic blessing.

## From the Silence

MAKE Thou my heart like unto a recording disc that receives impressions of melody upon itself and gives forth the same to those who desire to hear, but is equally unconscious of that which is received and of that which it gives forth.

Many people may listen to spoken words, but not everyone will recognize the voice of the speaker.

If you are treading the balanced path and can keep the center steady, then, as you aspire and can go forward, so will the power and activity increase on both sides.

Seek peace and joy; prepare for these the guest chamber; thus shall fear pass by your dwelling place.

It is possible to allow yourself to be used as a public house, where every kind of people walk in and out at will. Or you may be as an enclosed garden, where only invited guests of the owner are allowed to enter.

I have seen darkness, I have seen light, and now I know they both are one.

Love cannot be known in its fullness until control of the emotions is absolute.

Fear nothing, resent nothing.

If you can face and accept adversity, it will become your friend.

Faith can create from it own "substance of things unseen" whatsoever is desired.[1]

---

1 Hebrews 11:1.

If the shell of a coconut remains unbroken, the food it contains cannot be eaten.

Only in silence, deep and long, can I voice my true thanksgiving song.

Man is an expression of God, as a poem is an expression of a poet, or a picture of an artist, or a statue an expression of a sculptor.

Giving up our will means giving up a slight power for fusion with the great and all-powerful will of God.

May my mind become empty of fixed ideas, and my heart as an empty cup, that it may be filled with the wine of wisdom.

Religions and messengers of God must have a name and form for use in a formal world, but what do forms matter to those who have eyes to see reality underlying all forms: the One and Only Being? Nevertheless, names and forms are necessary for half-awakened and blind eyes.

We can never know ourselves as part of God until we first realize that every person is part of ourselves, and that we are part of every person.

It is in the ordinary, sometimes uninteresting, daily life that those who follow Jesus must bear the cross; not in some inner or occult (so-called) experiences, but amid the accumulated events with which we have to deal with our fellow humans every day.

The physical body is a form the soul uses to gain experience for the real self. When all experiences have been passed on, the form is no longer important.

When the field has been ploughed and the seed sown, what matter who reaps the harvest so long as the hungry are fed?

The heart is sealed by the desires of self. The one who would hear the voice of God must have courage to break the seal.

# At the Gate of Discipleship

# Foreword

*The words that I speak unto you,*
*they are Spirit, and they are life.*
*—John 6:63*

THE words of a messenger of God are living words, they can never die. They live to inspire, to give life to all whose rate of vibration enables them to respond, and may be interpreted in many ways; but even thousands of years after their utterance, will never fail to awaken response from one whose heart is tuned to receive them.

Words of life, words of power, words of consolation, words of healing, words of understanding, words of forgiveness, words of peace; these constitute the wisdom language spoken by all those who carry the message of God to humanity. It is called by mystics *the language of the heart.* And saints and sages of whatever religion, in all ages and in all lands, recognize and communicate with each other by means of this mystic language, known to and used by the fellowship of wisdom.

Blessed is the one to whom it is spoken.

June 1924

*Enter the path! there spring the healing streams*
*Quenching all thirst! there bloom th' immortal flowers*
*Carpeting all the way with joy! there throng swiftest and*
*sweetest hours!*

—*Edwin Arnold*
The Light of Asia

# 1

THE teaching of the saints and sages, that one upon the path of discipleship must surrender all of self and purify the heart of all save God, appears to many who are not yet prepared to tread that path a hard and difficult doctrine. It does, no doubt, seem a gospel of perfection, impossible of attainment by the ordinary person; but this is because they are looking at it from a wrong angle, viewing such a life as a constant renunciation, by obedience to the will of God, of something they wish to keep.

A seer has said eternal life is "the life of spirit without a body, it is attained by love, not by obedience."[1] Herein lies the secret: the essence of love is self-surrender. A great love cannot fail to eliminate self. Sacrifice by a mother for her child would be no sacrifice, not even the surrender of life itself. To the lover of God, nothing is worth a moment's thought that would stand as a barrier between the soul and the object of its desire. "When divine aspiration appears all desires melt away."[2] The human soul, while living on earth, knows itself in its immortal being, an exile ever seeking its source, the One Life of which it is part; but on the surface of life as a dweller in the body, it identifies itself with its humanity, which is fighting to retain an individuality and realize itself as a separate immortal being. This is the great illusion, the shadow in which humanity lives, until by love—inherent in

1 Sharaf al-Din Maneri, *Letters From a Sufi Teacher*. trans. Baijnath Singh (London: Theosophical Publishing Society 1909). p. 58.
2 Ibid. p, 45.

every heart—the fetters are broken by which the false self imprisons the soul, and it passes out of darkness into light.

The life of God, which ensouls every living thing from atom to human, must return to God. In reality, it has never left God; the human soul, one end of a ray of light, the other end God. When the realization of this truth comes to one—not knowledge but realization—the sole desire dominating everything else in life is to forget the small limited self in which one is restricted on every side by claims of the false ego; to reach the source of one's being and claim one's real inheritance: unlimited, eternal life, in which is perfect freedom. For verily, the human soul ever seeks its source as the river seeks the sea.

Whoever would understand the mysteries of life must search the scripture written by the hand of God: the book of nature, which will never fail to enlighten an awakened soul.

O! days and years of fleeting time what are ye?
*We are separated parts of eternity.*

Whither are ye going?
*Down the corridors of time to lose ourselves, where time is not.*

O ! restless rushing river what seekest thou?"
*I seek the ocean of my desire, to lose myself in its rhythmic ebb and flow.*

O! soul of man, thou too are restless, what seekest thou?
*I seek the source of my being, that as man I may cease to be.*

## 2

THE many warnings given and instructions written about the difficulties of the path do not produce any feeling of discouragement in disciples. They know the dangers and difficulties are but the exercises life gives in order to produce spiritual strength, and are given only in response to the demands of the disciples themselves for progress and efficiency. Even in the material world it is recognized that one cannot win a race depending upon the development of physical strength unless one trains and disciplines the body. One who is truly traveling in search of God is willing to face any difficulties upon the path, in order that the inner senses shall be developed, the eyes opened to perceive, and the ears opened to understand "The things which God has prepared for them that love Him."[1] The traveler knows that "weeping may endure for a night, but joy cometh in the morning."[2] In the dawn of a new day joy will meet each traveler upon the path to God, and the bliss of that meeting cannot be described; but one moment of such bliss is worth the whole long, toilsome journey with all its difficulties and dangers, for here time is not measured by days and years. "Beloved, be not ignorant of this one thing, that one day is with the Lord as a thousand years."[3]

> *To the strong difficulties are joy, and when they are conquered their strength passes into the conqueror.*[4]
>
> *—L. Adams Beck*

1 1 Corinthians 2:9.
2 Psalm 35.
3 2 Peter 3:8.
4 Beck, L. Adams, *The Key of Dreams: A Romance of the Orient.* (New York: Dodd, Mead, 1922). p. 241.

## 3

*Verily, verily, I say unto you, I am the door of the sheep.*
*—John 10:7*

IT is not easy for an aspirant to pass through the gate of discipleship; the gate itself is difficult to find. It must be sought and found alone, for in this task no one's help is possible, and when found, the disciple must pass through in silence.

There are many gates upon the path. The real one can be discovered by the light of intuition. Many are the mysteries surrounding it, for it is not stationary in one particular place so that pilgrims may be given a plan showing the way, or directed and guided thereto. Although there are many who think they are capable of guiding others, one moment it is seen in one place and the next in quite a different one. In reality, it is in the heart of the disciple and made objective by the disciple's creative thought, so that for each traveler its appearance is different; and yet there is but one entrance through which all aspirants to discipleship must enter. It is known only to the keeper of the gate, who passes through; to none other, not even to the disciples themselves in their physical consciousness, until they have been able to unify it with the higher consciousness that enables them to see with the light of true knowledge.

# 4

THERE is today much discussion about discipleship and the path, but very few know the reality of either; and those who do know are silent concerning it. True disciples are very hard to recognize, for they claim nothing and would never seek to appear in the eyes of others as different from ordinary people. If any power was developed within them, they would not speak of it to others but would regard it as a most sacred and secret trust. In outer life they are as others and may be a follower of any religion or of none, but in the inner life they are known as seekers of God. And the only thing that has any value for them is the search that, to a sincere disciple, is the vital reality beside which all else is unreal. This does not imply that ordinary life, with all its duties and responsibilities, is neglected. Not one responsibility can be avoided, not one duty left undone, not only the difficult and unpleasant ones but the easy and pleasant ones also. A seeker of God realizes that God must be sought through every condition and in every experience of life, for only through this constant seeking, with oneness of heart, will the realization come that there is no place in all the world, either great or small, high or low, good or bad, in joy or in sorrow, where God is not; that every atom in the universe is pervaded with God's life and upheld by God's love. But such a realization cannot be conveyed to another. For each one there is a different experience, which is for oneself alone.

The vision of God is known to those who understand the true meaning of singleness of heart, for the heart is one and can only receive one reflection at a time.

*The light of the body is the eye, if therefore thine eye be single, thy whole body shall be full of light.*
*—Matthew 6:22*

# 5

*Mind is the surface of heart, and heart is the depth of mind.*[1]
—*Inayat Khan*

BY a right understanding of this, the disciple will see how necessary it is that the accumulation of mental matter is cleared from the surface, in order that the heart, which is the abode of God, may be prepared to receive God. All the contents of mind received through the brain are useful while one is working on the surface, but when one begins to prepare for the birth of the Christ in the heart, "Until Christ be formed in you,"[2] one must see to it that all waste material be removed and only that which one wills shall remain. The disciple must, so to speak, make a clear pathway by which one is able to retire at will to the depths of one's being, and yet leave sufficient covering upon the surface that the entrance may be guarded.

The inner meaning of this teaching can be received by meditation; it cannot be given in words, which are but veils used to cover truth.

1 Inayat Khan, *The Gayan*.

2 Galatians 4:19.

# 6

A MASTER, one who has attained mastery upon the balanced path, has risen above the law of the pairs of opposites. The ordinary person cannot experience one without the other, can never know light without darkness on any plane until one has transcended the personality or false ego; for so long as one identifies with it, it will stand before the light that the true ego is seeking, and so create darkness by its own shadow. If people could realize that all darkness is caused by their own thoughts, which have built up this false ego, they would begin to withdraw their thoughts from things material and temporal, and strive to realize the part of themselves that is spiritual and eternal. Thus would the shadow grow smaller and smaller until it was dispelled by the light of their real selves. Balance can only be attained by experience and knowledge of both the real and the unreal, the light and the shadow.

> *Those of pure deeds in whom sin has come to an end, they, freed from the delusive pairs of opposites worship Me, steadfast in vows.*
>
> — *Bhagavad Gita*

A master upon this path understands that truth lies in paradox, and through the master's own experience knows that whoever would find light must walk through the gateway of shadows; that the mystery of sound is revealed in the silence; that the blessing of peace must be sought through the gate of sacrifice; that joy may abide in the house of pain; that knowledge walks upon the way of ignorance; and that only through the gate of time can humanity reach the eternal.

Whoever can reach these stages upon the road of life, remain in each until one has gained the necessary experience and then pass on, has mastered life and death.

# 7

THE secret of mastery and the object of humanity's creation is that one shall be able to stand in the middle kingdom or walk upon the waters, which lie between earth and heaven, to obtain mastery of both by controlling the kingdoms that lie below, and by rising at will to those that are above. The human being who is able to walk upon these waters can be surrounded by water and not be drowned by water, can live upon earth and not be buried by earth, can walk through fire and not be consumed by fire, and can breathe the air of heaven and yet not be held by heaven. But the first element to be controlled is water. In the mysteries of life, water represents the whole emotional and sensational life of humanity; and its waves must never rise above the feet of one who would obtain mastery of self. One must be able to stand above it with power to still its waves, which must never overwhelm but must be always under one's control or under one's feet.

When the aspirant has gained this control, the aspirant can also obtain the mastery of earth, which means power to control the physical body, its needs and demands. Mastery of heaven is gained by concentration and aspiration, which give power to free the thoughts so that they may be able to soar even through the gates of heaven and return at the will of the master, still singing their song of freedom. To be master of fire means control of life and death. To attain this, the aspirant must die before death, or lose the personal self in God. When neither life nor death has any dominion, the aspirant is "dead indeed unto sin, but alive unto God."[1]

1 Romans 6:11.

# 8

UNLESS the master has visited the heart of a disciple, the master could never be recognized in a physical body, even if a master were to walk the streets of your city, speak in your churches and halls, or even be entertained under your roof. All these things one might do and still remain unseen and unknown, although you may think the master is known unto you.

> *And hereby we know that we know him, if we keep his commandments; he that saith, I know him, and keepeth not his commandments is a liar, and the truth is not in him.*
>
> —*John 2:3–4*

# 9

EVERY action or situation in life can be made a help or a hindrance in the inner life of a disciple. To some extent this is true for every person, but to one who has begun to tread the return path it is very definitely and especially so. The teaching of the sages that the path is in yourself is thus understood: everyone upon this path must solve their own problems and their own peculiar difficulties in their own way, and for each these would be different, even although in some cases apparently the same. No person can solve another's problem. The solutions to the questions life holds before the human soul are not fixed and definite, nor set as an examination that all students must pass. Each one, as it arises, must be met and conquered within before it can be understood without; for the outer form is but a reflection of the inner truth, without which it could have no existence.

> *That only which we have within can we see within. If we meet no gods it is because we harbour none.*[1]
>
> —*Ralph Waldo Emerson*

1 Emerson, Ralph Waldo, "The Conduct of Life."

# 10

NO one can become a disciple upon the path to God until they have realized the non-importance of worldly knowledge. This does not mean that it should not be acquired; it is essential while living the outer life but must not be used as a guide for the inner life. To tread the path of return involves a complete turning round or turning away. Therefore, all that before seemed so important is now forgotten or left behind; but it must first be known, otherwise it would still be before and not behind the disciple. "The knowledge of all the sages culminates in the realization that they do not know."[1]

It is the culmination of knowledge that is important, not ignorance of it. When this stage of realization is reached, it is understood that self-knowledge is the only knowledge that will enlighten the seeker of God. And in turning round and facing the inner or real self, the seeker will receive illumination and, in the words of a Sufi teacher, will know that "It is thy existence that veils thee. Had there been the veil of a single activity, it could be uplifted by another opposite activity. But the whole of thyself being a veil, thou canst not be fit for divine vision unless, and until, thou vanish completely."[2]

1 Sharaf al-Din Maneri, *Letters from a Sufi Teacher.*
2 Ibid.

# 11

ANY experience the human soul contacts during its life in the world is a valuable lesson. Whether the experiences are pleasurable or painful, good or bad, they all contain important teaching; but on no account should they be indulged in after the lesson has been learned. In all the bodies of a person, both seen and unseen, continual and constant changes are taking place. Nothing is motionless that has life, and as life is in every atom of the universe, there is motion or change in every part, although uncomprehended by humanity.

Directly an experience is retained beyond the necessary period, then it generates a poison that affects the whole life and sometimes necessitates a very painful process of detachment from that experience.

It is most important for a disciple upon the spiritual path to realize the inner meaning of this teaching. Through a right understanding of it one will be able to solve many problems that would otherwise appear unsolvable.

# 12

EVERY action in the daily life of a disciple who has set foot upon the spiritual path and is striving to live the life of the spirit, should be made an offering to God. Disciples need not live a life apart from others; neither need they, in the outer life, appear different from others. But within themselves, their every act should be consecrated. It is not that they must only perform holy or sacred deeds, but that, in their thoughts, the ordinary, everyday duties should be offered as a sacrifice and be carried out in such a way that others may benefit rather than themselves. This is the real consecrated life and, if constantly practiced, will give the consciousness of the presence of God. Every act not thus consecrated or offered becomes an illusion and stands in the path of the disciple, blocking the view. This causes a bewilderment, as the disciple cannot now see the next step the feet should tread. And what before was perfectly clear to one's vision becomes confused by the clouds of doubt caused by illusion, which, unless they are dispelled, will entirely prevent further progress, as instead of pressing onward, one will continually trace and retrace the steps already taken.

Of course, people throughout the whole of their lives are surrounded by every kind of illusion; they could not otherwise live in this world of illusion. But those who can, by the power of God, realize and understand its nature, can always dispel the clouds which surround them by the light within their own souls.

# 13

IN every human heart there is the seed of goodness and truth, however covered over with weeds; but in order that this seed may grow, it must be believed in. Without this belief it can never grow. No matter how wicked some may be, if a firm belief in their goodness can be held steadily, they must, in time, respond; because the atoms of a person's subtle bodies always group themselves to the pattern held before the soul. In the same way, of course, if no one believes in the possibility of another's goodness, one cannot even believe in oneself; and the pattern presented to view being always wickedness, that person remains wicked.

It is, of course, difficult for ordinary people to believe in the buried goodness of another who is always acting wickedly, but by a close study of life, you will find that even the vilest person will show some kind thought or action if loved or believed in by only one person; even the love of an animal is able to call it forth.

The God-realized understand this and never condemn. Their way of dealing with the wicked would be to hold such a strong picture of the good to which it is possible for the wicked to attain that, in time, the atoms of their bodies would regroup themselves, and the wickedness would fall from them like a mantle for which they had no more use. For the God-realized it would be no effort thus to hold a picture, for from the heart in which God abides, nothing but good can be mirrored upon any other soul.

# 14

SORROW and happiness, pleasure and pain are the means used to awaken humanity from its long sleep in the prison house of material possessions. Humans must wake ere they can realize their condition of exile and rise to free themselves from the bonds that bind them and the lethargy with which the soul is drugged.

The means used to create emotion in the heart, either pleasurable or painful, is for the purpose of producing response: to make it so sensitive to vibration that it must, of necessity, seek harmonious conditions. The real use of emotion is to tune the heart to the keynote of the soul, in order that it may hear the voice of God. When this has been accomplished, the means used are of no further use and, if retained beyond this period, will cause discord. Of course, it requires the eye of a seer really to see this truth, but some degree of understanding may be attained by those who seek to tread the path of wisdom if they will endeavor to realize that nothing of itself, either good or bad, matters to the soul. The result produced is the only reality.

# 15

LIKE seeks like, and love begets love. In these ordinary, everyday phrases there is hidden a great truth. Directly the Christ has been born in any human heart, that person is capable of recognizing Christ in all others with whom one comes in contact; for the seed of such a birth is in everyone and can thus be discovered and also helped to expand, but it can only be seen by the eyes of Christ looking through the human heart. The God-realized person, in whom is the indwelling spirit of Christ, acts as a magnet; for as steel that has itself been magnetized can magnetize other steel, so can the magnetism of gaze of such a person draw to the surface the good hidden in the depths of the soul of whomsoever is gazed upon. For those who have themselves realized God in their own hearts cannot fail also to realize God in the hearts of every human being, however veiled by coverings of error. But although the God-realized can, for the moment, draw to the surface the hidden Christ in the heart of another, unless that other were continually in their atmosphere it would be liable to fall again into the depths from which it was, by recognition, called forth. It is only this recognition that can call it from the darkness into light; when deep calls unto deep the response is inevitable. It is for this reason that in the East the presence of holy ones is sought by those desiring to live the life of the spirit.

When Jesus was on earth, multitudes followed him from place to place; because in his presence they felt what perhaps never in their lives before they had felt: the stirring in the depths of their hearts of the living Christ.

# 16

THE only way that progress on the spiritual path is possible is by service to humanity, and it is just because of this that disciples have so many difficulties to meet. Insight and great understanding are needed, for unless they can see with the inner vision, this means of progress may become a stumbling block to their feet. If it is taken as a means of progress, it is useless as far as the disciples are concerned, though no doubt helpful to whatsoever or whomsoever the service is rendered. Words are not very helpful here; this teaching can only be comprehended by inner understanding. The service that is acceptable to the master is that of which the personality is not conscious. Actions that are passed over unnoticed, because seemingly unimportant and quite forgotten, are sometimes of greatest importance in the spiritual lives of the disciples; and often work that is seen by other people may become a hindrance. Only the master knows what progress is made and where each stands upon the path. The disciples can never know, until the master bids them look back on the path they have traveled; only then will they know what has been left behind.

The way of service is most difficult. It is natural for everyone beginning to live the spiritual life to want to work for the master, and all are eager to begin; but they have no idea of the reality of such service or even of the meaning of work for work's sake. The majority are working for results, which is a very different thing. The teaching that everything that in ordinary life is considered gain is, to the eyes of the master, but loss, cannot be too often repeated. Very few are capable of realizing this and so, meeting the disappointments inevitable upon this path, become often discouraged at seeing so little result for perhaps years of constant endeavor. They cannot yet understand that it is their endeavor that the master sees and which, in the master's eyes, is the only result of service that matters to the soul.

Result is the end of an undertaking. When we see a result upon the physical plane, it is something finished or dead; but endeavor is a constant striving, and so is a moving, living thing capable of carrying the disciples to heights undreamed of if they do not hinder their own progress by stopping to seek for dead results. Endurance and indifference must be the watchwords of those who would truly serve.

# 17

IT cannot be too often repeated that real spirituality cannot be seen upon the surface or expressed in outward acts, for every action that can be seen by others, or may appear in their eyes to be a spiritual action, can be equally well performed by those who possess no semblance of spirituality. Those whose lives have become spiritualized would guard the knowledge, as a treasure is guarded and hidden from the sight of all. The only way that it could be known to others is by the atmosphere that surrounds those thus spiritualized and the influence they have upon the people with whom they come in contact. This is the only proof of a spiritual life.

# 18

EVERY spiritual teaching, as well as every situation in life, has its true and its false value. And in order to understand these, disciples must develop discrimination so that they may not be deceived by false values; for upon the path there is always this danger. At every step they take, they must focus the light of insight or clear understanding upon it, for the true value of everything can only be discerned in this way. It is possible to be so enwrapped in heavenly visions as to be useless for work in the world. Even love, harmony and beauty may mislead the seeker after truth, unless they are seen and realized by means of the inner vision, which is very different from that of the world. The soul can wither in a love, however great, that desires possession and denies freedom; can be nauseated by earthly harmonies that shut out the cries of distress for help and aid; and become stifled in an atmosphere of beauty, artificially created. To the eyes of a seer, love, harmony and beauty may mean something quite different to those of a person of the world. A master upon the path would view discord as vibrations from which harmony could be produced; would see ugliness as material with which it was possible to create beauty; and hatred as a force that could be changed into love by holding in the heart the thought of God. A worldly person sees discord, ugliness and hatred as fixed and unalterable facts; but the seer knows that nothing is fixed, that every living thing is in flux, for constant motion is the attribute of life, either material, mental or spiritual, and it is, therefore, always capable of alteration and readjustment.

# 19

PROOF of spiritual truths cannot be given by one person to another, because the things belonging to the soul must be seen with the eyes of the soul; and for each the proof would be for oneself alone. It is impossible to explain spiritual truths to those whose spiritual eyes are closed. It would be exactly the same as trying to explain color to those born blind. The blind may believe what is said, but it would be an impossibility to give any physical proof of it; while if their eyes were open, the blind would at once see for themselves. This is so with the things belonging to the spirit. Nothing but spiritual sight can give proof, and one must remember that there are degrees of spiritual sight as there are of physical. Indeed, there are many more things invisible than visible, even to those whose eyes are open; and even many of those that are visible would not be understood without instruction.

Spiritual vision, most greatly to be desired, is the birthright of every soul; but the master's touch is needed to open the eyes. And when it is desired above everything else in life, when one is ready to sacrifice all the world holds to obtain one's sight, then will the master be there to give it.

> *When the cry of the disciple has reached a certain pitch,*
> *the teacher comes to answer it.*[1]
>
> —*Inayat Khan*

---

1 Inayat Khan, *The Gayan.*

# 20

IT is very necessary that the disciple should realize what is meant by treading the spiritual path. *Spirituality* is a word very much misunderstood by the generality of people, who confuse it with religion and religious practices. It does not mean continual prayers, meditation, or even the repetition of holy words; all these are for a purpose and are necessary and helpful, but they cannot of themselves make someone spiritual. By *a spiritual life,* the mystic means *a living life*, when every action, either mental or physical, is alive; and the incentive of every act is the spirit or life force within and not the dead form or outer appearance. When the spirit within becomes active or living, then every part of one is alive; and everything one touches in ordinary daily life in the world partakes of that life and becomes spiritualized.

Spirit, or the essence of life, arises from the soul and is the sign of that soul being awakened or living. Many assume a semblance of spirituality, or rather what generally passes for spirituality; for there are no necessary signs by which all may recognize the spiritual person, although those who are living the inner life will recognize one of the fellowship. But in the presence of such a one, everyone would feel the life force emanating from that person and would themselves, either consciously or unconsciously, become more alive. Even the greatest life-bringers, when they were on earth, were unrecognized except by the few. Jesus said "I am come that they may have life and that they may have it more abundantly,"[1]

1 John 10:10.

but only a few understood that he was offering them the living life, the real spirituality, which the majority still believed was only to be found in their religious forms. "Verily, the letter killeth but the spirit giveth life."[2] The more abundant the life within, the more spiritual or living one's atmosphere will become; and the more others will benefit by this passing on of the life force, which is flowing through that person, awaking to life whatever it touches.

2 2 Corinthians 3:6.

# 21

I WILL try to explain the inner meaning of what is meant by the terms, *the Master* or *the Christ*, although no words can really convey any meaning except to those whose eyes, to some extent, are opened to the mysteries of life.

The body of the Master (if one can use such a term—magnetic field would perhaps better express it) is composed of the perfected souls of those beings who, in every age since the beginning of this earth, have reached the stage of evolution known to mystics as perfection. The guiding, or informing, spirit is the same in every holy name and form and, collectively, they form the embodiment of the One Christ.

As individuals they have been, and are still, separate, distinct, and living; but their souls form one spirit, which is known as *the Spirit of Guidance.*

This will, in some measure, explain to those who have understanding the mystery of many masters, but only one Master; many religions, but only one Religion; many truths, but only one Truth. And there is still a further mystery: every soul that reaches perfection is an enrichment of that mystical Body, which, by the evolution of perfected souls, attains its own fulfillment. But of this, words may not be spoken; only to the closed senses can it be revealed.

The secret of all things is hidden in humans themselves. Search there, O student of life, if you would know of the mysteries; for in that book of nature is written all things necessary for your salvation. The breaths of God's body are the children of earth.

Humanity know thyself.

> *The peace of the Eternal lies near to those who know themselves.*
>
> —*Bhagavad Gita*

# 22

THE Spirit of Guidance is one without a second, as the sun is one but its rays can touch all people. Those who are able to perfect the personality are the messengers, and the personalities thus perfected will last to the end of the world, always as reflectors of the Spirit of Guidance; many reflectors but only one sun.

Every soul able to focus itself to the Spirit of Guidance may reflect the light to some extent, but only perfected souls are the great messengers able to give to the world the message of God for their age.

The great essentials upon this path of perfection are first, to keep the mind perfectly steady—this means absolute self-control; next, to break down and clear away everything that prevents the open vision; then the mirror of the mind must be rightly focused. An impossible task, do you think? It is, except to the heart capable of devotion. To the lover able to entirely forget the self's very existence, all things are possible. Therefore, the first step on this path is to cultivate the heart: to dig up, clear away and burn everything that has taken root in the garden of the heart, thus making an incense that will penetrate the whole being and will, of itself, open the door of vision. When once this vision has been clearly seen, then nothing can hold the soul back from God and it goes ever onward until it reaches perfection.

# 23

THE real meaning of initiation is a truth revealed within the soul. There are many initiations, but each one is a revelation of one aspect of truth. When all aspects have been thus disclosed, then shall the initiate know Truth. But let the aspirant remember that until a person knows the many, that person cannot know the One. Therefore all aspects are necessary, as all colors of the spectrum are contained in the white light and not one must be rejected. It is impossible fully to explain the mysteries to the human mind. They can only be revealed to those whose spiritual eyes are opened and their vision clear to behold the things which belong unto their peace.

# 24

THERE are many ways leading to the path, and each has a particular path by which that person travels. But there is only one path by which, when a person has set foot thereon, however many times one may turn back, one will surely reach the goal. The ways leading to the path are frequently mistaken for the path itself, although when this is so, it is always by means of self-delusion. Many wander up and down these ways who will never find the true path. Thinking that they are already treading it, they do not seek the entrance. Those who have the open vision can see that the reason for this is that they are self-deluded by their own thoughts about themselves. No one can take the first step upon this path until they can see themselves as they appear in the sight of God, and then remember themselves no more; for only through the gate of utter self-forgetfulness can the entrance be found. At the entrance there is a narrow gate, so narrow that none can pass until all has been left; for through this travelers can carry nothing, not even a garment to cover their nakedness, even though it be woven of their virtues. This teaching is not for everyone. Whosoever can perceive the truth, will receive it.

*Among thousands of men scarce one striveth for perfection;*
*of the successful strivers scarce one knoweth Me in essence.*
*—Bhagavad Gita.*

# 25

THE way of achievement in the spiritual life by the balanced path—the most difficult of all paths—is open to humans because, being made in the image of God, they alone possess the power to tread it. Human life, the great initiator of this path, weighs and tests each aspirant at every step of the way; for all, ere they pass from one stage to another, must be able exactly to balance the scales life holds. Not one part of a person must be in excess of any other part. The proportion must be exact, for before one can advance a step upon this path, the whole of one's being must be in equilibrium, or harmonious vibration. But once having passed, a person can never slip back again; that is the great promise to treaders of the balanced path. As they proceed, they take all of themselves with them and do not have to turn back continually for something lost or left behind upon the road; for life bars the way until they can balance the scales they hold. These scales are not the same for all. For every person, the size and shape is altered according to that person's capacity of balance, and at every fresh step is adjusted by the great initiator to the keynote of the vibratory chord to which the aspirant belongs.

To some this may seem a slow way of progress, and seeing many pass them on the journey, they feel dismayed and sometimes impatient at having to carry the many things life demands to balance their scales. Also, they cannot always understand the reason or the necessity for this, as others walk much more quickly when free from the burdens imposed by this initiator. Those who think thus must be content to trust their guide; for none can walk far upon this path except under guidance, until their own spiritual eyes are open and they are able to see for themselves the wisdom of the path of balance.

It is only upon this path that a human being can become perfect, or *hu-man*,[1] master of life and death, and realize within the words of Jesus, "Be ye also perfect, as your Father in heaven is perfect."[2]

---

1 *Hu* is one of the most ancient names for God.

2 Matthew 5:48.

# 26

IF the real work that is being done upon the inner planes by sincere disciples could be seen, there would never again be a feeling of discouragement at the absence of results. On the physical plane there does not seem to be much accomplished, but the form of the message that will raise humanity in every corner of the earth is even now being brought from the formless world to the world of names and forms. Thoughts, which are living things and will materialize in the fullness of time, are being born in every part of the world. It is for this reason that an army of selfless workers is needed. Those who are able to rise above the needs and thoughts of the personality can become instruments through which the thought from the higher planes may take birth upon the physical.

For many years these thoughts must be guarded, sheltered and nourished until the time of their maturity is come, when those through whom they were brought to birth will be no longer needed. The work of selfless disciples is far-reaching, for their thoughts can effect for many miles the district in which they live; and besides this, to themselves, the work they are doing is of the utmost importance to their own development and will take them many stages further upon the true path than if they are striving to perfect themselves by meditation and prayers. "The divine treasury is too full of prayers already. Put in a grain of humble devotion if you can."[1] If once the self can be lost sight of in the vision of God, then nothing but God and God's service has any real value in the eyes of

1 Sharaf al-Din Maneri, *Letters from a Sufi Teacher*.

such a one. Such a disciple then becomes what is known to mystics as virgin, or pure in heart, meaning free from all that would mar the image of God. And it is in the heart of purity that the message of God is able to be fashioned into a form intelligible to humanity.

# 27

FOR one who would seek the gate of discipleship, many things are necessary, the most essential being faith, trust, courage, and strength. Faith in the living God, beside whom is none other; trust in one's own judgment, in other words, an absolute unshakable conviction that what one is doing is right for that person; courage to stand alone and face all life's difficulties; and strength to overcome them. Without these qualities, although a person may spend a whole life in religious practices and good deeds but will never find the gate.

It is difficult, in a world that is everyday becoming more and more material, even to believe in its existence; but those who truly seek shall surely find. It is still more difficult, when found, for those living the ordinary life to pass through. For the path of discipleship does not lead onward; that is to say, it is not an extension of the way the aspirant has already traveled, not an increase of what the world calls greatness, goodness or success. This is the path of return and leads away from these things and means turning back, turning from self, including all that pertains to the personal life, to God. And unless the seeker is prepared to be misjudged by the world, who can never understand, it is useless to proceed further. Nevertheless, if one has courage, and can bear to hear one's highest motives distorted and ideals misunderstood, perhaps even jeered at, then will the seeker learn the mystic teaching of the heart; for the path of discipleship leads to the heart, which is the goal of the disciple. Those who have completed the turning are masters upon the path of wisdom and hold within themselves the power of turning or transmuting everything they touch to pure gold. But unless seekers are content to do without the approbation of their fellow humans, they will never reach this stage; for whosoever desires the approbation of God must do so with singleness of purpose. "No one can serve two masters."[1]

> *For as the heavens are higher than the earth, so are my ways higher than your ways and my thoughts than your thoughts, saith the Lord.*
>
> —*Isaiah 55:8*

1 Matthew 6:24.

# 28

THE Yoga teaching of killing out desire is difficult for a Western mind to understand. It does not mean that desire must be eliminated, but that the attitude of desire, or its rate of vibration, must be changed. Desire for the objects of sense cannot be conquered by asceticism or force. It can be kept away so long as the force is maintained, but directly this is in any degree relaxed, it immediately invades the human soul.

There is only one way of victory and that is by transmutation. Only by transmuting the substance of desire and raising it to its highest rate of vibration, can one transcend the desire for things temporal. The method is quite simple, although the practice is most difficult. If disciples can keep their thoughts always toward God, they will bring into activity a vibratory note in the astral body, or body of desire, which will keep all the atoms of which that body is composed at the highest rate of vibration of which they are capable; and while that note is sounding, they cannot respond to any other. When disciples can make this practice a habit of their daily lives, they will find that all desire for those things that once appeared so important has fallen away, and they have no more desire for them than they would have for a winter cloak when the sun is shining.

# 29

PEOPLE live in a world of illusion because they see all things outside themselves. If they could but look inward, they would perceive reality. Everything contained in the universe can be found within the human being. The worlds in which a person lives, physical, mental and emotional, are the shadows cast by the inner realities. This is the secret of illusion: one creates it oneself, and lives in the shadows one is continually making. No person can escape illusion while living in this world, but when the inner eyes are opened, one can recognize it for what it is and, once having recognized, would never again mistake it for reality. This is the great importance of living the inner life: to be able to distinguish the real from the false, to know that the appearance of any thing or person is no more its reality than the appearance of a person upon the screen of a cinema is the real person. There is, of course, much to be learned from appearances and, for a long time, it is the only way by which humanity can be taught. But to those who have eyes to see and ears to hear, an appearance would never be mistaken for the reality.

# 30

THE human soul identifies itself with what is before its view. Knowing itself as a separated part and aware of its incompleteness, it is constantly trying to unite with others, ever seeking completion. While the human soul is not awakened it can only see in half-lights, because the shadow of the false ego is held before its view, reflected by the mirror of the mind. And until the eyes of the soul are fully opened, it is unable to perceive that it is thus deluded; so thinking this false ego is its very self, it becomes united with it. In time, of course, it learns that this is not its true place; because the satisfaction and gratification of this ego can never satisfy the soul, or true ego, which becomes restless and unsatisfied at every fresh realization of its incompleteness.

The real self, the soul, can never be completed by anything but by identifying itself with God, in Whom alone it can find true completeness and peace.

When the mind is under the control of the soul, then will the soul see only that which it wills to see and not the false images presented by an uncontrolled mind.

The soul's endeavor is to draw the mind upward to its level of consciousness, to share its glorious vision. But the mind, when not thus held, is constantly striving to draw the soul down to its own level, in which only the things of earth can be comprehended. There is a constant struggle taking place within a human being, whose real destiny is to attain perfection in the middle kingdom, to be able to rise to the heights of consciousness and behold the true vision of the soul. And at the same time, to have such control of all the levels of consciousness below one that one may experience the life of those levels without being held by them.

# 31

A PERSON becomes confused when trying to understand the beginning and end of the soul. The mind cannot conceive the possibility of anything having no beginning and no end, which is the real history of the human soul; and until a seeker has risen above the limits of matter as opposed to spirit, and become one with all that is, the seeker will never realize it. The quickest means of attaining this state is by trying to lose oneself in God, to unlearn rather than to seek further knowledge, to as it were, strip off all the coverings under which the light of wisdom is hidden. "When the sun of divine knowledge rises ,all modes of knowledge become ignorance."[1]

It is extremely difficult to understand and, much more so, to realize that when a disciple begins to tread the path of return, everything—every action, every thought, every idea—must be looked at from a totally different viewpoint from that to which the disciple has hitherto been accustomed. To tread this path involves a complete turning round; consequently, all things appear upside down. Of course, the things themselves do not change or their appearance. It is that those who have changed their own attitude are able, for the first time, to see things as they are. But at first they cannot properly focus their sight, hence the confusion of thought; for upon the return journey, positive becomes negative and negative positive, and it is natural that, until they have thrown away their garments woven of accumulated error of thoughts, they should be bewildered. It is not at the beginning of the path

1 Sharaf al-Din Maneri, *Letters from a Sufi Teacher*.

that one can realize the mystery of manifestation, which is hidden in the heart of God and, deeper mystery still, reflected in the human heart so that in every human soul is the potential possibility of the realization of the whole in microcosm, which is the joy of the journey and the goal of the mystic.

When God inbreathes the divine manifestation, all souls are withdrawn from time into eternity when, as humans, they cease to be and merge again into that oneness of consciousness from which they came forth. But unless, as humans, they have attained illumination or realization, the whole of the long journey is made in the darkness of ignorance instead of in the light of wisdom.

At any stage upon the journey it is possible for one to turn round and face oneself. "He who has completed the turning and reached the heart is a master."[2]

---

2 Sharaf al-Din Maneri, *Letters from a Sufi Teacher*.

# 32

*He shall not be afraid of evil tidings his heart is fixed, trusting in the Lord.* — *Psalm 112:7*

*Thou wilt keep him in perfect peace whose mind is stayed on Thee.* —*Isaiah 26:3*

THE injunction, frequently given to disciples, to keep the heart fixed upon God, does not mean for one moment an empty life as far as human loves are concerned. This may sound a contradiction; it is a paradox, I will try to find a few words to give you, but the reality can only be understood by inner illumination.

The heart that is really fixed upon God sees every thing and every being, as it were, through God. It is impossible to find any true analogy for this; the best, perhaps, is to imagine yourself permanently surrounded by a radiant light, and every person you contact is seen through and becomes enveloped in this radiance, which reveals the God within. To fix the heart upon God does not mean that human life must be ignored, for that life, with all its joys and sorrows, its burdens and its privileges, is the great path upon which God meets humanity. But illumination here must be sought on the path of surrender, in the simple words of the master: "Who would save his life must lose it."[1] In this is hidden the power to create heaven or hell; ponder it in your heart unceasingly.

1 Mark 8:35.

# 33

AS the Christ Child is born in the heart, so is the heavenly person born in humanity. This earth is the womb in which we are formed. The birth of the Christ in the human heart is a reflection of this great mystery of the microcosm in the macrocosm: "as above so below."[1]

It is this new birth in the human heart that provides the material for the form of the heavenly person, the matter thus raised, or transmuted, forming part of the body of radiance. This is the real Easter message: from death to life, through burial to resurrection. Matter, when transmuted and raised to its highest capacity, is light. Light forms the body of the heavenly person, which then becomes a light to lighten our darkness, the Light of the World.

---

1 *The Emerald Tablet of Hermes Trismegistus.*

# 34

*Inasmuch as ye have done it unto one of the least of these, My brethren, ye have done it unto Me.*

*—Matthew 25:40*

IN these words of Jesus Christ is hidden a great mystery, which mystics of all religions recognize. It is the mystery of God buried in humanity, of Christ crucified on the cross of matter. In order to attain to a true understanding of the nature of God, the mystic strives to realize the ideal in the whole universe. The mystic seeks God under every cover that nature uses to shield the One Life in every form and every being. When one begins to hear God in every cry of pain, to see God looking through the eyes of every inhabitant of the human and animal worlds, realizing how the Christ is held in prison there, a daily and hourly crucifixion until the seventy thousand veils are removed and Christ may express His own Self; then one knows that every word of sympathy to fellow humans is for the God in humanity, every act of charity to others is something done for God; that in every stranger taken in, God is entertained. One begins to understand this mystery and to realize that, in the darkness of blind intellect, Christ is imprisoned; in the dumb suffering of animal life, it is Christ who suffers; and in the agony of human sorrow, it is Christ who sorrows.

If one could really realize this, that Christ is in very truth feeling all that is felt by the least of these, as one's own self feels the pain of every member of one's own body, would that person not hasten to relieve every cry of pain that is felt by Christ's heart of love, that one pain less may be spared it?

The Christ thus shut into, or buried, in humanity must be born again from humanity. The human heart must open, its outer shell of hardness must break in order that the Christ Child shall be born there, which is the true freedom of the soul.

> *When the heart breaks it gives birth to the soul.*
>
> *—Inayat Khan.*

# 35

*And I, if I be lifted up from the earth, will draw all men unto me.* —*John 12:32*

IN this saying of Jesus Christ, as in all his sayings, is hidden a deep mystery that is only very gradually comprehended by treaders of the spiritual path as they proceed. Those who sought and worshiped Jesus for the beauty of his personality and his physical presence remained upon the plane of that personality; but those who in their hearts were able to, as it were, lift him above personality—in other words, could realize his Godhead—were drawn upward even unto him. "Then said Jesus unto them, when ye have lifted up the Son of Man, then shall ye know that I am He and that I do nothing of myself."[1] Of course, words cannot really express the inner meaning of this teaching; at most they can but indicate a line of thought that each must follow for themselves.

The messengers of God in all ages and in all religions may be likened to living magnets whose work is to draw humanity upward. A magnet lying upon the ground would attract to itself any things capable of attraction within its magnetic field, but they would remain upon the ground. If, however, the magnet is lifted above the ground, all these things, by the power of attraction, are also lifted or drawn up.

The work of messengers of God is not to teach, although their words are living jewels, nor even to heal the sick or console the sorrowful, although many are healed and consoled; but to draw up unto themselves those whose rate of magnetism

1 John 8:28.

can respond to their own vibrations, to draw them upwards into the family of God. And everyone the masters thus uplift from the denseness of the earth can, in their turn, uplift others, as one magnetized needle can magnetize others. Only those capable of this response can be drawn upward. The others cannot move, however close they may be to the magnet. Teachers can only offer direction to their pupils, they cannot tread the path for their pupils or explain, in physical words, spiritual truths; neither can the messengers of God, however great, attract those whose spiritual eyes are not turned in their direction, as a magnet cannot attract even tempered steel, which is incapable of response unless it is turned towards the positive and negative poles of the magnet. So one cannot be drawn up unto God unless one is seeking or turned towards God.

# 36

"I AM the resurrection and the life"[1] is perhaps the most mystical of all the sayings of Jesus. In it is contained the great mystery of resurrection, which mystery was reflected in the death, burial and resurrection of Jesus Christ. It was symbolically enacted in the sacred rites of the ancients and also in the initiation rites of all the occult schools, even to this day.

That utterance of profound wisdom would give the information to all initiates of the greatness of the mission of Jesus and the stupendous task he had come to perform; that he was, in very truth, reflecting the Christ, the savior and redeemer of the world, not, as is believed by the unenlightened, to redeem or save people from the consequences of their wrong doing, which is quite another thing.

The cosmic Christ, who is the beginning and the end, alpha and omega, is bound to, or buried in, humanity until the whole of the matter of which that humanity is formed has been freed or raised from the bondage of death to the condition of life or light, which is the real meaning of resurrection.

The redeeming of the world is the task of the Christ: to raise every atom to its original condition; to fine, refine and purify the whole, until the four elements of which it is composed are alchemically resolved again into the ether from which they came forth. For the purpose of manifestation, the vibrations of ether were slowed down, as it were, until it appeared as solid form or material substance. In this condition, that of which all matter is composed is separable and

1 John 11:25.

knowable as earth, water, fire and air. In the etheric condition they are united and unknowable, except as light. Jesus, in his human nature, having redeemed, or raised to their original condition the atoms comprising his physical body, was able to appear, to those who had eyes to see, in his radiant body of resurrection, thus showing to all who were able to receive such teaching the completed task that it is the purpose of humanity to fulfill. "But now is Christ risen from the dead and become the first fruits of them that slept. For since by man came death, by man came also the resurrection of the dead."[2]

To dwellers in a material world, the process of raising dense matter to the condition of light seems an impossibility; because although the process of reducing ice to vapor is known, and solid earthly substance can, by fire, be reduced to ashes, still the ashes remain even though they may be scattered. But there is a resolvent by which everything known to man as matter can be changed into light. The secret of this, however, is known only to high initiates and cannot be given to a person until and unless one has reached the grade in evolution that would entitle one to receive it

The danger of such knowledge in the hands of those whose lower selves were not dead and buried would be too great. Only to those illuminated souls who have passed through crucifixion, death, and burial, is the secret of resurrection revealed.

2 2 Corinthians 15:20–21.

# 37

IN God—the manifest or limited God—is everything that ever has been, or can ever be conceived, or thought, or fashioned by any being in the universe. There is nothing new; everything has always existed. Before the beginning of time it was, and after time has passed away it will be; nothing can be added, nothing can be taken away.

What then is the purpose of creation? It is to create and destroy form; to rearrange, transmute and transform, over and over again, every atom and molecule belonging to the world in which we live, until the perfect form is fashioned, which then becomes the resurrection body, or body of radiance, of that great spirit that we call *Christ* or *the Spirit of Guidance*. That which comprises the body of the risen Christ is the essence of human evolution. As each soul is perfected, it passes on this essence, and by that much is the embodiment of Christ enriched. Until this body is complete, which means that every atom composing it is perfected, or raised to its original condition of light and occupying its own place in that body, the Christ is buried in humanity. Christ cannot rise or ascend to the Father until the stone has been rolled away.[1]

The mystical interpretation of the stone is that it is the accumulation of human thoughts, which through ages of erroneous thinking has become hard, concrete and fixed until it is almost immovable. But until it is removed, the Truth that is life cannot be seen. While Truth is held down to earth it can

1 Mark 16:4.

never be known; it must be set free. Only then, as it rises, can humanity see with true vision that whatever is held is lost.

While Jesus was on earth, even his nearest disciples could not realize his greatness and sorrowed that he should leave them. It was not until after he had risen in his resurrection body that they could understand. So long as he was close to them physically, and they could touch him and hear him speak, they could only know him as a human being. But when the body of earth no longer held him down, and he was freed from its limitation, only then, when they had apparently lost him, could they receive the truth that as he had risen, so they also could be lifted up with him inasmuch as they could realize the mystery in themselves. As the cosmic Christ rises in this mystical radiant body, that portion of humanity that has become perfect also rises with Christ to a further evolution. But here thought cannot follow, and any attempt at explanation would cause confusion. All that is perceived cannot be conveyed in words

# 38

THE story of Jesus washing the feet of his disciples has a very mystical interpretation. It is symbolical of the initiation of purification given by the master to those whom he was trusting to carry his message to the world. In the teaching of the mystics, the feet represent one's understanding; and the understanding of those who carry the message of God must be cleansed from the dust of earth. In the act of washing the feet of the disciples, Jesus gives to all who have ears to hear the teaching of the seers of all ages and of all religions. The necessity of cleansing the mind of all impurities, of washing away the error of thought that impedes right understanding, so that the heart qualities, wisdom and love, may henceforth rule the life instead of those of reason; this is only possible by the help of a master. A disciple upon the path of wisdom must unlearn all has been learned upon the path of outgoing and offer the self for the master's work, empty of all so-called worldly wisdom. For "Except ye become as a little child, ye cannot enter the kingdom of heaven"[1]; and only those who themselves know the way can lead others thereto.

1 Matthew 18:3.

# 39

*Blessed are the pure in heart for they shall see God.*
*—Matthew 5:8.*

IN these words of Jesus is contained the whole of the teaching necessary for travelers on the path of discipleship. To be pure in heart does not mean that the disciple has never known impurity or has never sinned. All those who are in the world know the shadow of the world; even the sun is sometimes eclipsed by the shadow of earth to the dwellers upon earth. The mystic interpretation of *pure in heart*, means a heart from which everything has been excluded but the vision of God. To attain to this purity of vision demands daily and hourly attention, for unless the heart is utterly empty it cannot be filled with God. Any thing or person in the life of a disciple causing the disciple for one moment to forget God claims a place in the heart, which to be pure, means that it holds one only, without addition of any other substance.

Disciples who have reached this stage are pure from distinctions, which divide and separate. They cannot help radiating love upon all with whom they come in contact. If their own hearts are filled with the love of God, they reflect that love upon every other heart they touch. Such as these would never condemn; they would have nothing but sympathy, understanding and consolation for the sorrows and shortcomings of others, and would rejoice in their joys. Having eliminated the image of self, they have become, as it were, reflectors of God. Blessed are they from whom self is covered; verily they shall reflect the light of God.

This stage on the spiritual path cannot be reached by striving and asceticism, but by substitution, or divine alchemy. Every time the mind offers a thought of hate, discord, or ugliness, it should be replaced by one of love, harmony or beauty. If this practice is persevered in until it becomes a habit of the daily life, it will, in time, enable the heart to reach purity of vision: the stage of purification when the pure in heart can see God. But to understand the vision, to know God, something further is necessary. To obtain a perfect reflection in water, the water, besides being freed from all impurities, must be absolutely still. So the surface of the heart must be utterly still, unruffled by the winds of illusion, or the image reflected there will be blurred. The slightest vibration of doubt, distrust or depression will disturb the equilibrium of perfect balance, which is only achieved when every atom of the being is vibrating in harmony. The disciple must see with purity of vision and know, in the silence of the heart. "Be still and know that I am God."[1]

*In quietness and in confidence shall be your strength.*
*—Isaiah 30:15*

*Let thy soul walk softly in thee as a saint in heaven unshod;*
*For to be alone with silence, is to be alone with God.*[2]
*—Samuel Miller Hageman*

---

1 Psalm 46:10.

2 Hageman, Samuel Miller, "Silence" (Brooklyn: D.H.Holmes, 1876). p. 29.

# 40

THE earnest seekers of God who find their paths strewn with obstacles should realize that they themselves have placed the obstacles there. The path to God leads to the human heart, and there the true seeker will find God. This sounds very simple and would be, if the path had not been blocked. "Mind is the surface of heart, heart is the depth of mind."[1] It is the contents of mind, reflected earthly wisdom, which bars the way. People are unconscious of this barrier until, urged by the desire of the soul to seek God, they turn round to find the entrance leading to that path is closed against them by life's complexities and complications, by doubts and worldly reasoning. Then the toilsome difficult journey begins, for they themselves must remove all the obstacles facing them that prevent even the first step being taken. If the seeker could realize that all these were the creation of one's own mind and, therefore, within one was the power to destroy them, the path would very quickly be cleared; but so long as a seeker thinks that some power outside the self, either God or devil, has placed them there and made the environment in which one finds oneself, the task is endless.

Created thought must be destroyed by its creator. From time to time, since the beginning of the world, messengers of God have been sent to earth to remind humanity of its inheritance, of its royal birth: that made in the image of God, we have within ourselves the God-like power of creative thought. But only a few have listened or even paused in

1 Inayat Khan, *The Gayan*.

their self-imposed task of blocking, by every kind of concrete thought, which in time becomes hard as rock and as difficult to move, the path leading to the heart, where abides the throne of God, the true home of the soul.

## 41

*God looked down from Heaven upon the children of men, to see if there were any that did understand, that did seek God.*
*—Psalm 53:2*

BEFORE a seeker can aspire to know God, the seeker must first know and understand the mystery of love. "He that loveth not, knoweth not God, for God is love."[1] But loving does not mean always living in a state of bliss, neither does it imply being loved. The true and inner meaning is complete surrender of self, the sacrifice of everything that stands between the soul and the object of its devotion. When such surrender is perfected, there will be no place for the desire to be loved; there would be no recipient if the merging is complete. One cannot love God until one knows how to love. That is the first lesson that life, the great initiator, tries to impart to everyone, for "Love has the power to open the door of eternal life."[2]

When disciples have learned love's innermost mystery of self-abnegation, they seek an ever-increasing greatness in which to lose themselves, until at last God becomes to them an absolute necessity. It is at this stage they realize their need and utter the cry of all true seekers: "O! that I knew where I might find God!" and, perhaps for the first time, understand the soul's longing to break the bonds of illusion and to escape from all that is holding it back from union with God.

*Self stands as a wall between man and God.*
*— Inayat Khan*

---

1 1 John 4:8.
2 Inayat Khan, *The Bowl of Saki*.

As no one can love unless one has found the object of one's desire, God must first be sought and then made a living reality to the seeker. Everyone's realization will be for themselves alone and cannot be communicated to another. "And ye shall seek Me and find Me when ye shall search for Me with all your heart."[3]

God can never be explained, because each soul would receive a different vision or realization; and if a seeker who had been privileged to lift even a corner of one of the seventy thousand veils of illusion were to attempt to explain, the lips would be sealed. Only those who are themselves ignorant of the true nature of God are anxious and willing to offer explanation to others.

Although, by the practice of loving to the point of self-forgetfulness, God can be made a living reality in the heart of all who seek with singleness of purpose to love and serve God—"For love is of God, and everyone that loveth is born of God and knoweth God,"[4]—ultimate knowledge cannot be attained until the Sacred Name is pronounced. The letters and syllables composing that most Holy Name have been scattered throughout the whole universe. They must first be sought and found, then arranged in their true order, ere the lost word can be uttered. Mystery of mysteries, how can it even be suggested without entirely obliterating the meaning? But each syllable found by one who is truly seeking spells God for that seeker; and one then has within the absolute conviction that can never be shaken: of the existence of God as a living reality. A Sufi sage has said, "Continue thy seeking until the seeking unveils itself and destroys thyself in thee."[5] The all-embracingness of God is so vast, including, as it must, the ultimate satisfaction and completion of every man's highest ideal of perfection, each one of which is necessarily different,

3 Jeremiah 29:13.

4 1 John 4:7.

5 Sharaf al-Din Maneri, *Letters from a Sufi Teacher*.

that it is an impossibility for any human being with a limited view even to imagine any other interpretation of perfection than that which it means to that person. Infinity cannot be grasped by a finite mind. Not until the many become One can God be known.

> *The secret of God is hidden in the realization of unity.*
> *—Inayat Khan*

# 42

THE solution, or solvent, of all life's problems is God, the one substance by which all things are made. Substance is the manifested or limited God, limited to a rate of vibration to which humanity is capable of responding; for the limited cannot comprehend the unlimited, or the manifested the unmanifest. The universe, or the limited part of God, is conditioned by God's thought to time and space. This process, to the human mind, is unthinkable. The only physical action that may suggest a line of thought is the process of reducing vapor by cold temperature or slow vibration to the condition of ice, which limits its freedom to a particular space and time. Humanity is limited by time, and so unable to realize the eternal. But if one could transmute the atoms composing one's being in the fire of love, which is God, one would be freed from this limitation of time and space. The whole universe will be thus transmuted in the end, but we have in ourselves the capacity to help or hinder the consummation by cooperation or non-cooperation with the Divine Will. Made in the image of God, we have within us, potentially, the power of becoming what we will to become; and everyone who, by the power of the Christ within, attains to the perfected state of *hu-man*, or divine man, by raising the vibrations of the atoms of one's own embodiment, helps to raise or redeem the whole.

Verily, no one lives to themselves alone; and no one can raise themselves without also helping others to rise, nor fall without taking others in the fall.

# 43

FROM the beginning of the world until the present day, God has never left it without knowledge of God. Always those through whom God's message could be given have lived upon earth, and the evidence of this lies in the fact that in every age people have worshiped God in some form, as a power greater than themselves, by whatsoever name they have called it.

Sometimes the message-bearers have been known to the world, sometimes unknown. But whether known or unknown, they all have completed the work allotted to them.

Those known to the world were the founders of the great religions, which are destined to give to humanity an answer to the questions it has been asking down the ages: *What is God?* and *What is a human being?* One finds this knowledge difficult to obtain when a person seeks it in one religion or one form of faith only, refusing to acknowledge the others. And if one form disappoints, the person will repudiate that one and seek another; one can never know more than half-truths in this way. The secret lies in the realization of the oneness of all the message-bearers of God and of their message; also that each form of worship that has been given to humanity is a partial expression of the One Truth, suited to the times and peoples to whom it was given.

> *The soul of all is One Soul and the truth is One Truth, under whatever religion it is hidden.*
>
> —*Inayat Khan*

The fierce white light of truth itself would blind those groping in darkness, so truth is broken into its colored rays that each one may find, through the color most suited to one's need, as much as one is capable of comprehending.

Mystics of all times and of all religions have always known that truth in its entirety cannot be understood until all the colors that constitute white have been united; in other words, until the half-truths contained in all the various forms of faith that God has given to the world have been accepted as making one complete whole.

> *All the disharmony of the world caused by religious differences is the result of man's failure to understand that religion is One, Truth is One, God is One. How can there be two religions?*
>
> —*Inayat Khan*

The work of the messengers of God has never failed; it could not fail. They work in the strength and by the power of God, whose message-bearers and agents they are. Although according to the judgment of the world there may be failure, those who have the understanding heart know that such failure means the final triumph of the Spirit, which transmutes failure into victory.

The work of Jesus when he was on earth culminated in his being tried and condemned as a disturber of the peace, to be executed as a common malefactor, the ordinary sentence of those days for such an offence. The multitude considered him a failure, as his only reply, to those who offered to believe in his message if he would perform a miracle and save himself, was silence—surely, the greatest example of transmutation of failure into victory the world has ever known.

# 44

*The beginning and end of all beings is the same,*
*the difference only existing during the journey.*
*—Inayat Khan*

*Each being is from Allah, and to Him each will return.*
*—Qur'an*

*As it was in the beginning, is now, and ever shall be.*
*—English Book of Prayer*

*As it was*
*As it is*
*As it shall be*
*Evermore*
*With the ebb*
*With the flow—Amen.*
*—From the Gaelic*

IF one could fully realize that the sum total of humanity is God, one would understand that every soul, being part of God, must necessarily be withdrawn again unto God at the end of manifestation, as the rays of light are drawn back into the sun after being received by the earth. People become bewildered because they confuse time with eternity, the limited with the unlimited. At the beginning there is only God, and at the end there is only God. It is the stage between, called by sages *the journey*, with which the human soul is concerned. In reality, there is no beginning and no end. Eternity is a circle, and the end and beginning are one; but the journey, taking place in time, has a beginning and an end. And the soul, while experiencing it, cannot realize any condition apart from end and beginning. This is natural, for the journey exists for that stage of being called *human*, midway between the highest and the lowest where one knows good and evil, heaven and hell, as separate and distinct. One is living, really speaking, in the condition of separateness; and so long as the soul lives in this state, it cannot understand the secret of unity. To do so, the seeker must rise above the bondage of the pairs of opposites and attain to union with that Divine Spirit that is the true center of being of every person. In the mystic sense there is only One who journeys, although, when reflected in many forms in a world of shadows, the One Life appears to be many and separate, each from each.

The personalities with which the soul clothes itself during the journey are important only so long as that time lasts. The real object of the innermost human spirit is to finish the journey and go home. It is interesting to take a journey, and if one never left home and came into contact with different peoples and experiences, one would know very little. But to whatever place, either beautiful or terrible, the journey may take any soul, and however far it may travel, there comes a time when it longs for the Father's home. Whatever may have been the experiences during the long journey, whatever one's shortcomings, one would still remain the child of the Father, and one's placc in the Father's home would still be one's own. Nothing can take away the birthright of the soul, but when it reaches that home, the garments it wore during the journey would not any more be needed; it has left them behind. If they were beautiful and well made, they may be used by some other journeying soul, altered perhaps; or added to possibly, if ugly; disintegrated altogether into their constituent parts, to be formed and reformed into other articles but, as a whole or a personality, lost.

The reason people find it so difficult to understand the truth about life is that they identify themselves with the garments they wear instead of with the innermost self. They must realize themselves apart from any clothing whatsoever, whether woven of physical, mental, or even so-called spiritual material; naked we came into the world of appearances, naked we must return. All souls come forth pure, having no distinctions or differences; the physical reflection of this truth is mirrored in the nucleus of embryonic life in the womb. They return pure, having shed all coverings that, although absolutely necessary during the journey in time, are no longer of any use in eternity.

The reason that mystics of all religions seek the path of wisdom upon which to travel instead of the path of ignorance, is that they may obtain knowledge of God and of humanity and, perchance, help other travelers also to understand. Because when one has, by traveling the path of wisdom, become master of life and death and all the other delusive pairs of opposites, one is able to transcend the stage in evolution called *man* and attain to that unity in which is perfect freedom. One then becomes *hu-man* and can, at will, enter the Father's house and also live among the human world. And for every person who attains to this state of perfection, thousands are helped; for by this uplift, they are enabled to leave the path of ignorance for the way of devotion. And by this means, the whole evolutionary process is made shorter in time, and the way more easy, even for those who are still treading the path of ignorance.

If all reach the same goal in the end, what does anything matter?

If a number of people started upon a journey, which they knew would last them a lifetime, it would matter very much indeed to themselves, and also to those with whom they were traveling, under what conditions that journey was made and whether they possessed a true map of the different paths by which they might reach their destination; whether they knew whither the various byways would lead, the kind of clothes with which they should clothe themselves, and who were their companions upon the road. Most of all, it would matter by which path they chose to travel and whether they carried a light to show the way when night fell.

If one understands that the mystic journey constitutes the whole of the life of a human being, which can be made by three paths—ignorance, devotion, or wisdom—the answer to this question is not so difficult.

In endeavoring to put eternal truths into language belonging to time, it must be remembered that only a fraction of reality can be conveyed. Words, at best, are but a cover for thoughts and sometimes convey quite the opposite meaning when used to express intuitive thought. No words, either written or spoken, should be taken in their literal sense only. The inner meaning should be sought by the light of intuition.

# 45

IF people knew how to interpret their own scriptures, they would find there, written in their own language, the answer to every question life presents to them that the mind is capable of comprehending and the solution of that riddle of the universe: *What is God and what is humanity?*

In the words of the Bible, "And God said, let us make man in Our image after Our likeness,"[1] is hidden the secret of the purpose of human evolution, which, for centuries, people have been trying to solve.

This great problem can only be reverently approached. Seekers must "loose the shoe from off the foot"[2] ere they tread this holy ground; in other words, must put off their ordinary manner of walking by uncovering their understanding. For the first thing necessary is that they shall have some knowledge of what is God before they can know what is the human being who is made in God's image. It is, of course, unnecessary to say that this knowledge cannot be given to another or that it cannot be found in books. Those who would find the truth must seek in the innermost depths of their own souls, for there, written in letters of light, it is clear for everyone to read for themselves when they have cleared away the accumulation of error with which it is covered. Sometimes the accumulation is so dense, that a solid wall, as hard as granite, stands between the person and the soul.

Although knowledge of God cannot be communicated to another, a thought may be suggested that each may interpret

1 Genesis 1:26.

2 Deuteronomy 25:9.

in one's own way. The seer thinks of God as the sum total of humanity, immanent in God's creation and yet transcendent. If this thought is meditated upon, one may gain some realization of the immanence of God.

> *I, O Gudakesha, am The Self, seated in the heart of all beings; I am the beginning, the middle, and also the end of all beings. And whatsoever is the seed of all beings, That am I, O Arjuna; nor is aught moving or unmoving, that may exist bereft of Me.*
>
> —*Bhagavad Gita*

If the power in the elements and the life of every moving or unmoving thing in all the kingdoms of the universe, from elemental substance or first cause, to the heavenly kingdoms and all the hosts thereof, are part of God's life, it implies that the atoms and molecules that comprise human bodies, a universe in microcosm, must touch every form of life from the lowest to the highest. How otherwise could people be made in the image of God, in Whom are all things whatsoever that have been made? This is the reason that they must tread the long pilgrimage, that as humans they may know these things of God; as humans, may be perfect as their Father in heaven is perfect; that everything in the whole universe, the macrocosm, may be reflected in miniature as the microcosm, for as above so below.

"The innermost being of man is the real Being of God."[3] In humility and with great reverence, O people, must this teaching be approached.

> *By Thee alone are filled the earth, the heavens and all the regions that are stretched between. The triple worlds sink down, O mighty One, before thine awful manifested form.*
>
> —*Bhagavad Gita*

3 Inayat Khan, *The Bowl of Saki.*

# 46

THE power of sex is the life of God manifesting in its dual aspect as positive and negative, or jelal and jemal. When these two aspects meet in the act of creation, then is kemal, or perfection, experienced, because having left the world of duality where it was separate and incomplete, it realizes oneness, the complete and whole life. The result and object of this union is a new birth on some plane.

When, in man and woman, the positive and negative seek each other in order to experience this perfection for the gratification and satisfaction of the physical body only, instead of for the purpose of passing on the life, then kemal would manifest as destruction instead of perfection. For the act of creation, which is the true purpose of the union of positive and negative, is frustrated and, in the end, results in pain instead of pleasure. The whole confusion and all the difficulties arising from the wrong use of this living force by both man and woman is the result of their failure to understand the law which governs it.

> *By the delusion of the pairs of opposites sprung from attraction and repulsion, O Bharata, all beings walk this universe wholly deluded.*
>
> —*Bhagavad Gita*

In man the sex force is positive, which urges him to seek the opposite, or negative, in order to give; and unless he understands how to control and use it for the purpose of creation or re-creation on some plane of his being, it will be claimed by his false ego for its own gratification. It cannot remain unused, for it is life itself; and the nature of life is movement.

In woman the force is negative, which urges her to demand; and unless this demand is satisfied, she feels incomplete, as the true work of woman is to mold, nourish and sustain new forms in which life may become objective. Men and women, therefore, seek each other in order that they may experience completeness.

There are many ways in which the two aspects of sex can meet in creative union upon planes other than the physical. All mental creative work is the result of such an union on its own plane; it results in physical creation on the physical plane, mental creation on the plane of mind. But the real union can only take place upon the spiritual plane, and when this has been achieved, both man and woman have complete control of this force on all planes of their being.

To restrict the power of sex to the gratification of bodily appetite is the degradation of God, and while humans do so they can never know its laws. It must first be raised to the spiritual world and realized as a spiritual force: the life-giving power of God. And when in one's own body the positive and negative aspects are balanced, man or woman can control the creative or sex force on all planes. Humanity works through mind, which must be negative to God. In other words, one must allow the mind to be controlled by the soul but must, at the same time, be positive to one's body, which must be under the control of the mind.

# 47

IF the human body could be seen as it really is, it would not appear as one complete and solid form but as millions upon millions of tiny living beings hard at work, constantly changing, continually passing out, and others simultaneously streaming in to take their place so that the pattern is always kept, although the size and shape alter as the child grows to adulthood. If this wonderful mechanism could be photographed, magnified and thrown upon a screen, it would reveal the greatest marvel ever beheld by the eyes: a whole world in miniature, containing millions of living beings, each intent upon and carrying on their own work, fulfilling the purpose impressed upon them by their Creator and, when their work is finished, passing away. Having no will of their own they exist only to carry out whatever is impressed upon them. When the thought impressed is steady, pure and controlled, then they all work in absolute harmony and, as a whole, unite in expressing the thought impressed. But when the thought is uncontrolled, impure and vacillating, then inharmonious conditions, which are the cause of all unrest, are the result.

It is in the body of the female—plant, animal or human—that the seeds of reproduction are grown. All female forms are negatively charged; I am speaking now about the physical bodies only. Seeds capable of reproduction must grow in a negative or receptive mold and cannot become either plant, animal or human form until they have been stimulated, or impregnated, by a positive charge. Life, light or heat in any form is produced by the positive and negative poles of electricity touching each other. The poles are not electricity but are only the means by which it manifests.

Electricity is the source of all life, but humankind, even the greatest scientists, are only beginning to learn the *ABC* of this mighty force, which brings all things into being. To the mystics, it is known as an activity of God.

The kind of plant, animal or man reproduced after its kind is determined by the form made on earth, not by the life or positive force that is the same in all: One, changeless and permanent. It is the mold that determines the finished product. God is no respecter of persons, and God's sun shines upon the just and upon the unjust. Upon whatever seeds the sun's rays fall, they will come to harvest, be they trees, flowers or weeds; and their falling upon the seed of an oak cannot make it a thistle, or upon that of a thistle cannot make it a lily. To humanity has been given the stupendous task of fashioning the human form, that God may give it life. Form is the outcome of thought; it is thought, its rate of vibration and color, that holds together in a particular form the millions of atoms of which a physical body is composed. A child is the result of the thought of its forebears but is not compelled to remain so, for as the atoms that compose a form are in flux and pass in and out of the body according to the thought of the inhabitant, it is the privilege of a human being, made in the image of God and so possessing the power of creative thought, to become whatever a person wills to become. This is one's true birthright, which ages ago was sold for a mess of pottage or the pleasures of the flesh. Today a priceless opportunity is offered humanity of redeeming the past error and exchanging the mess of pottage for one's true birthright.

It is true that life fashions the form in which the soul expresses itself according to the note of magnetism with which the soul is charged. But it is also true that the physical mold determines, to a great extent, the character of the person.

The matter the soul attracts to form its body is not pure matter, but is impregnated and saturated with the thought of the race and of the ancestors of the parents through whom it is born. The mold, fashioned by life in which to express itself, is formed in the womb of the mother; and her thought is capable of distorting and altering its shape. Also, if the hereditary history is bad, the child of such parents cannot fully express its real self until and unless its own thought is powerful enough to alter the rate of vibration of the matter forming its body. This really means tuning it to respond to the note of the soul. If parents, especially mothers, realized the importance of thought during the prenatal life of their child, and that its body is being built, to a great extent, in response to that thought, they would endeavor to generate thoughts of love, harmony and beauty, so that mold, which life has fashioned, would be as it was intended to be, and its shape would not be distorted by the evil thoughts of past generations.

# 48

THE soul is a center of magnetism and by the power of attraction draws around it the matter of each plane or world through which it passes and in which it sojourns on its way to physical life, where it fulfills its destiny as a human being. Its environment in all the worlds is determined by the rate of vibration of the magnetism with which it is charged, the rate being determined by the purpose it has to fulfill; predestined as to the purpose, but with free will as to the method of fulfillment and the length of time taken in its completion.

In the body of the Great Being in Which we live, every human soul has its own place; and that it may perfect itself to fill that place, is the reason of its existence.

Each unit must be completely perfected that the whole may be harmonious. The real purpose of every soul is to sound a particular note throughout its life. When this note is true, in absolute tune to the keynote, the atoms of each plane that form its various veils or bodies are grouped to the pattern belonging to that note. The bodies will remain in the same form or pattern so long as the note is sounding, although the atoms themselves are constantly changing. The matter of which all bodies are formed is the same. The difference is only in the grouping, hence the extreme importance of sounding a true note; when it is a false one, everything in the life is inharmonious. The pattern becomes distorted and cannot fit into the place to which, by virtue of its inherent purpose, it belongs. This not only affects itself; the whole body of which it is destined to form a perfected part remains incomplete until every part is in perfect harmonious vibration.

The keynote for this planet, with which all notes must keep in tune, is the Christ note. The sound is known to every soul, but by reason of the illusionary attributes of the matter that form its many veilings, the soul identifies itself with these and, listening to the confusion of sounds surrounding it on every side, becomes unable to hear the Christ note.

For this reason, it is necessary for those who realize the purpose of life to seek the presence of one who is sounding the triune chord of love, harmony and beauty; for in the atmosphere of that harmonious vibration, all discordant sounds are hushed, and the soul is enabled to listen to the keynote of its life. If one be wise, one will tune the heart to respond to the true note of one's soul.

# 49

THE question of human free will has always been a difficult one to answer. To be capable of fully understanding this, a person must first know oneself and what one really is. It is difficult to define a person, but as a human being, one is not an immortal being but could more accurately be described as a stage in the evolution of a human soul. Man—*manas*—mind. "God created man in His Own image, in the image of God created He him."[1] To humankind, therefore, belongs the power of creative thought on every plane on which one finds oneself, and of which one's bodies are formed. It is in this region of creative thought that humanity has free will. People are free to think what they choose to think and, as every thought seeks embodiment, every person is surrounded by a world of their own creation; and thought becomes the environment in which they live, on all the planes of existence. Whatever condition one finds oneself in is the result of thought. If a person's thoughts are turned towards God, and away from self, one creates a heaven; if entirely centered upon the self, a person can be literally living in hell. These are, of course, the two extremes; and between these two, most people live, experiencing fully neither one nor the other.

But the whole mystery of the human being cannot be solved in a few words. There are many factors to consider; for instance, everyone is impressed, more or less, by the thoughts of others, living or dead, although very few realize that they possess the power to control them or the importance of clear

1 Genesis 1:27.

thinking. The thoughts of the majority are confused, half-formed and muddled. They do not know what they think nor how to think; consequently, their lives are lived in confusion and unrest, "For as he thinketh in his heart so is he."[2] If one's environment is the reflection of one's thoughts, the supreme importance of a controlled and balanced mind will readily be seen by those who have eyes of understanding. "Even here on earth everything is overcome by those whose mind remains balanced."[3] The Immortal Self, which is using mind—and during that period becomes a human soul—is the real king or ruler. When mind is controlled by soul, there is complete harmony in a human life; but when there is absence of this control, it is like a chariot driver who, having lost control of the horses, is powerless to direct the course taken by them. In this situation, the ruler becomes slave. In the same way, the human soul, unless able to control mind, becomes its slave, being taken hither and thither without direction or purpose.

Creation and destruction are the positive and negative aspects of mind. What the mind creates, the mind can destroy. Therefore, when people realize that they are living in an undesirable environment composed of living thoughts of their own creation, they, if wise, will set to work to alter the condition by destroying all inharmonious forms. The life force, which gave them birth and by which they are also nourished and sustained, must be withdrawn by turning away the mind. There are various methods by which this can be achieved, but instruction in the application of whichever method is employed is necessary and must be given by one who knows. It cannot be found in books, although many are written upon the subject. Something more is needed by one who wishes to tune one's life to live in harmony with all others. To vibrate to the Christ note—the keynote for humanity—one must learn how to create as well as how to destroy. Protective thoughts

2 Proverbs 23:7.

3 Bhagavad Gita.

must be created in order to prevent undesirable thoughts of other people being impressed upon one's mind. There are also many ways by which the person who has control of mind can help those in need, but this is a vast subject and can only be touched upon here. Control of thought is an extremely difficult lesson for one to master. Fortunate is the person, and greatly favored, who has found a teacher.

The length of time necessary to destroy a thought varies according to the strength of the form, which depends upon the force and definiteness with which it was created. This is the reason why some people who most earnestly desire to alter their lives find such overwhelming difficulties facing them. The creations of the mind are living entities and do not wish to die. They will fight to the end for their individual life, so that directly anyone sets foot upon the path to God, one has to fight an army of one's own creating who, surrounding one on every side, are fighting to retain that person's life force for their own use. But if, before the battle begins, one has been able to create an army of protective thoughts and, while fighting, can keep the mind fixed upon God, the true desire of the soul, they will in time all fall dead upon the field, for they cannot live except by reinforcement of the thought, conscious or unconscious, of their creator.

The physical human body is formed of millions of physical atoms, separate, distinct and individual, all carrying on their own work but whose life depends upon the being of whose body they are a part, in whom they live and move and have their being. All the other bodies belonging to humans, emotional, mental, and spiritual, are made in exactly the same way. Millions and millions of living entities belonging to all the planes of existence are made by creative thought from the elemental essence of each plane, to form the bodies in which the human soul functions and by which alone one is able to express oneself.

The real self of every person is a silent spectator who creates an embodiment: a universe in miniature, children of the mind who exist so long as they are held in thought.

Humanity's free will exists in its power of creative thought, but humans are bound by necessity to the environment of their own creating.

# 50

*I form the Light and create darkness, I make peace and create evil, I the Lord do all these things.*

—*Isaiah 45:7*

*I am the gambling of the cheat; and the splendour of splendid things I.*

—*Bhagavad Gita*

WHAT then is the force we call *Satan*? Satan is the shadow of the Christ, that which obscures Christ, as darkness is the shadow of light. Where there is light, there must also be darkness. Wherever is the Light of the World, there also is the Lord of the Shadow. A sacrifice such as is impossible for the mind to conceive has been offered for humanity by the Lord of the Shadow, who must remain an outcast from the light throughout the manifestation of the world. This is the mystic interpretation of the crucifixion of Christ; for, mystery of mysteries, they are not two but one.

Evolution at that stage of being called *humanity* is only possible in a world of duality in the human kingdom. Man evolves into *hu-man* by mastery, control, and balance. The two forces, positive and negative, are combined in the human being; therefore, living in a world of duality, one cannot know anything without also knowing its opposite. Without a force that opposed and tested one's strength at every step, one could never become master of life, or a divine person, could never learn control if there were nothing to control, or become balanced if there were no opposition.

The opposing force is not the enemy of humanity, as is generally supposed. It is the illusion caused by and, therefore, part of, light; but one cannot reach or realize light until one has crossed over this illusion. The whole purpose of human evolution, made in the image of God, is that having the birthright of free will, one shall develop the power in oneself to choose reality and reject illusion; and by right of one's heritage of kingship and freedom of choice, shall conquer and possess one's own kingdom.

Humans commit sin when, having knowledge of light, they willingly remain in darkness, refusing to cross the illusion.

> *This divine illusion of Mine caused by the qualities is hard to pierce; they who come to Me, they cross over this illusion. He who seeth Me everywhere, and seeth everything in Me, of him will I never lose hold, and he shall never lose hold of Me.*
>
> —*Bhagavad Gita*

# 51

THE mystery of time is the greatest mystery of all. If humanity knew its secret, it would be free from bondage. Not knowing this, a person is a slave bound by its arbitrary laws impressed upon one from birth in a world where time is king. Those who would understand this mystery must learn through realization (knowledge is useless here) that time, as seen by humans, is an illusion; that past, present and future are not three but one; and that one is the present, in which both past and future meet and blend. Whoever is able, in the terms and meaning of the mystic, to live in the present carries no burden of the past; neither do they fear any future, for to them the three are one. They have in themselves become the balance of the scales of time and can stand upright and immovable whether the scales on either side of them rise or fall.

The reason that the mysteries of reality cannot be revealed to the human mind is because it can only see half-truths. It is beyond the capacity of its comprehension to realize that anything can be and not be at the same time. Even the words used in trying to explain this mystery are liable to be misunderstood; only to the inner eye can the real meaning be unveiled. To the seer, everything is and nothing is, time exists and yet there is no time. "The unreal hath no being; the real never ceaseth to be; the truth about both hath been perceived by the seer of the essence of things."[1]

Time in this world is the great illusion, and yet people could not live in the world without it. The only way they can

1 Bhagavad Gita.

free themselves from it is to realize it has no existence, no life except the life they give it by their own beliefs. No one living in time can know reality. Time is the shadow created by eternity, shadowed forth in physical life as the environment in which the soul lives. Humanity, really speaking, lives on earth in its own shadow.

The teaching of the sages and seers is that time is the shadow of the eternal that is within our innermost being. If we seek it within, we would see it as one eternal whole, unfolded before our view in miniature; but when we see it outside ourselves, it can only be perceived as separated parts that can never give a complete picture. Time and the secret of time is within your self; seek there for enlightenment. It is our perception of time that passes, not time itself, for "Time is God and God is eternal."[2]

---

2 Inayat Khan, *The Gayan*.

## 52

THE light of the sun, imprisoned and buried in the earth as coal, is the same substance whether manifesting as light or coal; one unlimited the other limited. Only through the fires of purification can the imprisoned light reach again the source of its being and be absorbed into the one light, from which it is separated throughout its life of limitation. As coal, it retains a separate individuality; but after being freed by the liberating fire, the symbol of purity—meaning pure from all that divides or separates—it loses for ever that burden of separateness and becomes one with, or identified with, the light that is its very self.

If one could think of coal as a living entity, able to feel and to suffer, what agony must it endure when shut into outer darkness with no power of movement; dumb, blind and restricted on every side; at the mercy of forces beyond its control; buried in the denseness of the earth. And if any memories of its real self were retained, and the realization of its heritage of light, would it not long with a longing unspeakable, at whatever cost—even of that consuming fire in which its coal individuality is reduced to ashes—for freedom for that self, which, through the ages, has been dumbly pleading to return to that from which it came forth.

It is only when the imprisoned light has been freed from its bondage that it can realize the reason for the long, long pilgrimage. Having returned to its original condition and knowing itself as light and not as coal, it can look back and see the necessity for the sacrifice of its freedom: the surrender of itself as light to the blackness of coal.

The sun, as light, could not help the dwellers upon earth to evolve into the civilized races that inhabit it today. So the supreme sacrifice of burial and imprisonment, for thousands of years, to the extreme limit of blackness was made; and what to the rapid vibrations of light is far worse, to inertia. It can now understand that when, as coal, it was through fire purified of black and became again white, it was not for its own salvation, although by this means it gained its own freedom, but for the helping forward of humanity in its efforts to gain the mastery of the elements. And by this sacrifice of its coal individuality, humanity had been enabled to obtain everything needed for the evolution of a great civilization: heat, light, food and clothing, dwelling places and means of transit, everything necessary to sustain life, to link nation to nation and race to race. By the quiet sacrifice of its life as coal through the fires of purification, which is so ordinary an occurrence that no one even considers it, humankind is helped to conquer the earth, sea and air, and even control fire itself. It now realizes that the sacrifice of itself as coal was not sacrifice but freedom, the passing from darkness to light; and that all the time its real self was not coal but light; that coal was its false self, the form that bound it to the denseness of earth.

Only by the power of the imprisoned light becoming active through sacrifice could humanity be helped; only by losing its life of limitation could the unlimited life be known. It knows now that all the time, it was not coal that had helped but light; for the real sacrifice was made by light, which voluntarily limited itself for the sake of humanity.

# 53

THE fact that some people are able to see long past events, and even to describe historical scenes, need not necessarily imply that in a former life they lived in those days. That may or may not be a fact, but there is another explanation: that they are the possessors of the clairvoyant vision enabling them to look back into the past. And the reason they see themselves as living and acting in those times and scenes, is because the soul identifies itself with whatever it is interested in. It is the nature of the soul so to do. When the attention is focused upon earth life, it identifies itself with body and mind, calling that *I*. But when it is turned away from the physical plane and is watching a panorama of past ages, it identifies itself with a character that appeals to it. Unless clairvoyants are highly developed souls, real seers, they are not powerful enough to hold themselves unidentified with the visions passing before them. Only the God-realized person, one who has identified oneself with the God Within, which is the soul's true identity, has the power of clear vision. Others are very easily deceived, as although *clairvoyance* means seeing through the eyes of the soul, unless that soul has reached a very high level, the vision is confused.

What should be impressed upon those willing to receive such teaching, is that it does not help the soul's progress in its journey God-ward to be continually trying relive the past. What is past belongs to the past. Jesus said, "Follow me, let the dead bury their dead."[1] The soul's concern is the living today, for whatever one thinks today, so will one's tomorrow be.

The results of experience, one's own and that of one's forebears, are in a person's own self, as shown by character, temperament and environment. All that one need concern oneself with is the best way of living daily life so that one may be enabled to take the next step upon the path to God: to learn the lesson that each experience brings; to pass from that experience, whether pleasurable or painful, directly the lesson is learned; never by word or deed willingly to hurt another soul; and to strive every moment of life to identify oneself with the God Within, the real Self of humanity.

1 Matthew 8:22.

# 54

SOUL, *atma*, or highest spirit, can never be anything but itself and must, therefore, be the same in every being. Differences exist not in the soul but in the forms or covers necessary for expression in a material world. As the covers used by the human soul are formed of every experience it touches or passes through, and of every impression received during its journey earthwards, the greatest differences among people arise in the world of thought, or mind, uniting highest spirit with lowest matter. The mind of each soul being peculiar to itself, its conception is that of a separate being apart from other beings: *I* as distinct from *You*.

As it is the nature of the soul to identify itself with whatever it beholds, being enclosed in covers formed of mental, emotional and physical matter, it identifies itself with either one or all of these bodies, which obscure its true source and origin; and the knowledge of unity is thus lost to itself, though always existing. "In heaven their angels do always behold the face of my Father which is in heaven."[1] It is difficult for the human mind to realize this mystery of unity in separation, of One yet many; and it can only be finally solved when the covers have been broken by suffering, the means by which the soul within is released. "Out of the shell of the broken heart arises the newborn soul."[2] But some measures of realization can be obtained if the covers can be refined, made thin and transparent instead of thick and opaque. In this way a window can be made through which the soul may obtain

1 Matthew 18:10.
2 Inayat Khan, *The Gayan*.

glimpses, as it were, of the nature of its own oneness with all that exists.

An analogy will sometimes help the mind to some understanding of things about which words cannot be spoken, if it is not pushed too far. For instance, the many-colored balls with which children play may serve as an illustration here. They are small bags or envelopes made from some physical substance capable of expansion when filled with air. It is the same air in all, difference of color, size and shape being in the envelope that contains it. They are each separate and distinct from the other and, in this condition, are called *balls*. Directly a cover is broken, the air or life with which it was filled is united with its source, uncolored and unchanged.

The soul no more partakes of or is affected by what is reflected in it or what it reflects than a mirror partakes of or is affected by the forms continually passing and repassing before it. After all the reflections have passed, it is the same as before the images were reflected. It is only during the time it is receiving reflections that there are differences. It remains the same always; it is only the reflections that alter and change.

The soul is changeless in a world of change, eternal in a world of time.

# 55

ANNIHILATION has a different meaning for the mystic to that which it has for the ordinary person, to whose mind this word presents a picture of the destruction and death of everything. Even the nirvana of the Buddhist has been pictured thus. A treader of the path of wisdom understands annihilation in the mystical sense, and for that person it means the attainment of bliss such as the world could never know. For in the light of that vision, everything fades into nothingness; even the personal self is completely forgotten.

In reality, it means annihilation of the barriers surrounding the soul on every side, which are the cause of the feelings of separation, exile, and unrest. And the removal of these enable it to find its true home; to become one with the whole to whom it belongs; to merge into and become part of that fuller, larger and deeper life in which is perfect freedom. In other words, it means absolute completion.

This mystic union of the soul with God has been experienced by saints of all religions. In all ages the inner experience is the same, although the outer expression may be different for each soul.

To the lovers of God, the ecstasy of joy is in the surrender of self. Even an earthly love is not complete while one thought of self remains as a barrier between the lover and the beloved.

Perfection cannot be experienced until barriers between the soul and God have been annihilated.

The prayer of Jesus for his disciples was, "That they all may be One, as Thou, Father, art in me and I in Thee."[1]

1 John 17:21.

If thou couldst empty all thyself of self
Like to a shell dishabited,
The might He find thee on the ocean shelf
And say, "This is not dead"
And fill thee with Himself instead.
But thou art all replete with very thou,
And hast such shrewd activity, that
When He comes He says, "This is enow
Unto itself,
'Twere better let it be.
It is so small and full,
There is no room for me."

# 56

WHAT becomes of the waste product, or ashes, of a world?

Essence ascends as one, but waste product, or ashes, is carried by the four winds and disintegrated into its constituent parts, into the ether from which it came forth and from whence it is recoverable, although not in the same formation, for it has lost forever its personality. This process is very, very gradual and, before the final disintegration, it is used again and again in countless ways. The whole of the matter forming a world belongs to that world and forms part of it as long as the spirit or essence remains. But after the essence has ascended, the residue is waste product and can never again, as a whole, form part of one living entity, although it may be distributed amongst many.

At the end of a world period, there remains a certain portion of matter that has not been redeemed, or raised to its highest rate of vibration. It then becomes waste product, or the ashes of that world.

The purpose of the evolution of a planet that has received the life impulse, is that the matter of which it is formed shall be raised to its original essence or spirit, as the seed of a flower that has received the essence of life from the sun evolves through the denseness of the earth until it becomes a plant; and at the end of its allotted task, the perfumed essence arises from the flowering, which is its perfection. It came to earth as seed; it returns as perfume, fulfilling the purpose for which it was created by leaving forms of other seeds capable of receiving the light of the sun, although not all of them do so. That part of the plant that does not become spirit, or essence, is in time disintegrated and becomes waste product, or ashes, as far as that particular plant is concerned.

In reality, nothing is lost, although everything is changed; but the beginning and the end of God's plan for the evolution of a universe is beyond comprehension by the human mind.

Is it the flowering or the fruit that is the perfection of a plant?

For everything there is the beginning, the zenith and the end. In a plant, the flowering would represent the zenith, or perfection; the fruit is the result of that perfection. In order to recreate after its kind, the flower must die, and the essence, or perfume, which is its life, ascend. And as the ray of ensouling light is drawn up, the form and color of the flower is impressed upon the seeds contained in the fruit, which remains as the womb in which they are brought to birth. In one sense, the fruit is the perfection of the plant. But strictly speaking, the fruit is the purpose for which the spirit, or life essence, came on earth; and each has its own perfection. But the perfection of a plant, as a whole, is its flowering, or expression of beauty, after which it begins to decay. The essence does not belong to the plant or to the flower, but is part of the One Life, a ray of light of the sun from which it came and to which it must return. Indeed, it has never been separate but the end of a ray of light, caught and held by the plant until its flowering when, as perfume, it is released to ascend again to the light of which it is a part. The act of expression of beauty, which is the ecstasy of the plant, causes the form and color of the flower to pass into the fruit.

In this fruit left on earth, the seeds, or forms of future plants, are fashioned. But the soul, or life, can only be received when the light of the sun falls upon them; that sun whose touch gives life to all seeds, whatever their form. Seeds are the fruit, or result of the union, of positive and negative forces. They are of earth, therefore negatively charged and cannot live or become active until touched by the positive, or life force. Those that are not thus touched, disintegrate.

The perfection of a rose tree is the color and perfume of its flowering. Not until this beauty has been expressed, or given forth, can the fruit of other rose trees be formed.

Fruit is of the earth; it can be seen, touched and handled. But the essence that produced it, no one can analyze.

## 57

THOSE who would gather seeds for planting must not desire the blossom. They may feel its beauty but seek not its possession, for whosoever possesses the blossom can never gather the fruit.

Leave your flowers growing, O traveler on the path, that their perfume may refresh the wayfarers. Thus shall your plants yield seeds for other sowing.

# 58

ETHER: the unmanifest beyond human thought or comprehension.

The four elements, earth, water, fire air: the manifested.

These elements are the syllables for the Sacred Name. The spoken or uttered word could not be sounded until broken or divided; the act of speaking breaks thought into words. One substance separated into four, by which all things are made manifest, from the greatest to the most minute, and without which nothing could be. The sacred four are divided and yet not divided. They are four and yet they are only One: the great Three in One, from which a new manifestation comes into being. But of this mystery of mysteries, more cannot be spoken.

# 59

GOD is not concerned with sin or pleased by virtue. Sin is its own punishment, virtue its own reward. Whoever sins must suffer the consequences sooner or later, and those who are virtuous always have the satisfaction that virtue gives; this is an unalterable law. But it is neither to gain satisfaction nor to escape suffering that the soul comes to earth. It is to master life and death, to become *hu-man*, or a divine man; and in order to do so, absolute mastery must be obtained over all the kingdoms in which one finds oneself. One must meet and conquer both sin and virtue, so that neither of these delusive pairs of opposites have any power over one; so long as a person is held by either, one is a slave.

"Whosoever commiteth sin is the servant of sin."[1] Likewise, the person whom virtue holds is the slave of virtue. Both are lessons given to us to teach us to know ourselves and gain the strength to rise above them. Sometimes people need more strength to rise above their virtues than to leave their sins; these should be regarded as valuable lessons that must be accurately learned, for people cannot pass from the elementary school of life until they have learned the lessons. But once having passed out, they do not need to continue the lesson. They retain within themselves the essence, or result, of the teaching, which qualifies them to receive knowledge of truth, in which is perfect freedom. "And ye shall know the truth, and the truth shall make you free."[2]

1 John 8:34.
2 John 8:32.

# *At the Gate of Discipleship 59*

*Religion is for the desire nature; the Path for the heart; Truth for the soul.*

*—Sharaf al-Din Maneri*

*Wherefore the law was our schoolmaster to bring us unto Christ that we might be justified by faith. But after that faith is come; we are no longer under a schoolmaster.*

*—Galatians 3:24–25*

# 60

A FEW words of explanation may be given about the teaching that disciples upon the path must turn away from their virtues as well as from their sins, as this sometimes causes a good deal of misunderstanding among those whose eyes are not yet open to the vision of truth.

Of course, as is so frequently repeated, neither this teaching nor any other pertaining to things of the spirit can be fully explained in words belonging to earth. Whosoever desires to understand must endeavor to do so by the light of intuition. It most certainly does not imply that travelers upon the path of discipleship need not consider their conduct, or that there is no necessity for them to practice the ordinary virtues of life common to all religious and ethical teaching. All these and many more must be acquired before an aspirant can pass through the gate.

The sages have said, "Thou must acquire all virtues, such as truth, purity and worship. When acquired, thou must scatter them in the air of supreme indifference."[1] The real meaning of this is that nothing must stand before the human soul as a something that belongs to it and from which it cannot separate. If any one thing, no matter how good or beautiful or holy it may be, is placed upon the throne of the heart, which place belongs to God alone, then the one who places it there is worshiping a false God. Until disciples have entirely forgotten their own personalities, they cannot be trusted with the knowledge of truth. When, by the help of a spiritual teacher,

1 Sharaf ad-Din Maneri, *Letters from a Sufi Teacher*.

the inner eyes are for a brief moment open to the vision of God, they become utterly and wholly unconscious of self, their very existence as a separate beings forgotten. Then in the light of that vision, both the memory of sins repented of and virtues acquired will fade into nothingness; for no other thought must remain to blur the image of God, which by this means is being impressed upon the hearts of the disciples.

Khwaja Bayazid was asked, "What is the way to God?" He replied, "When thou hast vanished on the way, then hast thou come to God."[2]

2 Bayazid Bastami.

# 61

TO understand the mystery of pain, you must understand the mystery of the pairs of opposites. While people live in this world of illusion, *maya*, they are subject to its laws and cannot experience heaven unless they also know hell. They cannot have life without death, nor joy without pain; they are living the separated life in the shadow world. If they could turn from this unreality to the real, for them, pain would cease; they would have crossed over the illusion and discovered the secret of the pairs of opposites. While these pairs are divided, they delude humanity; but when they can be united or balanced, they reveal the innermost mystery of being. "The Eternal is incorruptible and balanced. The knower of the Eternal neither rejoices on obtaining what is pleasant nor sorroweth on obtaining what is unpleasant."[1] But humanity has free will, and the experiences of every person are according to one's beliefs.

> *The faith of each is shaped to his own nature; a man consists of his faith. That which his faith is, he is even that.*
>
> —*Bhagavad Gita*

1 Bhagavad Gita.

## 62

AS each planet is self-contained, and its inner life hidden from any other, so is the inner human life. No one, however near, however dear, can know the hidden thoughts and aspirations of any other. They are known only to One Whose dwelling is at the center of our being in the innermost shrine.

We must always be alone in our inner life, which can never be shared with another soul. The only thing that can give us true companionship and real communion is union with God, Who is our very Self.

## 63

KEEP your faith and remember that thought is the greatest creative power in the world. Keep your mind free from any selfish desire, continually fixed upon God, and anything will be possible. Remember also that every thought, besides having form, color and life, has its own time.

# 64

THE chord to which humanity belongs is the threefold chord of love, harmony, and beauty. As the atoms of the body evolve and become finer and finer, so one is able to respond to the higher vibrations of this chord. From atom to solar system, the same process is repeated. The law imposed upon the universe is also imposed upon every single atom and electron of which it is composed. One substance—light; one law—vibration; one goal—God.

## Words of the Master Heard in the Silence

BLESSED are they whose eyes can behold the glory of the Lord; they cannot be held by the pleasures of earth.

Blessed are they whose ears are attuned to the voice of the Lord; verily, for them all other sound is stilled.

Blessed are they who understand the language of the Lord; verily, they are the knowers of wisdom.

Blessed are the steadfast in faith;
verily, they abide in peace.

Blessed are they who tread the balanced path;
upon a sure rock have their feet been placed.

Blessed are they whose hearts have the open vision;
in the days of tribulation they shall guide the homing souls.

Blessed are they who can steer their boats through the sea of doubt; for of all seas, it is the most treacherous.

Blessed are they who can tune their hearts to the keynote of their souls; verily, they shall hear the voice of God.

Blessed are they whose hearts are fixed upon God;
in the day of tribulation, they shall stand and fall not.

Verily, of all people they are most blessed,
whose eyes are closed to all save God.

Verily, those who rest in the thought of God,
have peace which passeth all understanding.

Blessed are they who can rise above earthly desire;
verily, shall their souls be satisfied.

Blessed are the humble-minded;
for theirs is the true exaltation.

Blessed are they who are empty of self;
for they have prepared for the birth of Christ.

Blessed are they who have conquered death;
for theirs is the life everlasting.

Blessed are they of the generous heart;
a thousandfold shall be their reward.

Blessed are they who care for the needy;
they shall receive the treasure of heaven.

Blessed are they who seek the lonely heart;
verily, they are companioned by God.

Blessed are they who pass through great tribulations;
they alone bind the broken heart.

Blessed are they who have walked through suffering;
they also know the way of peace.

Blessed are they in whom self is dead;
they shall be filled with the life of God.

Blessed are they from whom self is covered;
they shall reflect the light of God.

Blessed are they whose eyes are blind;
verily, they shall behold the perfection of beauty.

Blessed are they whose ears are deaf;
verily, they shall hear the perfection of harmony.

Blessed are they whose lips are dumb;
through them shall be given the words of Life.

Blessed are they whose hearts are attuned to the voice of God; verily they shall transmit God's Message.

# Between the Desert and the Sown

The Way of thc Disciple

# Foreword

THESE teachings are offered to travelers upon the path of discipleship. To others this may appear a path of sacrifice, but disciples would not so consider it, for they know that "the things which are seen are temporal, but the things which are not seen are eternal."[1]

There are, of course, many things that must be left behind by travelers on this path. They are traveling, and their objective is the journey's end. It is not a sacrifice to pass a momentary gain for one that is lasting, when they can see both with open vision. The sacrifice for them would be not to do so.

It is not wise for those who consider the life of a disciple one of sacrifice to try to live it. Life has many lessons, and there are many ways of finding God; each one must seek for oneself. Nothing but one's own intense desire can lead a person upon the path of discipleship, and then it would be no more a sacrifice than it would be for a child to leave a game when it hears the voice of a loved father calling it. The child just turns round and runs as quickly as it can to find him; the game is forgotten, it is only conscious of the father.

Those who are traveling the way of the disciple are often accused by those who cannot understand the disciples' actions of selfishly trying to save their own souls, regardless of others. There is a paradox here, for although it is true that each soul must find and tread the path to God alone, it is also true that by doing so one cannot fail to help others, consciously and unconsciously; consciously by the sympathy of

1 2 Corinthians 4:18.

an awakened heart, and unconsciously by the soul's atmosphere. There are many, weary and bewildered with life's difficulties, who would gladly journey to find peace if haply they knew where it could be found; but no one can help another to find the kingdom of heaven unless one has first found it oneself; no one can bring peace to another who has not oneself known peace. The God-realized ones radiate love, peace, and harmony by their presence, and only the traveler who has reached this goal is able to guide the feet of those who are seeking the way of peace.

July 1923

# Part One

## 1

THERE is a path that lies between the field of joy and the field of sorrow. It is on this path that the Beloved walks, and only in the silence between the desert and the sown can the Beloved's voice be heard.

## 2

EVERY soul returns to God by its own path, and each person's path is peculiar to that person; and yet there is but one path and one way for the seeking soul.

One road leading home, upon which all must travel; one gate, the gate of the master, through which all must pass to find the kingdom. But to each this path appears to be different, for whatsoever one sees within the heart is reflected outwardly in life, and becomes the environment in which one lives, and the path upon which one travels.

*As a man thinketh in his heart, so is he.*
*—Proverbs 23:7*

*Neither shall they say, lo! here! and or, lo! there!; for the kingdom of God is within you.*
*—Luke 17:21*

# 3

THERE is today much talk about the path and initiations on the path by those who are quite ignorant of the real meaning of such initiations; initiations into orders, such as Freemasonry and other occult societies, is another matter.

The disciple who knows the reality is silent; the one who speaks has not experienced. For each soul the path is different, and each one makes its own path. It is a mystery of mysteries and must be sought within.

The traveler on the way to God will, at some period of the journey, receive the torch of illumination, and by its light will be able to perceive the inner secrets of the traveler's own being. Then will one learn the great mystery of initiation and know that, at every step of the way one has traveled and still has to travel, life, the great initiator, tests and initiates each homing soul. The traveler realizes that the inner sanctuary, the abode of God that is in the human heart, is the real place of initiation. At this stage one also learns how every wave of emotion is used to refine and purify the soul who is consciously seeking God.

"Strait is the gate, and narrow is the way . . . and few there be who that find it," said Jesus Christ.[1] So strait the gate, so narrow is the path, that if anyone would go through, verily they must lose themselves.

The gate is within.

The path is within.

The kingdom and the king are within.

The one whose eyes are closed is the one who beholds the vision of these things of God.

---

1 Matthew 7:14.

## 4

THE tests that disciples must pass on their spiritual journey are experienced in ordinary daily life, and not in great ceremonies in halls of initiation on the astral plane; those are but symbols of the reality. The nearer the disciples are to the goal, the more will they find themselves surrounded by a sea of difficulties. This is a necessary test for a disciple's own safety, as before a person can pass on, one must be able to stand holding one's own note without vibrating to the sounds around one, however loudly they may call. The disciple must hold it clearly and steadily, for from henceforth the disciple must be able to respond to the higher vibrations that are heard in silence; and hearing in silence, may give forth in sound. This silence can only be obtained by eliminating all sounds that are not in harmonious vibration. But as one is living in a world full of every kind of vibration, both harmonious and inharmonious, one must know how to do this without being overwhelmed by them and tossed hither and thither on the ocean of vibrations.

The keynote for which disciples must listen is the Christ note, and when they can hear this through all the discords surrounding them on every side, they will have mastered that ocean and be able to walk upon the water with their master.

# 5

THE true path of discipleship is not an easy path to tread. During the probationary stage, the pupils may follow their own or another's light, and may weigh and compare many lines of development to their own advantage; but directly they become accepted disciples of any master, they must, during the time of discipleship, give to that master an absolute trust even to the extent of sometimes surrendering the personal will. It should be clearly understood, however, that this must be a voluntary surrender, as here there can be no coercion; and no one should accept as a spiritual guide a person to whom one is unable to give such a trust.

There are places upon the spiritual path where the disciple must walk blindfolded, and trust in the guide is a necessity; but this is for the protection and safety of the disciple, not for the glorification of the guide. No true spiritual teacher desires, or would accept, personal devotion or homage, but only for God to Whom all homage belongs. Faith and trust in the guide are the only means by which the disciple can reach the heights and attain to the soul's desire. There are many thousands upon this path who have gone halfway but cannot make further progress, because they are unable to give such trust. They will never reach the goal until they can do so, although they may travel a long way; but the guides understand and would never take a disciple farther than that disciple desired to go. They could not even if they would, because the faith and trust necessary at this stage of the journey must be spontaneous and cannot be forced. They know the eyes of such disciples are not yet fully open, and in infinite patience, await the complete unveiling.

# 6

WHILE the disciples identify themselves with the personality they will never be able to advance along the spiritual path. At this stage of the journey they must be free to satisfy the claims of the soul and carry out duties demanded by the soul, not continually turning aside to satisfy claims of the personality. Although, of course, these duties must be performed and debts incurred must be paid, they must be finally settled before any real advancement can be made, otherwise there is no end to the turning back. For real progress through all the difficulties touching the personality (practically the whole of the daily life in the world) there is only one way: keep the heart fixed upon God—not only the thoughts but the heart. The greatest love the heart is capable of must be there. "For where your treasure is, there will your heart be also."[1] Only then will every thought fly to God like homing birds to rest; and only when God is desired above everything else in life will life's difficulties cease to hinder the progress of the disciple. As "no man hath seen God at any time,"[2] it is through the gate of the master that love and desire for God will be realized.

1 Matthew 6:21.
2 John 1:18.

# 7

EACH soul has its own path upon which it must return to God; it can do so on no other. As soon as the return journey is begun, many and varied difficulties arise in the human life of such a soul. Disciples may themselves, at the moment of their realization, be upon another's path instead of their own. This would mean many changes in the outer life. Such changes are inevitable as, at this stage, one fully realizes in one's own being that each must tread their own path. Until the return journey begins it is of not much consequence what path the disciple is following; and many may attract one until that time comes, but when it does one knows. Another difficulty is the friends and companions made by the disciples in the various ways they may have trodden. Unless these too arrive at the stage of return simultaneously, which very rarely happens, the way is sometimes strewn with broken friendships, which is the cause of much suffering; for a person will never be understood except by those who have reached the same stage of development. Yet let the disciple remember that it is impossible for one soul to harm another unless there is desire to harm. Action without motive is nothing, and desire is the only force that can really affect another.

Every soul belongs to God, and God's help is the only help needed by any human being, however necessary one may seem to another. In reality, only God is necessary. In trying to take God's place in any human life, one may hinder instead of helping the progress of that life. God is quite able to take care of all God's children in God's own way and uses every blow of fate to open a door whereby divine love and divine light may reach them.

Once more, no one is necessary to the spiritual development of another. Only God is necessary.

# 8

FOR each life there is a place and a purpose, and until one has found it one cannot progress. Very often, when disciples begin to tread the path of return they will find that their own people, sometimes those nearest and dearest, become bitterly opposed. The more religious they are, the greater will be their opposition; and it is the cause of great strife and much suffering. It seems difficult to understand and strange, that those who have walked together happily on earth, should not also journey together to God. This has always been understood by the masters of wisdom, and there are many sayings of Jesus bearing upon this subject.

He who was called the Prince of Peace said, "I came not to send peace but a sword. For I am come to set a man at variance against his father, and the daughter against her mother, and the daughter-in-law against her mother-in-law; and a man's foes shall be they of his own household."[1]

These are hard sayings, and difficult to understand and interpret. There is an inner meaning for those who have ears to hear. In the ordinary life of the world, a person may walk side by side in unity with many without disagreement, but directly one sets foot upon the spiritual path there is a difference. Up till now one has had to meet every kind of difficulty and hindrance, and has found oneself in every sort of condition, good and bad, harmonious and inharmonious, in order that one may master them, or rise above them; for one cannot pass on until nothing has power to move or hinder one from

1 Matthew 10:35–36.

following one's life's purpose. One is now starting to return to the Father's house, the abode of the soul, and to find one's own place therein. This will necessarily cause a separation from all those who are not treading the same path of return; for there are many paths, and although they all lead to God, ultimately, each soul has its own place. "In my Father's house are many mansions,"[2] and all do not vibrate to the same spiritual note, although the complete whole makes the divine harmony. When disciples are sounding their own true notes, as they do when on the path of return, then the disciples can only vibrate in harmony with those who belong to the same vibratory chord. With others there will be a discord, for they can never agree upon spiritual truths, although in worldly matters they may do so.

This truth, or rather the misunderstanding of it, has been the cause of many tragedies and much religious persecution; because everyone believes one's path to be the only way to God. So it may be for that person, but not necessarily for another. Each one should give the freedom to others that is claimed for oneself.

2 John 14:2.

# 9

THE disciple should continually strive to realize the unreal and transitory nature of life in the world. In reality, it is but a shadow of the real or inner life, and without that inner life it could have no existence.

As the inner life of a disciple changes, so its shadow or outer life, alters, because the shadow must take the form of the reality that causes it.

> *When is the stick crooked and the shadow straight?*
>
> *—Al-Ghazzali*

When disciples have found God in their own hearts, their inner life, then they will also find God in the outer life, reflected in every being and every thing. When this truth is realized, that is, made real, then the whole mystery of life in this world and the next is solved.

The reason why people cannot understand this mystery is because they take the shadow for the reality. They are like the dog who was crossing a bridge over a stream with a piece of meat in its mouth and saw, reflected in the water, what it imagined was a much larger piece. The dog did not know that it was only the shadow of what it already had, so dropped the piece it was carrying in order to seize the larger one. Of course, directly it had done so, it lost both.

In the waters of illusion everything is thus presented to the human mind. The shadows are made to appear larger and more important than the reality. One can see the shadow with the outer eyes and it appears desirable, but the importance of that which creates the shadow one cannot see, because the inner vision is closed.

The sincere disciple on the path to God understands that where there is light there must also be shadow; but while worldly humanity turns its back to the light so that the shadow is always before its sight, the spiritual person faces the light and the shadow falls behind. Thus the eyes are filled with the vision of God, and for that person the worldly life is but the shadow of reality.

# 10

THE disciples must go forward without regret, never once looking backward, and remember that every sorrow and difficulty, and every joy was a necessary experience to teach some lesson that had to be learned before they could tread the path they had chosen. The disciples will need great strength, great courage, and a great faith; but the reward is more than it has entered into the human heart to conceive: it is the joy of service, the fullness of joy, which cannot be taken away.

## 11

DISCIPLES cannot receive real inspiration until they have ceased to desire anything for themselves. Until then, anything that is received is always colored, more or less, by the personality. Whatever vessel is offered to the master to fill must first be empty; only then can the master fill it.

## 12

WHEN the heart has reached the state of perfect stillness, which is the highest rate of vibration, then will every cry of suffering humanity find an echo there; for the still or empty heart is filled by God and attuned to God, without Whose knowledge not a sparrow falls to the ground. How much more then shall God hear the cry of God's own sorrowing children, which rises through the empty hearts of those who are called *the Sons of God*.

# 13

DISCIPLES cannot realize God while they are looking for God outside. They have not even yet begun to understand the meaning of the words of Jesus Christ: "The kingdom of heaven is within you."[1] It means that one must find God inside oneself,[2] for where the kingdom is, there also is the king.[3] It means also the new birth: "Ye must be born again of the Spirit."[4]

The Christ Child must be born in the heart. When this has taken place, as the Christ gradually fills the life, so the personality will fade and the physical vehicle will be used for a purpose, for whatever work Christ's wisdom chooses. The only thing necessary is to let the new birth take place; the rest is Christ's work, and the result with Him. If this could be possible to everyone, Christ's kingdom would have come on earth. This has always been taught by the mystics of all ages, but how few understand?

Of course, it is a great mystery, and few are ready to lose themselves to this extent; because before the new birth can take place, there must the death, or loss, of the personality, or rather seeming loss. Really speaking, it is a great gain, an enrichment of every part of the being; but this cannot be known until it has been experienced.

1 Luke 17:21.

2 "Seated equally in all beings, the Supreme Lord, imperishing with the perishing; he who thus seeth, he seeth." Bhagavad Gita.

3 "Yogis also struggling perceive Him established in the self; but though struggling, the unintelligent perceive Him not—their selves untrained." Bhagavad Gita.

4 John 3:3.

There is also another mystery. Before there can be a new birth, the soul must contact a master on some plane. The Christ Child cannot be born in the heart until love has been awakened there[5] and the heart opened by pain, the only thing able to open the heart. But again, that is another mystery, for where pain is, there also must be joy; the one draws its life from the other.

5 "Everyone that loveth is born of God and knoweth God; he that loveth not, knoweth not God;, for God is love." 1 John 4:7–8.

# 14

THE disciple should keep the feet steadily upon the spiritual path; turn neither to the right nor to the left; look not before nor after, but up and straight ahead; and walk in sure faith, keeping thoughts ever upon God. Then shall the disciple surely find God.

Only a master can safely tread the path of psychism. It is the illusion of illusions, a path leading to a world full of dangers and deceptions, delusions, false conceptions and false ideas. The warning must be given wherever possible, for the veil has been lifted between the two worlds. The demand has been made and must be met, but to all except the strong who are firmly established in the knowledge of God, it is a grave menace. The disciple must not desire psychic development, but only God and knowledge of God. "Seek ye first the kingdom of God, and His righteousness, and all these things shall be added unto you."[1] This is the only safe way of progress.

1 Matthew 6:33.

# 15

THE disciple should never cease seeking; it is the only way in which one can find God.

If any expression of the Christ were to walk the earth unveiled, everyone who came within Christ's atmosphere would be paralyzed, as they would be burnt if they approached near to the physical sun.

The messenger of God must always be veiled, with cover upon cover, in order that those who are really seeking may find.

Each soul must find for itself. No one can show another the Christ. For each Christ is different and yet is only One; for no one can see the Christ as He is, but only so much as one's spiritual sight can focus upon.

The veils of earth with which messengers must be hidden are necessary in order that they may reach those who are ready for a messenger's coming, without harming others. But it is always a crucifixion, like being buried alive; and every moment of physical life is a continual repression to prevent the light within the messenger from blinding those who are beginning to awaken.

# 16

THE disciples who would reflect the light of God to those who sit in darkness, which is the only way the light can be received by suffering humanity, must stand immovable and unshakable—unmoved by the cries of earth; unshaken by the waves of emotion that surge around their feet.

Those who would become a channel of light must be content to be nothing; to be misunderstood by a world that, hearing, understands not, and seeing, perceives not, for it can never understand what is beyond the range of its perception.

The majority, whose goal is goodness, is incapable of seeing trueness.

Unless the whole being of the disciple is turned God-ward, and no other thing is reflected in the heart, the reflection of God is blurred, and the light unsteady and wavering. How few are able thus to attain. It does not mean that the reflector of God becomes indifferent to the sorrows of others or deaf to their cries for aid; but one realizes that one in oneself can never heal the broken hearted, that only God can help them. One also realizes that, in order to reach the human soul, God requires a channel, which must be perfectly still and utterly empty that God may fill it with the Divine Self; and through God's disciple, emptied of aught beside, may God touch the sorrowful ones, speak words of peace and healing to the broken hearted and bring light to those who sit in darkness.

God sees not as humans see, and truth in the innermost parts is demanded of the disciple who would be the channel of God's love. The disciple must tread *the alone path*, for everything the world counts as good must be lost before God is found.

The prayer continually on the lips of this disciple should be: "Give to my heart, O God, the courage to lose all that I may find all in Thee, at Whose right hand are pleasures for evermore, and in Whose presence is fullness of joy."

# 17

IF, by an intense concentration of sympathy and understanding, disciples can focus their hearts on the heart of the teacher, whose heart in turn is focused upon the illuminated souls behind the teacher, who again are in touch with mightier beings still, the disciple may, for the moment, become a link in that great chain leading up in one unbroken beam of light to the throne of God. A great and wonderful privilege indeed, but to become a permanent link in that chain is not given to everyone to attain.

The first thing necessary is that the focus of the heart must be absolute, without shadow of turning. Then, before the soul can stand before God, the two must become one.

The eyes must be closed to good and evil, and see only the vision of God.

The ears must be deaf to pleasure and pain, and hear only the voice of God.

The lips must be silent in joy or sorrow, and utter only the name of God.

No other heart must be mirrored on the heart of the disciple who would reflect God.

No other voice must reach the ears of the disciple who would hear the voice of God.

No other name must be on the lips of the disciple who would speak the name of God.

All these things must the disciple attain before becoming a link in the divine chain of holy ones.

So long as life holds, it must hold, and duties must be faithfully carried out; but duties are for the personality. It is the innermost being of the self who would behold the vision of God; and before the soul can see God, the personality must be lost in God. But herein is the mystery of mysteries, the great paradox of life: for only that which is lost can be found.

The one who possesses is the one who has renounced.

The one who holds is the one who has loosed; and only by renouncing life is the power obtained to hold life.

The one who sees good and evil as truth, verily, that one sees with open vision.

# 18

WHEN a soul has chosen to tread the spiritual path and is accepted as a disciple by a spiritual teacher, the reason and the heart both must give assent. In other words, the positive and negative aspects of one's being must be connected with one's teacher.

The next step is to bring these two aspects together in the physical body, that light, or spiritual truth, may manifest.

The soul's knowledge, which is in the depth of the heart, must be brought to the surface in order that it may be reflected on the mind and so radiate through the whole body.

This process is repeated on every plane of being, but must begin on the physical. It is a great mystery and can only be learned very gradually.

When the union takes place on the spiritual plane, then all knowledge is as an open book before the soul. But the disciple must understand the laws governing the electricity in one's own body, and be able to bring together the positive and negative forces there, before being trusted with the knowledge of it working in the higher planes of being.

# 19

NEGATIVE to God and positive to other people: this is one of the most difficult lessons on the path of spiritual development and can only be suggested in words. The disciples must meditate upon it, and strive to realize the mystery within their own beings. A few words may be given, but they are only covers for the truth they contain, as a shell of a nut is a cover for the kernel it protects.

To be negative to God implies absolute emptiness when the soul is turned God-ward; but when it is dealing with people, then it must strike the note positively and fully, must realize itself as filled with God and thus able to reflect God to others. The soul that is negative to God is full, not empty, and because of this cannot receive into itself any other reflection. When this truth is fully realized by disciples, they know that they can never help any human soul except by being themselves so filled with God that all those within their atmosphere must feel God. And as others are able to tune their hearts to the positive note thus being sounded, so they will be able to receive the help they are needing.

Disciples, in the journey through life, will come in contact with all kinds of people who will make demands upon their sympathies; for good and bad alike will feel they have much to give. But when the disciples are able to keep permanently negative to God and positive to human beings, all those who are seeking truth will find help and healing in the disciples' presence, for they will radiate life and light. But those whose only satisfaction lies in drawing into themselves the magnetic life of another will go empty away, for the positive attitude prevents them from receiving any satisfaction. To maintain this attitude is as necessary for the protection of such people as for that of the disciples themselves, for if one allows the force with which one is charged to be drawn away by another, that other is in grave danger, as the other person's vampire nature becomes increased tenfold thereby. A great responsibility, therefore, rests upon the disciples thus charged.

# 20

THE eyes of those who would be spiritual teachers must always be turned inward if they would themselves safely tread the path to God and lead others thereon. The path itself is within, and it is the disciples and none other who make each step they must tread as they proceed. It is they themselves who place each obstacle in their own way, over which they find it so hard to gain the mastery. This is one of the last and most difficult of all lessons to be learned on the spiritual path. And at this stage, a guide is needed who is able to teach this lesson: that nothing in the whole world can affect one for good or evil that is not the result of one's own thinking. There is nothing else that can, and to those who are able to control their own thoughts, all things whatsoever are possible. The only way disciples can accomplish this with safety is to constantly allow their thoughts to rest upon God, and to obtain control of themselves by daily withdrawal of their thoughts from anything touching the personal life, and thus communing with their own souls in the silence. Then will they hear the voice of God and see, with open vision, the solution of all life's problems

# 21

THE disciple should think of life in the world as a journey that is taken for the purpose of experience. Of course, in reality one travels in a circle and in the end, arrives at the place from which one started plus the essence of one's experience, which enables one to proceed where thought cannot follow. Life is full of difficulties and dangers to be fought and overcome in order that a person may be conqueror and master of life; but there are many unnecessary sorrows and tragedies that one makes for oneself. Every experience that a person meets on life's journey is meant to be lived through and left behind. Trouble begins when one forgets altogether that one is only a traveler and must not tarry but continue the journey. Travelers find perhaps one experience so pleasant that they want to live it over and over again, holding it until they have to be detached by some painful process.

If people could only understand the meaning of life, they would realize that they are here to obtain mastery, not to become slaves. So long as they are held by even one experience of life, they are slaves. Directly one is able to let go, to rise above all experience, then one is master and has learned the real purpose of the journey: to retain in oneself only the results of experience. The experiences themselves are really dead or waste matter directly the essence has been withdrawn, and become a burden far too great for any person to carry. And so one is obliged to delay the journey until, by some means, this burden is removed. This happens many times in the life, as it is always difficult for someone to remember pain that is past when in the midst of some pleasing experience, for pleasure acts as a narcotic and drugs one to forgetfulness.

In the physical body, food is taken to nourish the body, which otherwise could not live; but only the essence of it is retained. The same process must be repeated in the astral and mental bodies, as they are also material and belong to earthly life, otherwise there is disease or unrest. God does not place unnecessary or unbearable burdens upon humanity. It is the human being who does so in ignorance of life's true meaning.

## 22

THE disciples who would follow the footsteps of a spiritual guide must be unconscious of the steps their feet are treading. They must be conscious only of the goal. If they were to stay to examine each step upon the path, either those they had trodden or those that were facing them, they could not, for one moment, stand upright upon the place they had reached. This stage of the journey, when disciples are treading the footprints of a guide, may be likened to someone walking upon a tightrope: one may only walk thereon in safety if the whole of one's being is conscious of the destination and the eyes are fixed upon the place one wishes to reach. If, for one second's time, the eyes were turned downwards, the person would fall to the ground. Upon whatever object the eyes are fixed, that object will be reached. The magnetism of gaze attracts the object gazed upon, as a steel magnet attracts a needle if turned in its direction. It is very necessary for disciples upon the spiritual path to meditate upon this teaching as applied to the inner vision, and try to understand the importance that mystics of all ages have attached to the realization of the constant presence of God. Blessed are they whose feet can tread in the footprints of a guide; verily, they shall reach the goal.

# 23

THE miracle of Jesus in turning water into wine has a very deep spiritual significance for the seer.

Water, in terms of the mystic, always represents the astral world, or world of illusions. In this region nothing has any real or permanent existence, and the forms in it change with every wind of thought. Even the forms themselves are never seen from a true angle: everything reflected in water is presented to the eye upside down, as the level of water is below that of humankind. The work of the mystic is to turn the water into wine, or pure essence. The fruit of the vine, ripened by the light of the sun, is already within the physical vessel and contains within itself the power of chemical change; but to accomplish the process of fermentation, the mystic must personally tread the wine press. Everything represented by water must be under the feet. The mystic must stand above it and walk upon the waters of illusion until fermentation is completed and the place of every atom has been changed or rearranged.

Then will the wine of Christ give ecstasy to the soul at the time of mystical union, or merging of soul with spirit. The disciple who has ears to hear, and eyes to see and understand, will also realize the extreme importance of control and balance at this stage upon the path. For even to obtain draughts of spiritual wine, one must not unduly tarry at the roadside inns, but must remember always that they are but *manzillha*, stages upon the path of perfection, and that the spiritual wine is for the soul's refreshment in order that one may be able to continue the journey and tread the path with sure and steadfast step.

# 24

THE light that is guiding the travelers upon the spiritual path is, in reality, the light that is shining from their own souls. When the inner eyes are opened, they will always see this light before them, lighting the path they are treading; and everyone they meet, and everything, animate or inanimate, becomes illuminated before their view. At first this truth is not understood by the disciples. They see a light, and because they see they follow, until they become bewildered by seeing it in so many places, which before were to them but darkness. This leads them into strange paths, and many truths are thus revealed; for everything upon which this light falls reveals its secret to the seer. But the disciples have not realized the mystery of the light of guidance until they have ceased to follow it outside themselves.

There comes a time in the spiritual development when the traveler to the goal closes the eyes. The meaning of this is that one seeks nothing, not even the light of guidance, outside oneself. When this stage has been reached, the traveler knows that the light, which so long had been before one's sight, leading one by so many ways, was a reflection of the light of God within one's own soul, which was turned Godward and so focused upon the only light.

## 25

WHAT is the use, except for one's own development, of trying to live the inner life? How can it help a suffering world?

What all those who try to live the inner life are really doing is road-making. Thousands today are trying to find the path to God. The majority know that somewhere it exists, but cannot find out where it is. Now the work of the road-maker is to make the road. The only way the road can be made is by treading it. When many feet have trodden a path, it will at last become clear to the view of all.

At the present time it is obscure, because only a few at long intervals have passed that way, and there has been time after their passing for the way again to become obliterated and overgrown with the thick undergrowth, so that even the entrance remains hidden. Steamrollers and mechanical contrivances cannot be used for making this road, because the way is too narrow, too steep, and too winding. It is also very difficult to follow, sometimes passing over chasms, sometimes beside precipices. There is only one thing able to make it a highway, and that is willing feet. These are difficult to find for this reason, that there are many thousands of devoted men and women who are willing and anxious to help their fellow humans to find God, but they want to take them by the hand and lead them along a path that is visible enough for all to see. They are ready and willing to help if the world understands their good and unselfish motives, and this desire is, of course, a helpful and useful thing at a certain stage of evolution. But no person can take another by the hand and lead the other along the real path to God. Each one must find and tread this for oneself. Today the opportunity is given to all who are willing to help their fellow humans, in spirit and in truth, to become road-makers of this path. Such a privilege has never before been given except to the few, but our planet has reached a stage in its evolution when it is necessary for the path to be open to all and a way made through the jungle of accumulated errors.

Who will offer themselves for the work? Strength and great courage are needed. It is sometimes very lonely work, and always the workers are misjudged by those who cannot understand. Sometimes they are even called selfish and accused of thinking only of treading their own path, and of being deaf to the cry of suffering humanity. Always the true road-maker will be so misjudged, always will be crucified, as was the Lord, by the judgment of the ignorant. But if the road-maker can work on and faint not, can bear to be so misjudged by the world and, what is far more difficult, sometimes by those nearest and dearest, the road will be made by which humankind will pass to God; and the entrance will be open and visible to all.

That is the reward, when at the end the road-maker shall turn and see thousands walking upon a great highway that the road-maker's own feet have helped to make. What greater reward than this can one have? One will have entered into the joy of the Lord.

# 26

THE injunction so often given to travelers on the path of spiritual development, that nothing be allowed to come between the soul and God, should not be interpreted by the disciple to mean that they must give no thought or time to the ordinary duties of life. On the contrary, unless these are faithfully carried out one cannot reach the soul's desire. "Be ye perfect as your Father in heaven is perfect,"[1] was spoken not to angels, but to humans living in a human world and does not imply leaving the physical body and life's duties uncared for and neglected.

Every part must be complete and balanced to obtain perfection on the path of wisdom, the most difficult of all attainments; but great indeed the reward, for the person who attains is the master of life and death.

The secret of success along this path may be found by following the words of Jesus Christ: "rendering unto Caesar the things that are Caesar's, and unto God the things that are God's,"[2] by keeping the feet upon earth and the eyes towards heaven; by holding the balance evenly, for the lower nature must be guided and controlled by the higher, not the higher dragged down to reinforce the lower. Neither must the lower be disregarded by the wise. It is only the unwise who would make such mistakes, thinking thus more quickly to arrive.

Those starting to walk with a definite goal must keep their thoughts upon the destination and their eyes focused in its direction. Then, if they had taken care before starting that

1 Matthew 5:48.
2 Mark 12:17.

their feet were properly shod, the feet will automatically obey the will without any attention on the travelers' part. But those who watch every step they take, keeping thoughts and eyes upon their feet, will walk in confusion; and as they cannot see the goal they are striving to reach, they can never find it. Sometimes even passing it unnoticed, they arrive at the place from which they started.

Likewise, those who start without care that the feet are shod will drop by the wayside footsore and weary.

Verily, the balanced path is the path of wisdom. Blessed are they who can tread it, for they shall reach the kingdom.

# 27

THE disciples on the spiritual path must not expect to have the approbation of their fellows because they are beginning to desire the approbation of God, and no one can have both at the same time. But the disapprobation of others, and especially that of those of one's own household, is a very heavy burden to bear. The only thing that is of help here is to try to tune one's heart to the note of the soul. God's approbation is the soul's true desire, and difficulties occur when the soul and heart are separate; for "where your treasure is, there will your heart be also."[1] When the heart of the disciple is in tune with the soul, thoughts will follow the desire of the heart, and the whole being will be in harmony.

1 Matthew 6:21.

# 28

A FEW words will perhaps explain some hard sayings in the Bible and other scriptures as to the need of an accepted disciple leaving all to follow a master. The inner meaning of these sayings is that when one offers oneself to be used as a channel through which the divine force may flow to those able to receive it, it is an absolute necessity, for the protection of one's own self, that nothing shall remain in the channel that would cause an obstruction. The force must flow freely and not be held for a moment. Its power is so tremendous that great suffering, and sometimes physical injury, may be caused unless there is a perfectly free passage. The channel becomes blocked by the thoughts and feelings being held down by any person or thing. To remain clear, the thoughts and emotions of the disciple must be fixed upon God.[1]

The soul must have absolute freedom to seek its own desire. Thus will the disciple become an empty vessel that the master can use to fill with living water of divine life, and thousands will be blessed. This does not, of course, mean that one must not give love or necessary thought to earthly ties and duties, but that none of these things must have any power to hold one. When one wills to forget, one must be able to forget, and remember when one wills to remember. In other words, the disciple must be master of thought, and the disciple's desire must be always to God. When this is so, no harm can befall one. One is at rest, for one's desire is satisfied.

1 "He who constantly thinketh upon Me, not thinking ever of another, of him I am easily reached, O Partha, of this ever-harmonized Yogi." Bhagavad Gita.

# 29

WHEN the Lord rides upon the whirlwind,[1] Behold! Who shall stand as the Lord passes? The upright and the strong shall be broken, and the weak scattered in a thousand pieces.

Those who bow low, they only shall remain and they shall the Lord uplift; for they are those who know the secret of the innermost places.

On the spiritual path, the whole of the journey is one of bewilderment from beginning to end, although until the spiritual eyes are opened, people do not know it. But directly they begin to see with the inner vision, then everything is a bewilderment; and they understand why the sages and seers have always taught that physical life is illusion—maya. If one could fully see the effect of a physical action on the higher planes, one would be more bewildered still. This is the reason that spiritual sight cannot be hastened but must be a gradual unfoldment, and cannot be fully awakened until the disciple is ready to follow the path of the whirlwind.

When the whirlwind comes, everything in its path is caught up from earth and whirled round and round in its mighty force, which never for one second's time is stationary. But as it passes only those atoms that are light as thistledown and strong as the wind can follow, the others sink exhausted to earth again.

Many are caught, but few there be who can follow.

There are many places of bewilderment on the path through which the disciple must go, but each gone through alone will

1 Isaiah 19:1.

help through the next. This is why one cannot be helped—guidance is another thing—but must oneself dispel the fog of illusion.

There is a light within the heart that can show the way through any fog, however dense. Once it has been found, no other guidance is needed. It is in order to help the disciples to seek for this in themselves that they are brought to this place of bewilderment; but they must look within for the light, not without. Nothing can help them here but their own inner convictions.

Remember, My path is the path of the whirlwind, only the strong can follow.

# 30

IN the lives of disciples who are beginning to live the life of the spirit, many things may need adjustment. In the outer life they are responsible for their own acts, and every mistake they make and every debt they incur must be settled by them. It is continual action and reaction, which goes on without ceasing; and they are "bound to the wheel of things."[1] But when a master really accepts as a pupil a sincere disciple, from that moment the master is responsible for the disciple.

In the inner life there is constant adjustment. No debt can be carried over to the next day but must be settled at once, so that each new day the disciples may be free; for they cannot now carry any burdens of past mistakes or these also would partake of eternal life and live forever. No one can travel this path except under the guidance of the master. The master is the gate through which all must pass, and at that gate all burdens must be laid down. This is the new birth of which Jesus Christ speaks, but before the birth can take place there must be the equivalent to what in the outer life is called *death*; and through the gate of death the soul can carry nothing.

At this stage of the journey the disciples learn that there is no such thing as sin: everything they have thought of as such is really experience. Every experience that the disciples brings with them, which they have lived through in their outer lives, is taken by the master, the Great Alchemist, and transmuted until only the pure essence remains. It is this essence from which the guiding light is produced, by which

1 Sir Edwin Arnold, "The Light of Asia," in *The Oxford Book of English Mystical Verse*, edited by Nicholson & Lee (Oxford University Press, 1917).

the disciples may proceed. If there had been no experiences, there would be nothing out of which the light could be made. When this transmutation is completed, the disciples are free to pass onward, free from the burden of accumulated debts of the past. But as no debt can ever remain unpaid, the master will pay all that is owing to others through a disciple's past mistakes, until the disciple has learned the lesson of true alchemy, by which everything one touches in the journey on the path may be transmuted to pure gold.

In the inner life as in the outer, the disciples are born as infants, and the master is responsible for them until they arrive at years of discretion. This is the real meaning of vicarious atonement and the forgiveness of sins; but just as a teacher of experimental chemistry is responsible for the pupils' mistakes and, therefore, would not teach dangerous experiments to those whom the teacher had not trained, neither does a spiritual teacher impart the knowledge of spiritual forces to a disciple until the disciple has been trained and tested by earth, water, fire, and air.

# 31

WHOEVER claims to have advanced upon the spiritual path has not even found the entrance and may be farther away than one who has not set foot thereon.

Whoever claims to have received illumination is walking upon the shadow path. Long and weary is their way, for at every step that they take, they are deluded by the shadows cast by their thoughts about themselves. Verily, one who is afar off and knows that one is, is nearer to the master.

Of accepted disciples there are few in any age. O! aspirant, the key that will unlock the gate of acceptance or initiation must be made by the disciples from themselves. It is a long and wearisome task to procure the material and difficult to fashion, for to do so one must pass through the great disintegration: the fourfold purification.

### The Purification of Earth

Into the crucible of truth the Great Alchemist places all the earth had given or could give; and the disciple watches disappear everything the world held of fame, honor, wealth, and the praise of others; of success, of pride of place and earthly power; the sins of the body, the pleasures and the pains. When all have been reduced to their true elements, nothing remains but a handful of dust.

Thus is the disciple purified of earth.

### The Purification of Water

Into the crucible is now placed every emotion and passion felt by the disciple through life: the loves and the hates, the feelings and the earthward desires; everything pertaining to the astral life; the sorrows and the joys.

As the disciple watches, they vanish into vapor, and the disciple is given the resultant: a few drops of tears.

This is the disciple purified of water.

### The Purification of Fire

Into the crucible of truth are now placed all the aspirations of the disciple: the efforts for self-development, the desires for achievement; the contents of the mind; also the sins of the mind, the pride of knowledge and power upon the spiritual path. When all these have been resolved, there remains a small heap of ashes.

Thus is the disciple purified of fire.

### The Purification of Air

For this process the master places in the crucible of truth the deep devotion of the heart of the disciple together with the handful of dust, the few tears, and the small heap of ashes. As the disciple watches the disintegration of innermost being in wondering awe, the disciple is given the result of this test: a key of pure gold that will unlock the gate of initiation; and the disciple is accepted in the Beloved.

Thus is the disciple purified of air.

Of the purification of ether, into which all these elements resolve, it is not permitted to speak, for the disciple may now pass through the gate; and ere one passes, the lips are sealed. A sign is given by which one will be known to those who have had the same experience; to all others there is no difference apparent.

Whoever claims to be an accepted disciple is making a false claim. The evidence of reality is silence.

## 32

ONLY when the heart has become indifferent to pain or pleasure, can the voice of the Beloved be heard.

Guide Thou my feet upon the path that lies between the desert and the sown, making me unconscious of either, that in that silence I may hear the voice of the Beloved.

# Part Two

# 33

*When thy mind shall escape from this tangle of delusion, then thou shalt rise to indifference as to what has been heard and shall be heard. . . .*
*He whose mind is free from anxiety amid pains, indifferent amid pleasure, loosed from passion, fear and anger, he is called a sage of stable mind.*

—*Bhagavad Gita*

# 34

PURE intelligence, which can be received by intuition, is never a burden to the mind; but it should be used for the moment only, held as lightly as a gossamer thread and let go when its purpose is accomplished. If you try to keep it, to put it into a mold and fix it, it will become a fact; and facts are very burdensome to the human mind because they are weighted by the thoughts of millions of people through millions of years.

Human intelligence is a continual reincarnation of ideas, and every mind through which they pass, which is strong enough, molds, colors, and adds to them. They are pressed into every kind of mold and shape, and added to until it becomes a wearisome thing to disentangle reality.

Truth is always perfectly simple. It is the accumulation and addition added by the human mind that makes it appear so complex and difficult of comprehension. It is for this reason the teaching is given to the disciple that one must unlearn all one has learned before advancement on the spiritual path can be made.

It is quite impossible to know the things of the spirit by the ordinary method of gaining knowledge of material things. Books or words may suggest but they cannot teach, because the germ of truth they contain is so covered over by the accumulated thoughts of many human minds, that it would mean the labor of many lives to undo the wrappings.

Reality can only be perceived by the intuition, flashed, so to speak, upon the mirror of the mind from which, for the time being, every other image has been erased. This flashlight only lasts for one second's time, and unless the mirror is perfectly clear, the truth cannot be correctly perceived. It is, therefore, necessary for the disciple to hold all thought lightly, that it may be easily put aside at the call of intuition.

# 35

THE burden of mind is reincarnated thought. Pure intelligence is no burden, it comes direct to the human brain without any coloring from other minds. All true artists receive their inspiration from this source. It is pure, original, creative, but is not held by any individual longer than is needed for the particular task upon which one is engaged at the moment. It is for this reason that the artistic temperament is such a difficult one for the ordinary person to understand and appreciate. Those who have it, in moments of real inspiration, touch the world of pure intelligence; and at that moment of time they become illuminated and are able to achieve without effort what others could not accomplish after many years of study and diligent application. And this is not only in the world of art. The artist may use this inspiration in any direction, in any task one is interested in, but the illumination will only last for the time in which the soul is interested. Directly the interest has gone, then the artist has no more, indeed rather less, ability than ordinary people. The artist is much more able to understand mysticism than is any other temperament.

# 36

NOTHING exists except what the mind creates. Everything created must eventually be destroyed. The use of the whole long journey is no more, from our finite point of view, than the games a person follows for the pleasure of excitement, or the dangers, difficulties, and privations one willingly faces for the sake of adventure and experience. One's own self it is who places obstacles in one's own path, for the sole reason of overcoming them.

So with the soul, the mind creates by the process of solidifying spirit to the condition of what we call matter, and then molding it by the power of thought to whatever form will express the idea.

It is extremely difficult for the mind to hold one thought long enough to mold the form completely; hence all sorts of wrong and misshapen forms fill the world. This is the cause of all unrest, confusion, and unsuitable conditions.

It is the human mind that makes one's environment, nothing else.

It is for the pleasure of mastering the mind that a soul undertakes the long journey, the divine adventure. But of course, as with those in the physical world who try to master the elements, climb mountains, hunt big game, or tame wild animals, the soul frequently fails and becomes mastered by the very thing over which it is trying the gain the mastery.

It is for this reason, and in order to help those who have failed, that masters of wisdom are sent to remind humanity of its divine origin, and that the human being is capable of mastering, and should not be mastered by, one's own mind.

But this cannot be taught except to those who can see.
The master can only light the lamp of wisdom in the human heart, so that each can see the truth for oneself.

# 37

MIND is a condition of spirit, not a separate thing.

Man (manas or mind) is a stage midway between heaven and earth, or spirit and matter. When a soul, to gain experience, conditions itself to the mental sphere, it comes into contact with all the mental images or thought forms there generated and becomes bewildered. It feels the attraction from both sides, spiritual and material, one moment pulled one way and the next the other. The human task is mastery in this middle sphere, that one may be able to remain exactly balanced.

A pair of scales may be taken as the symbol of mind, as in this stage, everything must be weighed; but a master of life will never allow one scale to be heavier than the other. If the scale of earth seems to be more weighty, then something must be added to the scale of heaven until both are in perfect balance. Absolute control is necessary; never for one moment must the balance be lost. To humanity alone belongs this stupendous power, the possibility of obtaining mastery of heaven and earth. One then ceases to be a man and becomes a divine man: *hu-man*, from *Hu*, God and; *manas*, man.

> *As we have borne the image of the earthly, we shall also bear the image of the heavenly.*
>
> —*1 Corinthians 15:49*

> *Till we all come in the unity of the faith, and of the knowledge of the Son of God, unto a perfect man; unto the measure of the stature of Jesus Christ.*
>
> —*Ephesians 4:13*

# 38

A PERSON'S thought is conceived as one thought, or one idea; but before one can utter or express it, it must be broken, divided into many words, producing results so far-reaching that it is beyond human power to comprehend, so innumerable that no one can number them. How then can a person presume to recognize or define the utterance of God, at Whose word of power all things were created: the heavens, the earth and all the hosts thereof?

Those who have lifted even the first of the "seventy thousand veils"[1] that cover the One Reality, realize how vast is human ignorance, how great is human presumption in seeking to uncover the things of God in order to satisfy the desire for knowledge. They begin to understand the meaning of the words of Jesus Christ: "Blessed are the pure in heart for they shall see God,"[2] for they know that not until everything gathered during the long pilgrimage has been laid aside, and only the essence of experience retained, can the soul stand free and pure. Only then can the last veils, in awe and reverence, be drawn aside. Only then shall we see God.

Pure from all thought, for upon the mirror of the heart only God is reflected; pure from everything pertaining to earth; pure from differences or distinction that divide and separate; pure in essence, being of one substance with the Father in heaven; thus and only thus, is it possible to see God.

---

1 "Between God, mighty and sublime, and creation are 70,000 veils." Hadith.

2 Matthew 5:8.

Truly, only the lowly minded, the one who has "loosed his shoes from off his feet"[3] may stand even upon the threshold of this holy ground.

3 Exodus 3:5.

# 39

AS the wind bloweth where it listeth, and no one can tell when it cometh or whither it goeth,[1] so no one knows the essence of life, whence it comes and whither it goes. Neither can one create a form of it, for it is utterly beyond the thought of a finite mind; and it is beyond the power of creative thought to realize the One Absolute Spirit. Every thought is necessarily limited to the capacity of the mind that produces it. The God of which you can think, is a created God; and everything created must one day cease to be. But remember that it is the mold that created and the mold that is destroyed. That of which it is molded is beyond the power of human beings to conceive, beyond the power of human thought to create. Shall the limited sense the unlimited? The dweller in darkness comprehend light? Or one who is bound by time realize the eternal? No more than an atom can realize the whole body of which it forms a part, can a person understand these things. How great is your presumption, O human! How vast is your ignorance! Nevertheless, keep the thought ever upon God, and as you grow in the perception of the spirit of truth, mold and remold your ideal of God. But seek not to limit the limitless within one of these ideals, for the highest ideal that can ever be conceived is but a cover that must one day be broken.

Reverence every person's ideal, for each soul has its own; and however small it may appear, never destroy, or seek to replace it by your own. Would a mother break the dolls her child loves because she herself who once loved them no longer

1 John 3:8.

has need of them, having conceived within her own being a living child?

To each there comes the time of awakening. Disturb no one's rest. Who is able to live up to a high ideal of God will radiate a light, which, an awakening soul perceiving, will reach out to share. More than this it is presumption on the part of humanity to attempt. Ponder these things in the heart in humility.

## 40

PAIN, disease, or suffering of any kind is always caused by the effort of the inner being of a person to refine the vehicles, to uncover or peel off the outer coverings of accumulated error that prevent the light of wisdom within from being reflected on the mirror of the heart.

The mental images, or thought forms, gathered during the long journey must sometime be broken—as must all created things—in order that the soul within may have the open vision. This breaking sometimes causes acute suffering, both mental and physical. The more complete and perfect the form, the more difficult the breaking. Emotion, either of joy and delight, pain or sorrow, is the great refiner used by the soul to produce that swift, ever-changing motion that means life, as inertia is death.

The God Within cannot find the God Transcendent until the error of the ages has been cleared away, and nothing remains between the soul and God but the light of vision.

# 41

THE important task for each soul is to become attuned to God. God is ever sounding the keynote, which is love. And when we can be in perfect tune with that, only harmonious vibrations can reach us; everything else must pass us by.

The way to really help the world is to be able to sound our own note in absolute tune. Then others may tune their instruments by it.

The only way we can give the note is by sounding it in purity of tone, not by trying to tune another's instrument. If we try to sound another's note there is at once a disharmony.

All notes are necessary with their millions of combinations, but all must be in tune and give forth each their own note. Then will our earth be able to sound the Christ note in the divine harmony, the Christ note for which purpose it was created; and the unstruck music will then sound through the universe.

# 42

WHAT is the best way of helping the world in these difficult times? First, a fresh ideal of God must be built up in the thought world so that the matter of that plane, which is continually passing through the brains of those living this earth, may be stamped with it. This has been done again and again in the history of the evolution of our planet by those who can sense the ideal in the spiritual world. It is then passed through their master minds and molded into a form intelligible, more or less, to the human mind when expressed mentally; and many times has it been broken, as must every ideal of God, in time.

The ideals of God held by humanity have differed according to the collective capacity of human beings to interpret and express in words the ideal existing in the world of thought. Each race would necessarily have a different interpretation, and so many different religions have been established in the world; and each thinking they had the only true one, tried to convert every other with more or less success. During the late war[1] many of these ideals were broken.

The reason that at the present time there is such chaos and godlessness is because the ideal that had been built had to break. The time has come when humanity generally has evolved to the stage of being able to understand a higher ideal, which hitherto has only been possible to very advanced souls: the ideal of the oneness of human life in the divine. It is this ideal that must be built up in the mental world: that God

1 World War I.

is the sum total of humanity, and that every being is part of God's life and belongs to God and cannot be separated from God; that if one part suffers the whole suffers; that no human being can live to oneself alone. If this ideal can be firmly held in the world of mental matter, then it must so permeate that matter that every brain will, in time, become impressed, according to its capacity to receive impressions. This is a partial explanation of a scientific law.

This idea is being sensed very imperfectly by those who can only see half-truths, and is resulting in the teaching of a oneness or human fellowship. Apart from God, this is an impossibility. One may just as well teach that all the atoms of a person's body are one, independently of the person. There can be no human fellowship without the family of God. The task of those who can, even in the smallest degree, understand this truth is to fit themselves to become builders in the world of thought of this great ideal, to know without any shadow of doubt that it is the only thing able to help the world, and to be content never in this life to see the result of their work.

## 43

IF the disciple wants to find the truth, that disciple must first of all clear the mind of all prejudices—all—just as one must cut all the ropes holding a balloon to earth if one wants it to rise.

The disciple must make the journey alone; none of the things that may hold the disciple are bad—there is no good or bad—but because the mind must be free in order to soar, and it can only do this when untrammeled.

Everything perceived by the mind on this plane, when attached to the earth by cords, is illusion, mirage. Even though it may last thousands, nay, millions of years, still it is only illusion, and reality can never be perceived in this way. The disciple must be free from all preconceived ideas before the real search for truth begins.

# 44

IF you desire to get an answer to a question from a spiritual source through intuition, you must remember that the answer will be for that moment only and cannot be applied in the same way at any other time. Each moment has its purpose, which is different from every other moment. The difficulties of a particular time can always be answered from the spiritual plane when the intuition is developed; but after the difficulty of the moment has been settled, the answer is like a spent match. The illumination was meant for a particular moment of time, as was the match; and neither can be used again in the same way. This truth is seldom understood and is almost impossible to explain in words, but it really means that truth cannot be held for more than a fraction of time, in one particular form or color, and live. Its nature is constant change, perpetual movement. It can, for a moment, be sensed but not held. There is no life without change; the higher the life, the swifter will be the change.

# 45

THERE is a deep occult significance in the proverb, "A place for everything and everything in its place." There is also a place for every being, as well as for every thing, and the whole training of life is to enable each to find their right place and to make them fit to fill it. When this has been accomplished, one is harmonious and peaceful, which is otherwise quite impossible. This is the sign that one has found one's own place.

Of course, until people realize that each has a place in the universe of the great body of God, they do not try to find it, but wander aimlessly on, seeking peace in this place or in that and finding none, feeling equally lonely among crowds or in desert places; for nothing, however dear, can satisfy the craving of the soul for its own place in the Father's house and the companionship of its own kin. It is as though some atoms in the body belonging to the hand were trying to find a place in the ears or the eyes. The great magnetic power, which sooner or later draws all things to their appointed place, from chemical affinities in the laboratory of the chemist to the souls of humans and of angels, is the love of God. The whole universe is held together by this power: the trees in the forest, the sand in the desert, the seas in their appointed places, and the stars in the heavens. There is nothing that cannot feel this drawing power. Humans, having free will, sometimes try to resist for a time, but in the end "neither death, nor life, nor angels, nor principalities, nor powers, nor things present, nor things to come, nor height nor depth, nor any other creature shall be able to separate us from the love of God."[1]

1 Romans 8:38–39.

# 46

RELIGION is a shade over the light of truth. If it were not for the shade, the light would blind the eyes of awakening souls. Only when they are fully awake can they face the light without the protection of this shade. In every age some form of covering has been necessary, and it is also necessary today. The shades may vary in form, color, and size, but the light they cover is One without a second, eternal in the heavens, from everlasting to everlasting.

# 47

THE doctrine of reincarnation, as it is generally understood in the Western world, is one of the greatest hindrances to spiritual progress; for like all truths upon the path of return, it is true and not true. Its truth can only be understood by those who have ceased to vibrate to any note struck by the personality. Its *not truth* is what is being taught and understood by people who are teaching this doctrine. Those who know the inner meaning would never teach it; they understand that it cannot be taught, but can only be realized by the awakened soul. When taught to the unawakened, the effect is like being in a maze: the soul wanders up and down its many paths, attracted this way and that way, always feeling fresh allurements and ever seeking unexplored paths, which are specially attractive to the curiously minded. When once a soul has started upon this investigation, it may go up and down the winding paths for countless ages before it finds the way out, returning again and again to the place from which it started.

One of the greatest dangers of this teaching lies in the so-called recognition of old ties; if the disciple only knew how this idea is used to drag one back from the true goal. Directly any soul takes a definite step upon the path to God, everything in this world and the next tries to prevent it going forward; and entities of the astral world find it very easy to impress living personalities with the idea of past relationships. It is one of the subtlest of illusions of that world of illusions and seldom fails to arrest the steps of a returning soul, as in these astral impressions the idea of a karmic debt is always suggested. The more spiritual the soul the more it feels its obligations to pay to the uttermost what it owes; but a truly accepted disciple should remember that karmic debts have been remitted unto the disciple, and realize that these suggestions are always from the shadow side and are only phantoms, having no more reality than the figures moving across the screen of a cinema.

Take heed therefore, you who are seeking God, that this truth be not a stumbling block in your path.

# 48

SEEKERS of truth! How few people there are who are really seeking truth. Although thousands believe they are truth seekers, they are only seeking their own ideas about truth and are quite unable to recognize the reality when they see it. Truth is round about us all the time, but because of its familiarity and simplicity, it is passed over by those who are seeking the mysterious.

Humanity's love of mystery has been traded upon by priests of all religions for their own profit or love of power, and has never failed to hold in subjection millions in all ages.

True mysticism is a very different thing. It is really a recognition of the wonder and glory of the common everyday things of life, a discovering of the stupendous marvels of nature, and the working of nature's laws. But the way of the mystic, or real seeker of truth, is not an easy way nor one likely to satisfy those who eyes are filled with their own vision. On this path every idea or vision of truth previously held must be abandoned, for the eyes of the soul may behold one vision only. If it were not so, nothing but confusion could be perceived.

Only the one who is ready thus to abandon may proceed.

# 49

THE spiritual significance of wireless telephony is that in this age God is speaking to humanity without wires (priests and mediums). And each can, in one's own home (the heart), oneself receive God's messages, which are constantly being broadcasted, if one will first tune one's receiving apparatus to the right wavelength and then listen in.

# 50

EVERY communication received through a medium is colored by the personality of the medium. This is the difficulty of getting anything really reliable. The personality and bias must always be taken into account. To hear the inner voice, the mind must be kept absolutely clear and be prepared, as a mirror, to reflect what passes before it. Unfortunately, the slightest thought will blur the image; that is the trouble. Words cannot adequately express eternal truths, and that is why symbols are so frequently used, as they can sometimes convey a message to the higher mind even if the lower does not understand them.

# 51

PSYCHISM has to come, as the pressure of all those lately passed on is great. From both sides it is pressing and cannot longer be delayed. Yes, it is good for those attuned to good, but very evil for those attuned to evil.

What I want to impress upon you and upon all those who can understand is that union with God is the only reality. That is the real life everlasting; everything else is but a passing shadow of the real.

The astral life is just as impermanent as the physical. Of course, it is true that there is an astral life; but if one rests content with the idea that it is the whole of the life after death, how much better off is one?

Life after death does not mean another life after physical death, although that may be a fact. The real meaning, Christ's meaning, is that only after the death (crucifixion) of the personal self can one obtain the everlasting life of God by being merged into, becoming part of, God.

By calling back those who have passed from the physical body, either by trying to get into communication or by unrestrained longing for their presence, we prevent their souls from throwing off the burden of the mind. While the pull from earth is strong, either by their own desire or the desire of those still upon earth, they cannot drink the waters of oblivion, which give to the soul eternal youth.

When people can find and communicate with their own spirits, then they can safely communicate with the spirits of their loved ones, either in the body or out of the body.

# 52

THE sacred center of the heart is the organ, or instrument, of the higher self on the physical plane. Only when the heart center is open can the voice of God be heard.

# 53

IF disease is the lack of life, how can one keep health?

By an intense realization of the presence of God, Who is life, not by merely thinking about God, but a realization of God's nearness, every moment of the day. To realize God means to lose one's small self in God, and so partake of God's life, which, when once realized, will flood the whole being and bring into harmony every part of one's body.

# 54

THE ideal of love, harmony, and beauty must be carried into every corner of the earth. It is the only way that evil can be overcome and humanity inherit the kingdom of God.

We must realize that we are the creators of our environment, not God; by our thoughts we create. Made in the image of God, we have God-like powers and are free to create whatever we will.

This is an answer to the questions so often asked, *Why does God permit evil? Why are some people born in luxury and some in slums?*

The divine in human beings, that which makes them living souls, is exactly the same in every person born into the world.

Each is a ray or spark of the One Light, "Which lighteth every man that cometh into the world."[1] The differences are caused by the forms; the key to the problem is on your side.

The law is that whatever form (thought form or physical form) made by a person must, when the form is complete, receive the life of God. But the expression of that life is limited by the form on every plane.

If every child could be born as the result of pure love, how different would the world be. Of course, there would be differences, it is variety that makes unity; but all could be happy and harmonious if the keynote of their lives was love.

It is in the realm of mind that we must begin our work. The life must be withdrawn from the evil thoughts humanity has created and kept alive by continual reinforcement. If

1 John 1:9.

there is not reinforcement by thoughts of a like nature, they will, in time, die out. The life having been withdrawn, the thoughts will be unable to seek physical embodiment.

It is humanity that is making humanity, it is humanity that is making the world; it is humanity that makes heaven and humanity that makes hell. That which is of God is life or light: that which cannot be made, but is always. Always it has been and always it will be; it has no beginning and no end. Every form made by human beings receives the life of God, as every seed in the earth receives the light of the sun, whether it be good or whether it be evil, whether it sends forth the perfume of a flower, or the noxious gases of a poisonous weed.

Take heed, therefore, what forms you make and what seeds you sow, for God is no respecter of persons but "sendeth His rain on the just and on the unjust,"[2] that all may grow together until the harvest.

2 Matthew 5:45.

# 55

THIS is the day of the dawn of unity. The One, the universal Christ Spirit, has expressed part of Himself, from time's beginning, in all the great religions of the world. But now has dawned the day when the eyes of all shall be opened to the mystery of the oneness and allowed to realize how all the aspects of truth are but parts of One Truth, as all colors of the spectrum are rays of the pure white light.

This is the beginning of the great return, of the union with God; not in some faraway, dim future, but here and now beginning.

Once a soul has realized this mighty Oneness, it becomes incapable of seeing the separated parts. It sees always the One in Whom all that is exists. When this vision has become a reality, its eyes are opened; and never again can it know itself as a separated part. The small part of the soul is merged into the great whole.

First the One, then the many; now the many gathering again into the One. Thus and ever thus is the great law.

Blessed are they whose understanding is opened to this truth, for they have entered the path that leads from the unreal to the real, from darkness into light.

# 56

*Be still and know that I am God.*
*—Psalm 46:10*

GOD must first be known in solitude before God can be found in the crowd; must be heard in the silence before God can speak in sound; must be realized within before God can be seen without. When you have found the kingdom within, then surely shall the King walk with you without, and in everything shall you see God. God's light shall guide your feet, and darkness cover you no more forever.

# 57

A FEW words may be given to explain what is meant by union with God, although it is almost impossible to put a mystical idea into ordinary language. It does not mean that one is merged into something outside oneself, or that a person becomes nothing and no more functions as an individual. If the disciple has realized that the kingdom of God is within and that the Christ is born in the human heart, the disciple will also realize that the mystical union with God must take place within the human heart.

One of the most important things to be remembered is that unity is not uniformity. There will always be quite distinct differences between those who have attained to this union. Until a person has thus attained, there is within one a constant struggle, as though there were two forces striving for possession. As long as this continues there can never be peace or harmony in the life. The peace of God can only be realized when, within a person's innermost being, there is a unity of every part, and no part is striving or warring with another part. One is then, as it were, made whole and complete, *hu-man*; and wherever one goes, one will radiate peace and harmony, for in unity is completeness.

# 58

"I AM the way, the truth, and the life,"[1] is one of the greatest utterances of the Christ; so often on the lips of people, so little understood by them.

Verily, their ears hear these words, and their lips repeat; but their hearts comprehend not at all.

The "I AM" that is the way, the truth, and the life, is to be found in the human heart, which is the shrine of God where dwells the great "I AM."

How many are seeking for signs outside, forgetting the words of Jesus Christ, "The kingdom of heaven is within you."[2] When the kingdom is found, then also is found the King, Who is the way, the truth, and the life: the way to God, the truth of all things, and the life everlasting.

1 John 14:6.
2 Luke 17:21.

# 59

*Seek and ye shall find; knock and it shall be opened unto you.*
*— Luke 11:9*

TO every soul that knocks the door is opened, but many do not recognize the answer to their knocking, because sometimes it is Pain who opens the door to them.

Pain it is who is the opener of closed doors, the Great Deliverer, for only when the door of the heart is opened can the vision of God be seen, in Whose presence is fullness of joy.

# 60

HOW is it possible to let the Christ Child be born in the heart?

Not by an outer, but by an inner change. The disciple must consecrate every act of daily life and purify all the bodies, until the temple is fit to receive the Christ Child, who can only be born of purity and sincerity.

Of course, all the ordinary daily work must be done and the business of life attended to, more if possible, certainly not less. But if the thoughts are continually upon God, outer activities must be permeated with God's life, and the disciple will find every duty easy instead of difficult.

The light will radiate from the inner sanctuary directly the door of the heart is open, and will flood the whole being, no part of which will be left in darkness. Therefore must every part be purified, in order that the illumination may be complete.

As the sun shines upon the just and the unjust, so will this light shine upon all the actions of the disciple, increasing their power for good or ill.

# 61

THE Christ cannot be explained to a human being any more than light and heat can be explained to an animal, however great the desire to do so. It could be brought into a lighted room, it could be made to feel the warmth of the fire, but these things could never be explained to it.

# 61

THOSE who really desire to help humanity and are content that their work shall be unrecognized, should try to make of themselves mental architects. They are specially needed at this world crisis, when new thoughts and ideas must be given in order that humanity, as a whole, may be helped to take a step forward in evolution.

When something from the heavens must be brought to the earth, it is done so through those souls who are sufficiently balanced to stand between the spiritual and material worlds, and hold the thought so steadily that neither the winds of heaven nor the waters of earth can move it. A thought thus held becomes as a model, upon which those who are attuned to the same vibratory note may build. The mental architect must bring a thought from the formless to the world of form, by making a plan or model upon the material plane so that the details may be seen by the builders. What the world will see is the builders at their work and the completed buildings.

Those who hold the ideal in thought work unseen and unknown of others, but known to God, Whose agents and messengers they are. After their ideas have materialized, the plans, the models will be forgotten; there is no more need of them. But without the architect, the great monuments of God's promise to humanity could never have come into existence. For those who would become mental architects or molders of thought-stuff, many things are necessary. The most important are that they are attuned to God and have absolute control of themselves and their thoughts. They must be attuned to God in order that they may receive, within their own beings, the ideals from the spiritual world. They must have complete control of themselves to be able to hold those ideals against everything in the material world that is trying to prevent them. In this middle sphere where thought is held, only those able to tread the balanced path can stand for one moment; for gathered together in that place, the two great opposing forces meet in the zenith of their strength, and nothing but the power of God in them can keep them upright in that plane. One's faith in oneself and trust in God must be absolute; the slightest divergence in either direction would cause one to fall.

Pray without ceasing that you may be able to stand when your God shall require you.

## 62

THE plans are made by the master minds and impressed upon those who are able, in a more or less degree, to carry out the designs. The object is to create creators, able in their turn to create, design, and plan, in order that beauty may be expressed after being impressed. The time for which a created object lasts depends upon its beauty and the kind of material used in its formation. The marble statue sculptured by a master-hand may last for centuries; it entirely depends upon the skill of the worker, the concentration upon the work, and the material used. Of course, eventually everything created must once again be resolved into its constituent parts or, as people say, destroyed.

What is the purpose of it all? The purpose is the joy of creation. The joy of the artist is in painting, in the creation of a picture, the visible result of an invisible idea. But when artists have achieved this, they do not spend the rest of their lives in looking at it; they wish to create again, something better. The true artist never rests content with what has been achieved but wants to do more, and always better, work. Joy is in the act of creating. If you give a child a box of bricks, its pleasure is in building; and directly it has built something it knocks it down in order that it may build up again. It would not be the same pleasure to the child to have an object already built. The child wants to build; that is its joy, in building. Possession is a passing pleasure, to create is joy.

# 63

ICE is a condition of water, not a different substance. It can, by the application of heat, become steam or vapor. Sound is the breath of God; when solid, it is called *matter*. In this condition it has no motion and may be described as imprisoned or buried: the God buried in humanity. When matter is raised from the solid state to its original conditions, then shall the lost word be uttered.

By sound worlds came into being.

First there was silence, then was the word. From silence and sound was born light, "and the darkness comprehended it not."[1]

1 John 1:1.

# 64

SPIRIT is not separated or individualized until it has clothed itself in a garment of mental material, which is its vehicle on that plane. In this garment it is a soul. The physical environment and the physical body both are determined by the rate of vibration of the mental images in which the soul is first interested.

In spirit is absolute free will. A soul has also this attribute in its spiritness, hence its freedom of choice in what it is interested in. But it becomes limited directly it is clothed in mental material, to the rate of vibration of the material chosen.

The choice lies with the spirit, the soul carries out the result of the choice.

# 65

THE purpose is in the Universal Soul, not in the individual soul. Division or individuality is caused only by action or motion; in rest there is no separation. If water is poured through a strainer from one vessel to another, it is separated only while it is being poured, conditioned as to size and shape by the holes in the strainer. In the first vessel the water is one, and after it has fallen into the second it is one. The outbreathing of the Universal Soul expresses itself in diversity, the inbreathing is rest; and there is no separateness. Then all is again One.

# 66

IT is in the great problem of sex that you will find the key to God's plan for human evolution.

This world is subject to the pairs of opposites; a divine human cannot fully manifest without a perfect physical body. The whole training of life is a series of initiations on the path to God. God teaches the pupils while they are unconscious of God in the ordinary life of the human family, so that although they are not yet capable of comprehension, they may begin to learn God's lessons.

In the lives of human beings, the whole evolutionary plan of the universe is repeated in miniature. They who have eyes to see, they see. The most sacred trust in the world has been given to man and woman: the task of passing on the life of God and making of forms for an ever fuller and fuller expression of the beauty of God. The secret of life in a world governed by the pairs of opposites is balance; neither one extreme nor the other must be allowed. Humanity has forgotten this lesson, and it is this that must be taught today. It is the keynote of the message: not tolerance, but balance. One can have and enjoy all things in the world if the balance is complete.

> *Even here on earth everything is overcome by those whose mind remains balanced.*
>
> —*Bhagavad Gita*

# 67

BALANCE must be achieved by developing equally the positive and negative elements in a person's own being. One or the other is latent in most people, but to obtain a perfect balance it is necessary that both be equally developed: the heart or feminine attributes, and the head or masculine qualities. Not until these two forces, in their inner meaning, are in absolute equilibrium is it safe for a disciple to advance on the spiritual path. For this reason, on this path a person must necessarily come in contact with very highly charged centers of magnetism, both magnetically and electrically charged. And if in one's being these two forces, of positive and negative electricity, were not in absolute balance, one would be drawn to whichever one was lacking and be held there, utterly unable to proceed. The law of attraction and repulsion holds good on every plane, and cannot be ignored; but if the disciple has both the positive and negative qualities in exactly equal proportion, it follows that the disciple could not be attracted by either, and thus could pass in safety.

# 68

GOD is hidden by many veils of illusion in order that God may be found. The only way to find truth is to seek it in the most unlikely places. It is only by drawing away the veils, one by one, by letting go illusion after illusion, even at the cost of our heart's blood, that will finally open the inner eyes by which we can perceive truth. And when the last illusion has gone we find that, after all, God was never hidden, but it was we who were blinded; for all the time God was close beside us, although we could not see.

# 69

AT the manifestation of a world, all the matter that will eventually form the completed whole is already in existence, but in a state of chaos; the number and arrangement of every atom has yet to be made. It is not that any new thing or world or being is to be created, but that there shall be a rearrangement of all the parts until the whole is complete. Every electron and atom of electricity must take its own appointed place. This is the great evolutionary process.

The God buried in humanity must be uncovered and placed on the divine throne in the human heart. The difficulty is that all, from atom to human being, are continually trying to fit into a place to which they do not belong. The upheavals of nature, the great unrest, the world revolutions, the shedding of bodies, the separations and divisions among people, all these things are caused by the parts trying to stay in a place to which they do not belong. Directly one is in one's own place, then that person has peace. Until then one cannot have it.

A world in the making can be likened to a great jigsaw puzzle whose separate parts have life and are capable of independent movement. Each part has its own particular place and its relation to every other part, and no thing or being can live to itself alone; but if they are in their wrong places, the hand of God must move them before the complete picture can be revealed.

The way by which humans can find their own place of peace, is to tune their instruments to the keynote of the chord to which each belongs. Sound is the force that groups all things, from atoms to worlds. The chording vibration sounds in the innermost being of a person and can only be heard in the silence. When one can go into the inner chamber and shut the door to every sound that comes from the life without, then will the voice of God speak to the soul and one will know the keynote of one's life.

# 70

THE Divine Being at the head of this planet is not expressed by one form, but by myriads of forms. God is One and yet God is Many. You have no words in which I can make you understand this mystery.

> *Behold, Oh Partha, a form of Me, a hundredfold, a thousandfold, various in kind, divine, various in colors and shapes. . . . There, Pandava, beheld the whole universe divided into manifold parts, standing in one body of the Deity of Deities.*
>
> —*Bhagavad Gita*

This soul of the planet is expressing itself in countless forms for the purpose of evolution and is conscious in every single one, as a human being is conscious in every atom of the body. "For as the body is one and hath many members, and all the members of that one body, being many, are one body, so also is Christ."[1] These forms, when ensouled by the specialized part of the One Life, or God, are, during the time the form lasts, separated or individualized souls again for the purpose of evolution and, as such, cannot realize God, or the One Life. They can only do so by fusion. In order to do this, the separated or individualized soul must, by the mighty power of love, lose its separateness, so to speak. This is the only way Oneness can be realized. "I in them and Thou in me, that they may be made perfect in One."[2]

The power of love is the strongest thing in the world and the only thing that can draw the many back into the One.

1 1 Corinthians 12:12.

2 John 17:23.

The divine life force is love, and only love; but this is very different from the human love that seeks possession. Divine love is fusion, or losing.

In order to realize God, you must go through the gate of the master; and the only thing that can take you through that gate is devotion. "I am the door; if any man enters by me; he shall be saved and shall go in and out and shall find pasture. I am the door of the sheep,"[3] The universal Christ spirit uses the human form for this purpose: to create devotion in the heart of the devotee, first for the teacher and then, through devotion to the teacher, for the Christ within, of which the teacher is but the veil or cover. "The foolish disregard Me when clad in human semblance, ignorant of My supreme nature, the great Lord of beings."[4]

"No man cometh unto the Father but by me,"[5] said the Christ, speaking through the lips of Jesus. And through the lips of Shri Krishna, "By devotion, he [the disciple] knoweth Me in essence, Who and What I am; having thus known Me in essence, he forthwith entereth into the Supreme."[6]

3 John 10:7–9.

4 Bhagavad Gita.

5 John 14:6.

6 Bhagavad Gita.

# 71

IN the beginning of the world, God endowed it with the essence of life. It was, as it were, a seed of a world, able to reproduce its kind with every living thing that formed part of it. God fashioned from its material the human form that should eventually evolve into *hu-manity*. The essence of life is the God essence, or spark of the divine life, inherent in every thing as well as every being. By the essence alone can a world come into being and evolve into its prototype.

The progenitors of a world are the sun and moon. From them is the seed of a world produced, and through them it is created, nourished and sustained until its evolution is perfected. That which brings to birth, nourishes, and sustains the embryo life given by the sun and ripened by the sun, is of the moon and is hidden in the earth, as every living thing must come into being through darkness.

Everything needed for the sustenance of humanity is in the earth, and by its alchemy are produced fruits and plants for human food and healing, gold and precious stones, animals for toil and pleasure, protection from heat and cold, and the bodies of human beings. Everything known to us and by which we live is contained and enclosed in a sphere of matter traveling through space, held in its appointed place by the rate of vibration or magnetism with which it is charged.

How great is the work of Thy hand O God. How wonderful Thy ways.

# 72

TO realize God, human beings must identify themselves with all that is beautiful and all that is lovely, all that is unlovely and all that is ugly, and try to feel themselves as a part of one great whole. There is no place upon which the eyes may rest where one cannot see God; there is no sound in all the world in which one cannot hear God; and nothing at all that one can sense in which one cannot feel God, in good or in bad, in saint or in sinner. Because all that lives and moves, lives because there is only one life; and every thing or being that moves, does so by the life that is in it. Without movement, there is no life. Life is ever moving, ever changing, producing fresh forms and ever fresh forms, remolding the same material again and again. And whether the forms are good or bad, they are each the expression of the life that molds them; and the same life that produces a bad form can mold and remold, again and again, until the perfect form is produced.

All is the life of God working through matter, and when the whole is permeated with God's life, then will begin the great withdrawal, or inbreathing: the night of Brahma.

# 73

THE only way people can know anything about the great All-Father is by assimilating into themselves one of God's attributes: love, beauty, or harmony on the subjective side; or nature, God's objective and created work. This is the only way people can possibly know anything about God: by making one of these part of themselves and living it, taking in and giving out again.

The disciple must try to understand. It is difficult to express the meaning in words. No soul can tell another; this does not mean that no soul can help another.

# 74

THE human forms in time pass away, but that which became humankind in order to experience, cannot pass away. It is One, separated only while imprisoned in the form. When they shall all fade away, the One remains.

The physical form is one, but its members and its functions are many. It is through them that the inhabitant of the body experiences physical life, but when this has been experienced we have no more need of these. We ourselves are the result of what we have experienced through them. To retain the forms beyond this period would be a burden.

## 75

VIRTUES and service to humanity will keep someone standing upright on the earth, but they of themselves will never take a person into another state of being. Only the passionate desire for things spiritual and the absolute surrender of every part—body, mind, and spirit—can supply the necessary conditions for a new birth.

# 76

FROM time's beginning, in all places and under all conditions, the human spirit, which is a ray of the divine light, has ever been seeking the source of its being, ever striving to find an open door in its prison house of matter by which it can escape. It may not do so finally until the task for which it came to earth is finished, and that portion of matter that forms its prison house has been redeemed or raised to its original condition. Mystics in all ages have sought, and many have found, a key to open the door to temporary freedom through spiritual ecstasy, or intoxication of the soul. The wine that can thus intoxicate is the wine of Christ—Christ's life, or blood. When a soul is able to drink this wine and return at will to its prison house, it is possible to so refine its earthly vehicles that they may be drawn up, as it were, to partake of the spiritual ecstasy until the whole body of the person is redeemed and one's earthly task finished.

This key to freedom cannot be bought but must be patiently worked for and diligently sought, sometimes through sorrow and bitter pain. And oftentimes it means that in the search a person must leave everything dear and journey through the desert alone. Few are prepared thus to search.

Thousands seek to find the way through intoxication of the mind, and millions more through intoxication of the body. And although by such artificial means as alcohol or drugs, the door can for the moment be opened, the effect upon the soul is disastrous, as by this means it is dragged downwards to partake of the body's intoxication. Every time this happens, the matter of the body and vehicles of the spirit become coarser and coarser, until the whole is in danger of disintegration. But more harmful to the human soul because more subtle, is psychic intoxication, which today is causing untold suffering to thousands of human beings. The astral world, whence this intoxication comes, is full of the subtlest deceptions. There are many disembodied entities there that are longing for a chance to enter a physical body by turning out its lawful tenant, in order that they may gratify their desire for physical life; and these will not scruple to use even spiritual means in order to lure them to do so. Beware of this intoxication, for verily, of all it is the most deadly.

Alas! These unfortunate victims of artificial intoxication are unable to realize that what their souls are craving is the wine of the Christ. This vision has become distorted, and they see all things upside down. The need of these unhappy ones for compassion is great.

## 77

THE part of a human being that is *I*, that says, “I can do this” or “I think this,” is the mind. When the mind can be merged in another, a fusion takes place; and there is only one where before there were two.

When the mind can become so absorbed in God that only God’s mind can be realized, then there is no more *I*, and *I* does not exist. There is only God.

# 78

MEMORY belongs to the stage or phase of the soul called *man*—mind, *manas*, man—and this phase lasts as long as there is any remembrance. So long as two people who love remember each other, so long will they exist and love as separated beings, both during the life and after the death of the physical body conditioned by the law of the pair of opposites. But the true love of the soul can only find satisfaction in the realm beyond mind, where spirit meets with and merges into spirit, and realizes oneness, where there is no memory of past pleasure or pain and where sin cannot exist. For the consciousness of wrong belongs only to mind, the separated state of being.

If memory could be taken by the soul to the realm of spirit, all past mistakes and shortcomings would partake of eternal life and live forever. Forgiveness of sin means that it is erased from the mirror the mind is holding before the soul. In the state of pure spirit there can be no memory of things past. It is the state of eternal youth that philosophers all down the ages have searched for, and which has been materially interpreted as meaning the renewal of youth and love in the physical body.

The mystics call this state *annihilation*, which, if materially interpreted, appears to mean nothingness and repels rather than attracts a seeking soul who is beginning to tread the path. In reality, it is a state of bliss too great to be understood by the human mind and so, to it, appears undesirable.

There are no words in which an explanation can be given to describe this, but perhaps an illustration may suggest a line of thought to a thoughtful soul. Sometimes when life's difficulties seem overwhelming and memories of the past become unbearable, a person seeks some form of distraction or dissipation that will give, even for a few brief moments, forgetfulness of the self. One wants, as one terms it, to be taken out of oneself. The burden of memories is greater than that person can bear; it is the soul seeking to escape from its bondage. The bonds that hold it to earth are memories, and it is longing for that freedom that is the goal of the mystic of every religion.

Heaven and hell are both stages of consciousness that belong to mind. Each soul creates its own, and they last as long as the soul remains in the world of opposites or separateness. And for that soul there must always be heaven and hell, good and evil, positive and negative, pleasure and pain, sorrow and joy. This is the state in which the soul exists and lives as a person, in this world and the next. But when the soul has freed itself from bondage by becoming the master of mind, then it has placed all these things under the feet. It has become a divine man, or *hu-man*. This is the stage of the masters, prophets, and saviors who have conquered the world ruled by the pairs of opposites and are no more under its law. They have become one with all that is; one with God, that oneness of which words fail to convey any adequate meaning to the mind. "The mind is the slayer of the real, let the disciple slay the slayer."[1]

> *By the delusion of the pairs of opposites, sprung from attraction and repulsion, O! Bharata! All beings walk this universe wholly deluded. . . . But those men of pure deeds in whom sin is come to an end, they, freed from the delusive pairs of opposites, worship Me, steadfast in vows.*
>
> *—Bhagavad Gita*

1 From *Voice of Silence*, Nargis Dowland's own inspired aphorisms.

# 79

HUMANS must meet their destiny—that they cannot escape. And life will bring experience after experience, which they must go through. The mistake they make is in not passing through. They remain in the experience, either to enjoy the pleasure or bewail the pain. A person is not obliged to stay in any of these experiences—that is how all life's difficulties arise. One stays in a pleasant experience until one reaps the bitterness, and it is this that hinders the progress of the soul towards its goal. Destiny brings the lessons necessary for each soul to learn, in order to accomplish the purpose of its earth life. Humanity has free will as to the time one takes in learning and the method one uses. If one could realize that everything life brings is but transitory, and that no person or thing can really be possessed by another, the path would not be set with thorns of one's own plants; nor would one have to reap the harvest of one's own sowing, but could proceed upon the journey, unshaken by pleasure or pain, and finding peace and joy.

## 80

NO human beings can escape their destiny. They must meet whatever it brings. Over this they have no control, but they have absolute free will as to the way in which they meet it and the effect it has upon them. Whether they make of this life a heaven or a hell is entirely within their own choice. The freedom is in thoughts: as a person thinks, so a person becomes. If your thoughts are only upon money, you are claimed by money; if only upon evil, you become one with evil. But if they are constantly upon God, then you are absorbed in God and become one with the Father.

The greatest power in the world is creative thought. If one knew how to use it one would have power to put all things under one's feet. Such a force in the hands of the ignorant would be disastrous, as they could destroy themselves, body and soul. One can see this in the case of those whose thoughts are always upon money. Their whole being becomes obsessed with money until their souls are drowned in it. These can never find God. The person whose thoughts are only of evil creates the devil, but the thoughts of a person constantly upon God, create God.

# 81

THE human being is the most wonderful creation of God, composed of highest spirit and lower matter. Humanity is able to touch life at every point, both earthly life and heavenly life. Humans possesses, by virtue of the inner centers of their being, the power to function on every plane of the spiritual universe. But to use this power, they must obey the laws of all living things and beings. They must pass through darkness into light.

In order that the inner centers may be opened (and it is by means of these that one becomes conscious in the spiritual realms), the outer centers, or physical senses, must first be developed and allowed to function normally, according to the will of God. It is by going through this process of development that one becomes capable of responding to every experience of life, material or spiritual. And just as a seed cannot become a flower until development has taken place within the darkness of the outer coverings, hidden away, that is, from the light of the sun until mature; and just as these outer coverings are shed when of no more use to the growing flower, so it is with the physical senses. They, being the means of growth, must be used as such. But, just as surely, they must be shed as the spiritual flower becomes mature and ready to open to the sun of truth.

The Christ uses the souls of those who have reached the state of perfect flowering, of perfect bloom, as His representatives on earth. For only through humanity can the knowledge be given to humans of their divine heritage, their royal birth, the knowledge that they alone, of all created beings, have been made in the image of God.

# 82

HUMANITY is the greatest expression of the life of God in the world; but human beings are created beings and therefore, as humans, will one day cease to be. They are more capable of expressing the beauty of God than any other created being, and until they have fully expressed the triune nature of their Lord—love, harmony, and beauty—for which purpose they were created, they have not fulfilled the purpose of God's creation, as the caterpillar has not fulfilled the purpose of its creation until the essence of beauty within its form has emerged as a butterfly.

With the ultimate expression of beauty of which the form is capable, the purpose for which it was created is achieved. And although retaining the possibility of endless reproductions of itself in time, in the end as in the beginning, there is only God. Humankind and the whole created universe, in time, cease to be; but in eternity the essence of all created things exists in God, capable of re-expression.

> *The dust of the rose petal belongs to the heart of the perfume seller.*
>
> —*Abul Fazl*

# 83

WHENEVER the message of God comes forth in any age, it is always by means of a mystic birth.

The beginning of the mystery is in the soul's great passion of desire for union with God. But before this consummation there must always be the intoxication of divine passion, which alone burns away everything but the one desire. It is also the great fire of purification, which leaves the soul virgin, or pure, from all difference and distinction.

Then is the sacramental marriage: an absolute surrender, or fusion of the personality, in this mystical union with God. The result of the consummation is the conception of the idea. And from that time onward until the birth of the truth takes place, is a time of great burden and suffering for the messenger, the bringer of life, until the actual time of birth or giving forth the message, which must always be a time of agony and crucifixion.[1]

After the truth is born, born in a stable—the place where the "animals," or bodies of earth, live—other hands can tend the newborn child; but always they must clothe it (wrap it in swaddling clothes), for the naked simplicity of the truth must not be shown except to the few who understand.

---

1 "The solar cross is the symbol that must ever express crucifixion— the effort of spirit to penetrate matter, the light to illumine darkness, and that which is 'inner and sacred' to express outwardly in the life." Harriette Curtis, *The Key to the Universe* (New York : E.P. Dutton, 1919).

# 84

THE crucifixion—the messenger must always bear the cross. Every vibration, both spiritual and material, must pass through the messenger's body, suspended between heaven and earth.

The messenger must stand firm, nailed to the cross, while all the crosscurrents of earth and heaven surge around. The messenger must disentangle and set them in the right direction. Only so, can harmony be created out of discord.

# 85

WHAT is God, and what is humanity? It is impossible to answer fully this question, because there are no words in the physical human brain with which to clothe the idea. Until the inner senses are opened, a person cannot perceive or receive spiritual truth. There is no way of communication.

Spiritual truths are fluid, not fixed. They are scintillating with light and colors. By passing an idea through the brain it at once becomes set in a mold, fixed to one color and one shape. When this happens, a truth becomes a dead fact (facts are always dead), instead of a living truth.

To be alive connotes continual movement. Therefore a spiritual truth can never become a fact, because it belongs to the realm of life, the life of God, the only reality, which is continual movement, continual change, ever giving forth, constantly changing color as the diamond under the light. And it is just that constant movement that is life and color. This is the reason why it is so difficult for very intellectual and learned people to know the truth; they pass every thought and idea through the brain and fix it, thus making it impossible to find living truth.

Truth! That most illusive of all illusive things; one moment seen as one thing, and the next as something totally different.

*Whose secret Presence through Creation's veins*
*Running, quicksilver-like eludes your pains:*
*—Taking all shapes from Máah to Máahi, and*
*They change and perish all, but He remains.*

*—Omar Khayyam*

# 86

IT is difficult for people to realize that all experiences in this world and the next are the result of their own thoughts and desires. If they understood the laws of magnetism, they would know that every thought acts as a magnet and attracts its own unto itself.

The thinker is surrounded by materialized desires, which the thinker's own thoughts have attracted. In this atmosphere of one's own creation, one must live until, by a stronger magnetism or thought, one can dispel or change it. This is how a human being becomes a slave who should be king. The great masters of wisdom in all ages have given this teaching to their disciples, and in every scripture it is written for those who have ears to hear and comprehend. But in this age, when humanity as a whole has reached the point in evolution when it is possible to seek the path of return, it must be given to all who are willing to hear. The great need of humankind today, in every part of the world, and the solution of all life's difficulties—personal, social, and political—is that people should think about God. Thinking, they shall know; knowing; they shall realize; and through realization they shall enter into kingship.

## Part Three
## 87

*Prepare ye the way of the Lord!*
*Prepare ye the way of the Lord!*
*—Mark 1:3*

O PEOPLE of the blind eyes.

If you cannot see God can you not hear the signs of God's coming?

God speaks in the silence and in the voice of many waters. The Lord rides upon the whirlwind and walks upon the waves, and thunder and lightning are the Lord's power and glory, "For as the lightning cometh out of the east and shineth even unto the west, so shall also the coming of the Son of Man be."[1]

Be not sleeping when God comes, though your eyes may not behold, your ears may hearken to God's footstep, O people of the blind eyes.

1 Matthew 24:27.

## Words of the Master Heard in the Silence

BLESSED are they who hear My voice amid earth's discords;
verily, they hear.

Blessed are they who seek Me in the heights and in the
depths; verily, they see.

Blessed are they who know Me, though veiled with many
forms; verily, they know.

Blessed are they whom I have called;
verily, they shall partake of the mysteries.

Blessed are they who hearing, have renounced;
verily, they shall inherit the kingdom.

Blessed are they who for My sake are bereft of all;
verily, they shall be crowned.

Blessed are they who in My service are as outcasts among
humanity; verily, they shall sit upon a king's throne.

Blessed are they who give their earthly treasure for My work;
verily, they shall receive the treasure of heaven.

Blessed are they who walk in darkness, seeking light;
verily, shall their feet be guided.

Blessed are they who humble themselves before God;
verily, shall they find the heart of truth.

Blessed are they who, comprehending light,
yet remain in darkness to guide the feet of the unawakened.

Blessed are they who pour out their treasure before the Lord; verily, with joy shall their lives be crowned.

Blessed are they whose faces are ever toward Me; verily, they see no evil.

Blessed are they whose hearts are lonely for My sake; verily, I abide with them.

Blessed are they who carry the water of life to the parched and fainting; verily, they shall never thirst.

Blessed are they who show a light in the deep darkness; verily, their feet shall never stumble.

Blessed are they who have found Me in great tribulation; verily, their reward is great.

Blessed are they who keep their robes of purity yet seek Me in the foulest places; verily, they are pure.

Blessed are they who seek the face of their Lord in every face; for they shall be satisfied.

Blessed are they who hear the voice of God in every cry; verily, they hear.

Blessed are they who make their hearts the abode of God: verily, verily, they have peace.

Blessed are they who are dumb before God; verily, shall they speak the word of power.

Blessed are they to whom wisdom speaks; for they are companioned in solitary places.

Blessed are they who thirst for God; they shall surely drink the wine of Christ.

Blessed are the unsatisfied; for they rest only in God.

Blessed are they who receive My teaching in their hearts
and treasure it.

Blessed are they who hear My words in silence,
and in silence speak them again.

Blessed are they who seek the heart of My message,
for it is covered by many petals, as is the heart of a rose.

Blessed are the truth seekers;
for their desire shall be satisfied.

Blessed are they who work for Me, seeking no results;
verily, they shall receive love's crown.

Blessed are they who endure;
verily, their strength shall be as a lion.

Blessed are they who can patiently wait;
verily, for everything there is a time.

Blessed are the humble of heart;
to them shall be shown the greatness of God.

Blessed are they who walk softly lest they wake those who
sleep; verily, they have the understanding heart.

Blessed are they who sow My seed in the darkness;
verily, it shall multiply in the light.

Blessed are they who for My sake have renounced;
verily, their treasure no one takes away.

Blessed are they who perceive My teaching under many
forms; verily, to them is given the light of truth.

Blessed are they who are hungering for Me;
for with the bread of life shall they be satisfied.

Blessed are they who hear My voice in many waters;
verily, they shall never drown.

Blessed are they who remember their own heart-wound;
  they shall console the broken and troubled ones.

Blessed are they whose hearts are illumined;
  they are as torches in a dark place.

Blessed are they whose faith is immovable;
  verily, to them all things are possible.

Blessed are they who can feel the presence of God;
  verily, they shall fear no evil.

Blessed are they who seek help only from God;
  verily, their feet shall never stray.

Blessed are they who know their own shadow;
  verily, they shall not be afraid of the terror by night.

Blessed are they who have conquered fear,
  for their eyes shall behold the vision of God.

Blessed are the harmonious ones;
  verily, they are the makers of peace.

Blessed are they who daily tune the strings of the heart,
  that the hand of God may bring forth melody.

Blessed are the consolers,
  for they shall be called the friends of God.

Blessed are they whom silence calls;
  to them shall be given the mystery of sound.

Blessed are they whose hearts have understanding;
  verily, they shall walk in peace.

Verily, only the empty heart can echo the word of God.

Verily, they are blessed who can rest in the thought of God.

Verily, they are blessed whose eyes have seen the beauty of God.

Verily, they are twice blessed who speak of God with closed lips.

## Index

### A

abode 13, 16, , 72, 257; abode of the Lord of Light 72; abode of God 37, 141, 249, 362; abode of the soul 257. *See also* dwelling place; *under Father, God the,* Father's house.
absorption 93, 219; in God 93, 349, 353
Abu Fazl 355
Abu Hamid Muhammad ibn Muhammad al-Ghazzali 258
acceptance 47; gate of acceptance 290
achievement 91, 110, 165, 291, 355. *See also* attainment, completion, fulfillment, satisfaction, success.
action 29, 34, 45, 47, 57–58, 75, 146, 149–150, 153, 155, 158, 175, 195, 245, 286, 288, 327, 334. *See also* motive, movement, purpose, task, worker.
adversity 83, 126. *See also* bondage, difficulty, limitation, obstacle, oppression.
advice 48, 54–55, 78–79. *See also* guidance, instruction.
agony 57, 179, 219, 356. *See also* anguish, pain, sorrow, suffering.
air 32, 67, 86, 125, 184, 220, 224, 231, 234, 289; air of heaven 144; purification of air 291. *See also* wind.
alchemist 288, 290. *See also* alchemy.
alchemy 58, 183, 189, 289, 342; alchemy of God 20. *See also* alchemist, crucible, fermentation, transmutation.
alcohol 347
alpha and omega 183
altar 14
angel 19, 32, 106, 115, 223, 282, 310; angel's food 19; angel voices 24. *See also* Angel of Pain, archangels.
Angel of Pain 43. *See also* pain.
Angelus Silesius 37, 85
anguish 27. *See also* agony, pain, sorrow, suffering.
animal 63, 150, 179, 206, 207, 297, 328, 342, 356
annihilation 85, 112, 225, 350
archangels 32. *See also* angels.
Arnold, Edwin 133, 288
Arnold, Matthew 102
artist 21, 127, 296, 331. *See also* creation, creator, sculptor.
asceticism 171, 189
ashes 184, 219, 227–228, 291. *See also* fire, flame.
aspirant 7, 12, 35, 78, 83, 91, 110, 114, 138, 144, 163, 165, 169, 203, 234, 290. *See also* aspiration, disciple, pilgrim, seeker.
aspiration 38, 60, 144, 237, 291; divine aspiration 135. *See also* desire, goal, purpose, quest, search, seeking.
astral plane 54, 171, 250, 276, 291, 317; astral world 278, 312, 348
atma 223. *See also* spirit.
atom 34, 41, 44, 65, 95, 136, 139, 148, 150, 171, 183–185, 189, 195, 203, 207, 209, 213, 239, 278, 286, 302, 307, 310, 338–340

at-one-ment 17, 60. *See also* unity.
attainment 19, 37–38, 45, 49–50, 60, 84, 101, 103, 110, 135, 142, 140–151, 160, 173, 175–176, 179, 188, 193, 195, 199–200, 225, 251, 282, 324. *See also* achievement, fulfillment, success.
attunement 73, 240, 242, 262, 305, 317, 329–330. *See also* keynote, note, tuning.
awakening 12, 27, 112, 114, 131, 151, 266, 286, 303, 311; awakened heart 245, 246; awakened soul 13, 136, 158, 173, 311– 312. *See also* realization.

## B

badness 90. *See also* cruelty, evil, sin, wickedness.
balance 38, 49–50, 59, 70, 91–92, 103, 111, 121, 142, 165–166, 189, 205, 212, 215, 217, 236, 278, 282, 299, 329, 335–366; secret of a successful balanced life 38. *See also* duality, equilibrium, harmony, pairs of opposites, path of balance, scales.
balloons 86, 308
barrier 43, 135, 190, 225. *See also* difficulty, limitation, obstacle, problem, tribulation.
Bayazid Bastami 235
beauty 8, 14, 19, 38, 52, 76, 79, 124, 156, 181, 189, 199, 208, 210, 228–230, 234, 239, 320, 331, 335, 343–344, 355, 364; perfection of beauty 21, 241
Beck, L. Adams 137
belief 15, 22, 26, 30, 51, 54, 59–61, 70, 109, 118, 121, 150, 157, 159, 169, 183, 197, 218, 236, 257, 314. *See also* religion, scriptures, trust.
beloved 109, 225
Beloved, The 137, 247, 291–292. *See also* love, lover.
Beresford, John Davys 29
bewilderment 22, 24, 81, 149, 175, 198, 246, 279, 286–287, 299. *See also* confusion, doubt.
Bhagavad Gita 30, 50, 52, 58, 74, 142, 161, 164, 203–204, 212, 215–217, 236, 263, 285, 293, 335, 340–341, 351
Bible 202, 285. *See also* Christianity.
bird 38, 253
birth 5, 26, 31, 34, 115–116, 124, 152, 167, 178, 180, 190, 204, 212, 217, 228, 342, 354; birth of Christ 53, 141, 178, 241; mystic birth 356; new birth 346, 263–264, 288; second birth 51, 60. *See also* rebirth.
birthright 19, 157, 199, 207, 216. *See also* heritage, inheritance.
Blavatsky, Helena 44
blessing 75, 125, 142
bliss 8, 137, 192, 225, 350. *See also* ecstasy, happiness, joy, nirvana.
blossom 230. *See also* flower, rose.
body 34, 36–37, 39–40, 46, 51–53, 55, 57, 75, 86, 95, 112, 114, 127, 135, 137, 140, 144–145, 160, 179, 185–186, 204–209, 213, 221, 239, 271, 276, 282, 290, 302,

307, 310, 317, 319, 333, 335, 340, 345–348, 350, 353, 357; astral body 171, 276; body of God 209, 310, 340; body of emotion 93, 213; body of radiance 140, 178, 184–185; mental body 51, 93, 108, 213, 276; mystical Body 160; subtle bodies 150. *See also under resurrection,* resurrection body; embodiment; form.
bondage 15, 39, 40, 52, 73, 84, 183, 199, 217, 219, 351. *See also* imprisonment, limitation, oppression, prison, slave.
Brahma, the night of 343
brain 36, 95, 98, 116, 141, 296, 306–307, 358. *See also* mind.
breath(ing) 32, 34, 39, 46, 160, 176; 332; inbreathing of God 334, 343; outbreathing of God 334
Browning, Robert 20, 54, 65
Buddhist 225
butterfly 355

## C

candle 99, 122. *See also* flame, light.
Catholic Church 26
centers of magnetism 37, 336; inner centers 354; outer centers 354. *See also under heart,* heart center.
chain, of holy ones 269
channel 285; channel of light 267. *See also* instrument.
chaos 108, 306, 338
charity 179
chemist 310
child(ren) 11, 21, 34, 63, 90, 118, 135, 160, 187, 192, 199, 206–208, 224, 245, 302–303, 320, 331, 356; children of God 73, 121, 254, 262; children of the earth 12; children of the mind 214. *See also under Christ,* Christ Child; infant; son.
chord 10, 165, 210, 239, 257, 338–339. *See also* harmony.
Christ 17–18, 45, 49, 51, 53, 59–60, 88, 90, 114, 117, 141, 152, 160, 179–181, 183–185, 195, 215, 233, 241, 249, 263, 266, 278, 282, 288, 299–300, 317, 322, 324–325, 328, 340–341, 347, 354; Christ Child 178, 180, 263–264, 327; Christ note 65, 210, 212, 250, 305; cosmic Christ 18, 84, 183, 186; false Christs 7; love of Christ 108, 115, 122; wine of Christ 278, 347–348, 262. *See also* Christianity, cross, crucifixion, Easter, Jesus, Light of the World, Lord, Lord of Light, Prince of Peace, resurrection.
Christianity 22, 118. *See also* Bible, Catholic Church, Christ, church, Easter, Jesus, Nicene Creed, Protestant faith.
church 16–17, 30, 32, 72, 117–118, 145. *See also* Catholic Church.
circle of influence 100
civilization 15, 112, 122, 220

clairvoyance 221. *See also* psychism; messenger; prophet; seer; sight, spiritual; vision.
clouds 21, 31, 89, 117, 120, 124, 149. *See also* cover, veil.
coal 219–220
color 56, 86, 116, 163, 197, 224, 228–229, 294, 309, 311, 322, 340, 358
completion 10, 52, 59, 173, 193, 209, 225. *See also* achievement, fulfillment, satisfaction, success.
concentration 34, 110–111, 144, 269, 331
confidence 83, 101, 189. *See also* faith, trust.
confusion 38, 78, 89, 103, 149, 158, 175, 186, 198, 204, 210–211, 212, 221, 283, 297, 314. *See also* bewilderment, discernment, doubt.
conquering 14, 118, 137, 146, 171, 216, 220, 232, 351, 364; conquering evil 24; conquering death 51, 53, 241. *See also* conqueror, mastery, victory.
conqueror 88, 137, 275. *See also* conquering.
consciousness 8, 11, 50, 73, 80, 83, 85, 92, 138, 149, 153, 158, 173–174, 176, 190, 213, 245, 249, 277, 340, 350, 354; God-consciousness 49; higher consciousness 138, 154. *See also* knowledge, realization, self-consciousness.
control 37, 40, 49, 72, 110, 126, 144, 162, 173–174, 204–205, 215, 219–220, 274, 278, 282, 299, 329–330, 353; control of emotion 12, 35, 51, 126; control of the mind 37, 55, 173, 205, 212–213, 299; control of thought 34, 206, 211, 213, 274. *See also* mastery, self-control.
courage 46, 52, 58, 81–83, 88, 112, 124, 127, 169, 260, 268, 281. *See also* strength.
cover 13, 32, 41, 43–44, 61, 67, 75, 86, 120, 122, 141, 150, 164, 179, 188, 201, 223–224, 241, 266, 272, 294, 300, 302, 311, 323, 341, 363; coverings 82, 152, 175, 200, 304, 354. *See also* clouds, form, garment, mask, veil.
creation 5, 26, 37, 19, 41, 45, 49, 51, 65, 67, 92, 95, 106–108, 113, 118, 126, 142–144, 151, 156, 172, 177, 185, 190, 203–205, 211–213, 215, 211–214, 218, 227, 258, 297, 300, 302, 304–305, 320, 328, 331, 341–342, 345, 351, 3543–355, 357, 359. *See also* artist, Creation, the; creator; Creator, the.
Creation, the 5, 16, 212, 300, 358
creator 34, 67, 106, 121, 190, 213, 320, 331. *See also* creation, Creator, the.
Creator, The 34, 44, 206. *See also* Creation.
cross 50, 60, 127, 179, 216, 356, 357. *See also* crucifixion.
crown of life 60, 102, 112
crucible 58, 68; crucible of truth

290–291. *See also* alchemy.
crucifixion 84, 179, 184, 215, 266, 281, 317, 356–357. *See also* Christ, cross, Easter, Jesus, resurrection.
cruelty 16–17, 106, 118. *See also* harm, pain, wickedness.

## D

danger 33, 54–56, 88, 112, 121, 137, 156, 184, 265, 273, 275, 297, 312, 348. See also difficulty.
darkness 12, 16, 21–22, 24, 32, 36, 44, 50, 59, 61, 64, 69, 72, 78, 92–93, 118, 122, 126, 136, 142, 152, 176, 178–179, 196, 215–216, 219 220, 267, 279, 302, 322–323, 327, 332, 342, 354, 356, 361–364. *See also* shadow, illusion, Prince of Darkness.
dawn 20, 137; dawn of a new age 117–118; dawn of unity 322
death 24, 31, 41, 44, 51–53, 55, 59–60, 106, 112, 118, 120, 124, 131, 143–144, 154, 158, 166, 178, 183–184, 200, 211, 213, 221, 225–226, 228, 232, 236, 241, 263, 275, 282, 288, 304, 310, 317, 321, 350, 358. *See also* resurrection.
debt 45, 89, 253, 288–289, 313; karmic debt 312
deliverance 32, 115; the Great Deliverer 326
delusion 56, 265, 293; delusion of the pairs of opposites 52, 58, 204, 351. *See also* illusion.
dependability 103, 110. *See also* reliability, steadfastness.
depression 35, 91, 189. *See also* sorrow, sadness. suffering.
desert 13, 247, 292, 310, 347
desire 26, 43, 50, 54–56, 75, 93, 103, 110, 126–127, 135–136, 156–157, 170–171, 190, 192–193, 213, 230, 233–234, 238, 241, 245, 251, 253–254, 261, 265, 280, 282, 284–285, 291, 300, 309, 317, 328–329, 346, 348, 356, 359, 363; earthly desires 11. *See also* aspiration, goal, purpose, quest.
destination 200, 277, 282. *See also* goal, purpose.
destiny 49, 71, 88, 173, 209, 352–353. *See also* fate.
destruction 41–42, 49, 108, 204, 212, 225; destructive force 50
detachment 148, 275. *See also* indifference.
development 56, 100, 110, 137, 167, 251, 254 265, 280, 354; spiritual development 77, 255, 272, 279, 282. *See also* evolution, growth, progress, self-development, stage.
devil 5, 58, 78, 106, 190, 353. *See also* Satan.
devotion 162, 167, 192, 200–201, 251, 291, 341; devoted love 62. *See also* faith, love, service, worship.
difficulty 13, 27, 33, 47, 57, 83, 88, 91, 94, 103, 137, 146, 153, 169, 204 *(cont. overleaf)*

difficulty *(cont.)* 213, 246, 250, 253–254, 256, 260, 275, 284, 297, 309, 316, 338, 351–352, 359. *See also* adversity, barrier, danger, limitation, obstacle, oppression, problem, tribulation.
disciple 12, 14, 53, 103, 137–139, 141, 145–149, 153–154, 156–158, 167, 169, 171, 177, 186–189, 192, 225, 234–235, 245, 249–254, 256–261, 263, 265–269, 271–275, 277–279, 282, 284–291, 294–295, 308, 312–313, 324, 327, 336, 341, 344, 351, 359. *See also* discipleship, initiates, pupil, seeker.
discipleship 83, 91, 114, 135, 138, 139, 169, 188, 234, 245, 251. *See also* disciple.
discipline 137
discouragement 19, 137, 154, 167
discovery 20 87, 138, 152, 236; rediscovery 19. *See also* realization.
discrimination 78, 156
disease 276, 304, 319. *See also* healing.
diversity 334
divine man 195, 215, 232, 299, 335, 351. *See also* hu-man.
Dodd, Catherine 88
dog 258
door 12, 18, 70, 77, 138, 162, 192, 255, 339, 341, 347; door of the heart 326–327. *See also* gate.
doubt 9, 33, 69, 82, 91, 135, 149, 153, 189–190, 240, 307. *See also* bewilderment, confusion.
Dowling, Levi H. 17
dragon of evil 118
Drake, Sir Francis 52
dream 6, 28, 123
drugs 276, 347
duality 41, 49, 92, 204, 215. *See also* balance, pairs of opposites.
duty 7, 139, 149, 253, 269, 282, 285. *See also* responsibility, task, worker.
dwelling place 89, 126; dwelling place of God 14–15, 72. *See also* abode; *under Father,* Father's house.

## E

earth 5, 11–12, 18, 21, 24, 26, 30–32, 44, 47, 53–55, 65, 67, 71, 73, 77–78, 88, 92, 98, 109, 111, 113, 115–116, 118, 120–122, 135, 144, 152, 158, 160, 167, 170, 173, 178, 181–182, 184–188, 190, 196–198, 203, 207, 212, 218–221, 227–229, 231–232, 234, 240, 256, 263, 266–267, 282, 286, 289, 299–300, 305–306, 308, 317, 320–321, 329, 335, 342, 346–347, 351–352, 354, 356–357, 361; earth's travail 112; earth symphony 65 earthbound 5, 50; new earth 19; purification of earth 290. *See also* form, materialism.
earthquake 5, 30
East, the 152

Easter 178. *See also* Christ, crucifixion, Jesus, resurrection.
ecstasy 21, 59, 225, 228, 278, 347. *See also* bliss, joy, nirvana.
ego 32, 93, 142, 173; false ego 14, 67, 100, 136, 142, 173, 205. *See also* individuality, personality, self, separateness.
elders 84, 121–122. *See also* great ones, masters.
electricity 61, 207, 271, 336, 338
elements 34, 44, 67, 183, 203, 213, 220, 231, 290–291, 297, 336. *See also* air, earth, ether, fire, water.
embodiment 54, 65, 84, 195, 211, 214, 321; embodiment of Christ 160, 185; embodied thought 34. *See also* body, form, manifestion.
Emerson, Ralph Waldo 87, 146
emotion 27, 35, 40, 51, 55, 86, 144, 151, 173, 223, 249, 267, 285, 290; body of emotions 93, 213; control of emotion 12, 35, 51, 55, 126. *See also* control.
emptiness 9, 127, 177, 187–188, 226, 241, 261–262, 267, 272, 285, 364
endurance 14, 43, 46, 60, 88, 119, 137, 154, 219, 363
equilibrium 49–50, 92, 165, 189, 336. *See also* balance, harmony.
error 152, 175, 187, 202, 207, 281, 304. *See also* failure, misdeeds, mistakes.
essence 34, 39, 50, 58, 70, 97, 135, 158, 164, 185, 213, 217, 227–229, 232, 275–276, 278, 288, 300, 302, 341–342, 355
eternity 21, 85, 113, 136, 176, 198, 200, 218, 224, 245, 302, 311, 355; eternal, the 142, 160, 195, 218, 236, 316; eternal life 51, 106, 135–136, 192, 288, 350; eternal now 20; eternal youth 19, 39, 317, 350. *See also* immortality.
ether 31, 67, 183–184, 227, 291
evil 5, 16, 24, 26, 29, 46, 58–59, 68, 75, 92–93, 96, 106–108, 112, 115, 120–122, 177, 199, 215, 269–270, 274, 317, 320–321, 351, 353, 362, 364; evil thoughts 108, 111, 118, 120–121, 200, 320, 353. *See also* badness, cruelty, dragon of evil, sin, wickedness.
evolution 5, 41, 49, 59, 84, 109, 120, 160, 184–186, 200, 202, 211, 215–216, 220, 227–228, 239, 280–281, 306, 329, 335, 338, 340, 342, 359. *See also* development, growth, progress.
exile 39, 70, 135, 151, 225
expansion 38, 41, 224. *See also* growth.

## F

failure 51–52, 89, 94, 197, 204. *See also* error, mistakes.
fairies 21
faith 12, 26, 37, 56, 61, 78, 88, 90–91, 121, 126, 169, 196–197, 233, 236, 238, 240, 251, 260, 265, 299, 330, 364; *(cont. overleaf)*

faith *(cont.)* creative faith 26; faithfulness 110, 112, 269, 282. *See also* confidence, devotion, religion, steadfastness, trust.
falsity 55
fate 91, 255. *See also* destiny.
father 11, 245, 256
Father, God the 16–18, 34, 47, 49–50, 59–60, 70, 73, 84, 92, 106, 121, 166, 185, 203, 223, 225, 282, 300, 341, 344, 351, 353; family of God 117, 182, 307; Father's house 39, 49, 52, 60, 70, 199–200, 257, 310. *See also* abode of God.
fear 8, 20, 27, 52, 69, 112, 124, 126, 177, 217, 293, 364
female 206; feminine attributes 336. *See also* mother, women.
fermentation 278. *See also* alchemy.
fire 67–68, 106, 144, 184, 219–220, 231, 289, 328, 356; fire of love 195; purification of fire 219–200, 291. *See also* ashes, flame.
flame 5. *See also* ashes, candle, fire, light.
flowering 227–229, 354
flower 21, 44, 99, 133, 207, 227–228, 230, 354; spiritual flower 354. *See also* blossom, perfume, rose.
fog of illusion 287. *See also* cloud, illusion.
force 26, 43, 50, 54–55, 103, 108, 111–112, 118, 121–122, 156, 171, 204–205, 207, 213, 215–216, 219, 228, 251, 254, 271, 273, 286, 324, 330, 336, 338, 353; constructive force 26, 43, 50; divine force 37, 285, 341; ensouling force 37; spiritual forces 110, 205, 289. *See also* electricity, god of force, life force, magnetism, power.
forests 13, 30, 310. *See also* trees.
forgiveness 50, 59, 131, 289, 350
form 5–6, 16–18, 23, 26, 29, 36, 38, 41–44, 55, 61, 65, 70, 73–74, 98–99, 105, 113, 116–117, 127, 146, 158-160, 167–168, 178–179, 183, 185, 196–197, 199, 203, 205–210, 212–213, 215, 220, 223–224, 227–228, 238, 258, 278, 297, 299, 302, 304, 306, 309, 311, 320–321, 329, 335, 338, 340–343, 351, 355, 361, 363; breaking of a form 34, 38–39, 41–43, 61. *See also* body, cover, earth, embodiment, garment, manifestation, form-makers, thought forms, vehicle.
form-makers 74
freedom 24, 27, 34, 38–40, 45, 52, 70, 73, 84–85, 111–112, 118, 122, 136, 144, 161, 156, 165, 168, 180, 183, 185, 195, 200, 216–217, 219–220, 225, 232, 253, 257, 285, 288–289, 293, 300, 308, 320, 333, 347, 351–353. *See also* free will, liberty.
Freemasonry 249
free will 45–46, 48–49, 54, 70, 209, 211, 214, 216, 236, 310, 333, 352–353. *See also* freedom, liberty.

friend 33, 83, 126; friends of God 364. God as the Friend 17, 33.
fruit 9, 44, 80, 124, 184, 228- 230, 278, 342; fruit of the spirit 80
fulfillment 10, 42, 80, 160, 209, 227, 355. *See also* achievement, attainment, completion, happiness, purpose, satisfaction, success.
future 20, 123, 217, 228, 322. *See also* past, present.

## G

garden 126; garden of the heart 162
Garden of Eden 67
garment 38, 67, 107, 164, 175, 333. *See also* cover, form, vehicle, wedding robe.
gate 11, 18, 21, 24, 50, 83, 124, 138, 142, 164, 169, 234, 249, 288, 290-291; gate of the master 248, 253, 341; gates of heaven 24–25, 50, 59, 91, 144; gates of hell 50, 59; keeper of the gate 138; seventh gate 24–25. *See also* door.
gifts 8, 20, 46, 49
glory 5, 19, 21, 52, 60, 63, 173, 240, 314, 360; glorification 50, 251
goal 8, 12, 56, 84, 164, 169, 176, 200, 239, 246, 250–251, 267, 277, 279, 282–283, 312, 351, 352. *See also* aspiration, desire, destination, journey, path, purpose, quest, search, seeking.
God buried in humanity 179, 332, 338
God-consciousness 49
God-identification 85
god of force 118
God-realization 49; God-realized man 150, 152, 221, 246
God Transcendent 304
God Within 14, 18, 36–37, 46–48, 84, 177, 221, 222, 279, 304
gods 5, 146. *See also* god of force.
Goethe, Johann von 81
gold 30, 117, 170, 289, 291, 342
goodness 15–16, 26, 29, 58–59, 68, 75, 90, 96, 108, 120–121, 148, 150–152, 169, 199, 256, 267, 269–270, 272, 274, 280, 308, 317, 321, 327, 336, 343, 351. *See also* morality, righteousness, virtue.
goodwill 113, 115, 121
great ones 78, 84, 109, 124. *See also* elders, masters.
growth 21, 38, 75, 354. *See also* development, evolution, expansion, movement, progress.
guardians of the path 9
guidance 47–48, 78, 115, 138, 166, 279, 282, 287–288, 361. *See also* advice, guide, instruction, Spirit of Guidance, training.
guide, spiritual 7, 25, 48, 59, 147, 166, 240, 246, 251, 274, 277, 292, 323, 361; guiding star 16; guiding voice 16. *See also* guidance, guru, master, murshid, mystic, sage, seer, teacher.
guru 124. *See also* guide, master, teacher.

## H

Hageman, Samuel Miller 189
happiness 37, 39, 52, 89–90, 124, 151, 320. *See also* bliss, fulfillment, joy, pleasure, satisfaction.
harm 50, 54, 100, 254, 266, 285, 348. *See also* cruelty, pain, poison.
harmony 52, 65, 95, 151, 156, 165, 189, 206, 208–210, 212, 239, 241, 246, 250, 256–257, 284, 305, 310, 319–320, 324, 344, 355, 357, 364; Divine Harmonist 65; harmonious discords 65. *See also* balance, chord.
harvest 109, 127, 207, 321, 352. *See also* fruit, reaping.
hatred 92, 120–122, 156, 189
healing 35, 108, 110, 121, 131, 133, 181, 267, 272, 342; health 35, 95, 112, 121, 319. *See also* disease, life force, vitality.
heart 3, 9, 14–15, 17, 25, 36–37, 43, 45–46, 48, 51, 53, 55, 70, 72, 75–76, 78, 81– 82, 84, 89, 96, 115, 118, 120–121, 125–127, 131, 135, 138, 141, 145, 150–152, 156, 162, 169, 176–180, 187–191, 193, 197, 203, 210, 212, 233– 235, 240, 242, 248–249, 253, 258, 260, 262–264, 268–269, 271, 284, 287, 291–292, 298, 303–304, 315, 324–325, 327, 336–338, 341, 355, 361–364; awakened heart 245–246; broken heart 27, 180, 223, 241, 267; door of the heart 326–327; heart center 124, 209, 318; heart of God 176; language of the heart 131; pure in heart 168, 188–189, 300; singleness of heart 110, 139. *See also* love.
heaven 19, 25, 30, 47, 49–50, 59, 65, 84, 91–92, 105, 144, 156, 166, 170, 177, 187, 189, 192, 199, 203, 211, 223, 236, 241, 282, 299–300, 310–311, 321, 329, 351, 353–354, 357, 361; gates of heaven 24–25, 50, 59, 91, 144; kingdom of heaven 105, 187, 246, 263, 325 *See also* nirvana.
hell 5, 24–25, 50, 59–60, 69, 177, 199, 211, 236, 321, 351, 353
heritage 21, 216, 219, 354. *See also* birthright, inheritance.
Holy Grail 13–14
holy ones 152. *See also* messenger, mystic, prophet, saint, sage, seer.
hu-man 70, 166, 195, 200, 215, 232, 299, 324, 351; hu-manity 342. *See also* divine man.

## I

ice 29, 68, 184, 195
ideal 21, 34, 58, 79, 81, 98, 169, 179, 193, 302–303, 306–307, 320, 329–330. *See also* image.
idea 32, 36, 56, 81, 94, 98, 116, 127, 265, 294, 308, 312, 314, 324, 329, 358. *See also* mind, thought.

identification 37, 67, 85–86, 135, 142, 173, 199, 210, 219, 221–223, 252, 343
ignorance 32, 43, 78, 89, 137, 142, 147, 175–176, 193, 200, 201, 249, 276, 281, 300, 302, 341, 353
illumination 12, 19, 36, 59, 147, 176–177, 184, 249, 269, 279, 290, 296, 309, 327, 356. *See also* light, radiance.
illusion 7, 55, 81, 86, 97, 135, 149, 172, 189, 192–193, 210, 216–217, 236, 258, 278, 286–287, 308, 312, 337; illusion of illusions 56, 265; secret of illusion 172. *See also darkness,* delusion, maya, mirage, shadow, unreality.
image 99, 173, 188–189, 224, 295, 299, 304, 316, 333; image of God 29, 34, 49, 65, 73, 87, 108, 165, 168, 190, 195, 202–203, 207, 211, 216, 235, 320, 354. *See also* ideal.
immortality 27, 29, 86, 133, 135, 211–212. *See also* eternity, life everlasting, resurrection.
impression 126, 223, 307, 312
imprisonment 39, 43, 73, 179, 219–220, 332, 345; imprisoned soul 27, 136. *See also* bondage, limitation, prison.
Inayat Khan 9, 23–24, 27, 46, 53, 56–57, 73, 79, 85, 89, 123, 141, 157, 180, 190, 192, 194, 196–198, 203, 218, 223
incense 162
indifference 35, 80, 154, 234, 267, 292–293. *See also* detachment.
individuality 86, 135, 219–220, 334; individualization 86, 333, 340. *See also* ego, personality.
infant 115, 289. *See also* child.
inheritance 49, 136, 190. *See also* birthright, heritage.
initiates 163, 183–184, 249. *See also* disciples, initiation, initiator.
initiation 77, 80, 163, 183, 187, 249–250, 290–291, 335. *See also* initiates, initiator.
initiator 83, 165, 192, 249. *See also* initiates, initiation.
insight 34, 47, 75, 112, 153, 156. *See also* intuition; mind; vision.
inspiration 36, 131, 261, 296
instruction 13, 48, 105, 110, 137. 157, 212. *See also* advice, guidance, lesson, training.
instrument 37, 104, 167, 305, 318, 338. *See also* channel, vehicle.
intellect 81, 179. *See also* brain, intelligence, mind.
intelligence 294, 296. *See also* brain, intellect, mind, insight, intuition, knowledge, wisdom.
intoxication 347–348, 356. *See also under wine*, wine of Christ.
intuition 7, 24, 63, 78–79, 92, 138, 201, 234, 294–295, 309. *See also* insight, mind.

## J


Jalal ad-Din Rumi 5, 17, 29, 45, 63, 106

jelal 49, 204

jemal 49, 204

Jesus 7, 17–18, 22, 26, 37, 50–51, 53, 59–60, 92, 108, 113, 117–118, 120, 127, 152, 158, 166, 179, 181, 183–184, 186–188, 197, 221, 225, 249, 256, 263, 278, 282, 288, 299–300, 325, 341. *See also* Christ, Christianity, cross, crucifixion, Easter, Lord, Lord of Light, Prince of Peace, resurrection.

journey 9, 11, 13–14, 25, 39, 47, 49, 84, 124, 137, 165, 175–176, 190, 198–201, 221, 223, 246, 249–251, 253–254, 256, 272, 275, 277–278, 286, 288–289, 297, 304, 308, 347, 352; journey's end 8, 245; outward journey 13, 39, 81–82. *See also* goal, path, pilgrimage, purpose, quest, search, seeking, stage, traveler, wayfarer.

joy 11, 23–24, 27, 39, 50, 52, 57, 59, 66, 86–88, 93, 103, 124–126, 133, 137, 139, 142, 176–177, 188, 225, 236, 247, 260, 264, 268–269, 281, 291, 304, 326, 351–352, 362; joy of creation 331; joy of seeking and finding 19. *See also* bliss, ecstasy, happiness.

justice 106, 111. *See also* law, morality, penalties, punishment.


## K


kemal 49, 50, 204

keynote 65, 95, 151, 165, 209–210, 212, 240, 250, 305, 320, 335, 338–339; keynote for this planet 210. *See also* attunement; under Christ, Christ note; note; tone; tuning.

king 21, 111–212, 217, 249, 263, 323, 325, 359, 361; kingship 216, 359. *See also* kingdom, throne.

kingdom 21, 144, 173, 203, 215–216, 232, 249, 283, 323, 361; kingdom of God 10, 18, 51, 56, 59, 70, 89, 248, 265, 320, 324; middle kingdom 144, 173. *See also under heaven,* kingdom of heaven; king.

Kipling, Rudyard 72

knights 118

knowledge 9, 27, 39, 43, 50, 58, 73, 81, 92, 98, 100, 102, 110, 123, 136, 138, 142, 147, 155, 175, 184, 193, 196, 216–217, 223, 262, 271, 289, 291, 294, 299–300, 354; knowledge of God 9, 56, 85, 196, 200, 202, 265; knowledge of truth 43, 73, 105, 232, 234. *See also* consciousness, intelligence, self-knowledge, wisdom.

Krishna 341


## L


law 90, 92–93, 204–205, 216, 232–233, 236, 239, 271, 307, 320, 322, 350–351, 354,

359; law of attraction and repulsion 336; law of the pairs of opposites 92, 142, 350–351; laws of balance 50. *See also* justice; morality; *under nature*, nature's laws; penalties, punishment, rules.
lesson 14, 27, 35, 38, 43, 52, 70, 89–90, 105–106, 110, 148, 192, 213, 222, 232, 245, 260, 272, 274, 289, 335, 352. *See also* instruction; life, school of; life the great initiator; life, school of; training.
liberty 45; liberation 84, 219. *See also* freedom, free will.
life, consecration of 149, 327
life, daily 47, 57, 80, 91, 100, 106, 127, 149, 158, 171, 189, 222, 250, 253, 327. *See also* experience.
life, drama of 45, 82, 97
life everlasting 51, 52, 84, 241, 317, 325. *See also* immortality.
life force 41, 55, 158–159, 212–213, 228, 341; life-giving power 73, 108, 205. *See also* healing, quickening, vitality.
life, inner 14, 91, 100, 110, 139, 146–147, 158, 172, 237, 258, 280, 288–289
life, mystery. *See under mystery*, mystery of life.
life of God 30, 136, 204, 241, 317, 320–321, 335, 343, 355, 358
life of the soul 57
life of the spirit 39, 109, 149, 152, 288. *See also* spirit.
Life, the One 30, 135, 179, 199, 228, 340, 343; oneness of all life 107
life, school of 96, 106, 110, 232. *See also* life, daily; lesson.
life, the great initiator 83, 165, 192, 249. *See also* lesson.
light 7–8, 13–14, 16, 21, 24, 30, 36, 43, 61, 69, 72, 78, 82, 85, 92–93, 100, 105, 116, 118, 122, 126, 136, 138, 140, 142, 149, 152, 156, 162, 175–177, 183–185, 198, 201–202, 206, 215–216, 219–220, 225, 227–228, 235, 239, 249, 251, 259, 266–267, 269, 272, 287–289, 302–304, 322, 327–328, 332, 347, 354, 356, 358, 361–362; all-seeing light 124; light of eternal now 20; light of God 36, 188, 241, 255, 267, 279, 321, 323; light of guidance 28, 279, 288; light of intuition 7, 24, 138, 201, 234; light of the sun 36, 219, 227–228, 278, 321, 354; light of truth 77, 196, 271, 311, 363; light of wisdom 175–176, 298, 304; One Light 320; ray of light 36, 136, 198, 228; uncreated light 5; white light 163, 196, 322. *See also* candle, dawn, fire, illumination, Light of the World, Lord of Light, radiance.
Light of the World 178, 215. *See also* Christ, Jesus.
limitation 6, 45, 85–86, 175, 186, 195, 219, 220. *See also* adversity, barrier, bondage, difficulty.

listening 47, 55, 104, 118, 126, 210, 250, 315. *See also* sound, voice.
loneliness 50
Lord, the 15–16, 19, 24, 28, 30–31, 60, 67, 117, 119, 137, 170, 177, 240, 263, 281, 286, 341, 355, 360, 362. *See also* Christ, Jesus.
Lord of Light 72. *See also* Christ, Jesus.
Lord of the Shadow 215
love 8, 10–12, 16, 19, 43, 50, 52, 61–63, 85, 92–93, 118, 120–122, 124–126, 135, 139, 150, 152, 156, 177, 187–189, 192–193, 208, 210, 225, 239, 246, 253, 255, 264, 267, 285, 290, 305, 320, 340–341, 344, 350, 355; all-pervading love 17–18, 115, 122; limitless love 85; love of Christ 88, 108, 115, 117, 122 179; love of God 63, 118, 137, 139, 188, 192, 195, 310, 314; love of power 314; love's crown 363; mystery of love 192; spiritual love 124. *See also* Beloved, devotion, heart, lover.
lover 162; lover of God 135, 225. *See also* Beloved, heart, love.

## M

macrocosm 34, 178, 203
magnet 152, 181–182, 277, 359
magnetism 181–182, 207, 209, 272, 336, 342, 359; magnetic field 160, 181; magnetic power 310; magnetism of gaze 152, 277
manas 211, 299, 350. *See also* mind.
manifestation 18, 29, 34, 41, 85–86, 92, 97, 176, 183, 185, 195, 198, 203–204, 207, 215, 219, 231, 271, 335, 338; manifestation of love 61. *See also* embodiment, form.
manna 19, 20
manzillha 278. *See also* stage.
masculine qualities 336. *See also* men.
mask 29, 63. *See also* cover, veil.
master 11–12, 24, 26, 37, 56, 59–60, 65, 75, 77, 88, 103–104, 110, 113, 115–116, 118, 124, 142, 144–145, 153–154, 156–157, 160, 169–170, 176–177, 182, 187, 213, 215, 248, 250–251, 253, 261, 264–265, 275, 285, 288–291, 298– 299, 306, 331, 341, 351; master builder 113; master-hand 331; master of life and death 166, 200, 232, 282; Master of masters 114; master of wisdom 13–14, 59, 256, 297, 359; master's aura 75; master's work 103–104, 109–110, 114, 187; master workers 115; One Master 160. *See also* guide; great ones; guru; elders; holy ones; mastery; messenger; *under mind*, master mind; prophet; saint; shining ones; Spirit of Guidance;

teacher.
mastery 35, 40, 59, 81, 88, 92–93, 110, 142–144, 215, 232, 256, 274–275, 297, 299; mastery of the elements 220. *See also* conquering, control, master, self-control.
materialism 78. *See also* earth, matter; world.
maya 236, 286. *See also* illusion.
maze 312
meditation 7, 34, 48, 84, 100, 110, 141, 158, 167, 272, 277. *See also* mysticism.
medium 315–316. *See also* psychism, séances, spirit messages.
melody 126, 364. *See also* music.
memory 235, 350. *See also* remembrance.
men 63, 97, 115, 118, 121, 204, 280, 335. *See also* father.
mental plane 116, 158, 172, 200, 223, 306–308; mental images 299, 304, 333; mental material 98, 141, 333; mental sphere 299; mental work, 205. *See also under body,* mental body; mind; thought.
message of God 73, 109, 112, 131, 162, 168, 187, 196, 242, 315, 356, 363; Easter message 178; message of Jesus 197. *See also* messages, messengers, prophet.
messages 54, 109, 315, 317, 335. *See also* message of God, spirit messages.
messengers 73, 109, 127, 131, 162, 181–182, 190, 197, 266, 329, 356–357; message-bearers 196–197. *See also* master, prophet, seer.
microcosm 34, 176, 178, 203
Mighty Whole 25
mind 29, 37, 39–41, 45, 48, 54–55, 56–57, 63, 72, 81, 91, 94, 98–99, 102, 107, 113, 115, 118, 127, 141, 162–163, 171, 175, 177, 187, 189–190, 194–195, 202, 205, 211–215, 217, 221, 223–225, 228, 238, 258, 271, 291, 293–294, 296–297, 299, 302, 306, 308, 316–317, 320, 335, 346–347, 349, 350–351; control of the mind 37, 55, 173, 205, 212–213, 299; divine mind of God 98; master mind 34, 116, 306, 331, 351; mental architects 329; single-mindedness 8, 109. *See also* brain, consciousness, idea, intellect, intelligence, knowledge, manas, mental plane, realization, thought, wisdom.
miracle 51, 197, 278
mirage 11, 308. *See also* illusion, unreality.
mirror of the mind 162, 173, 294. *See also* reflection.
misdeeds 27. *See also* error, mistake, penalties, punishment.
mistakes 39, 89, 164, 172, 282, 288–289, 350, 352. *See also* error, failure, misdeeds.
molecule 185, 203
money 91, 353
moon 30, 342

morality 15, 93. *See also* goodness, justice, law, righteousness, virtue.
mosque 16–17, 32
mother 34, 51, 135, 208, 256, 302
motive 26, 111, 169, 254, 280. *See also* action, purpose.
movement 41–42, 116, 205, 219, 309, 338, 343, 358. *See also* action, growth, expansion.
murshid 124. *See also* guide, mystic, teacher.
music 65, 305. *See also* melody, sound, tone, tuning.
mystery 36, 58, 67, 70, 84, 86, 138, 160, 163, 176, 178–179, 180–181, 186, 217, 236, 263–264, 271–272, 279, 314, 322, 356, 361; mystery of eternal youth 19; mystery of initiation 249; mystery of life; 136, 144, 160, 258; mystery of love 192; mystery of manifestation 176; mystery of man's being 211; mystery of mysteries 193, 215, 231, 249, 270; mystery of oneness 17, 322, 340; mystery of pain 236, 264; mystery of resurrection 183; mystery of sound 142, 364; mystery of time 217; mystery of unity in separation 223; mystery teaching 86. *See also* mystic, paradox.
mystic 13, 37, 56–57, 85, 131, 158, 160, 168–169, 176, 179, 187–188, 197, 200, 207, 217, 225, 263, 277–278, 314, 347, 350–351. *See also* guide, guru, holy ones, murshid, mysticism, sage, saint, seer, shining ones, Sufi, Yoga.
mysticism 56, 296, 314. *See also* meditation, mystic.
myth 13

## N

name 18, 72, 90, 99, 117, 127, 160, 166, 196, 269; Name of God 269; Sacred Name 193, 231
nation 29, 31, 72, 106, 114, 117, 124, 220; community of nations 111
nature 41, 44, 179, 205, 258, 338, 341, 344, 355; book of nature 136, 160; nature's laws 15, 41, 314
negative (energy) 55, 92–93, 175, 182, 204–207, 212, 215, 228, 271, 336, 351; negative to God 205, 272
neutralization 49–50, 92–93, 120, 122
new age 111, 115–117, 122
Nicene Creed 51
night 3, 5, 30, 69, 72, 83, 113, 117, 137, 201, 343, 364
nirvana 124, 225. *See also* bliss, ecstasy, heaven.
note 65, 75, 171, 207–210, 212, 250, 257, 272, 284, 305, 312, 329. *See also* attunement, keynote, sound, tone, tuning, vibration.

## O

obedience 90, 135, 283, 354
obstacle 13, 190, 274, 297; stumbling blocks 12. *See also*

adversity, barrier, difficulty, problem, tribulation.
occultism 9, 56, 75, 100, 127, 183, 249, 310. *See also* psychism, medium, séances, spiritualism.
ocean 5, 67, 136, 226, 250. *See also* sea, water.
Omar Khayyam 64, 358
Only Being, the 34, 58, 63, 68, 127
opportunity 21, 34, 49, 77–78, 114–115, 207, 281
oppression 118, 120. *See also* adversity, bondage,
original condition 67, 183–185, 219, 332, 347
overtone 65. *See also* sound, tone.

## P

pain 24, 27, 35, 39, 43, 46, 51, 59, 70, 88–90, 112, 115, 142, 148, 151, 179, 204, 222, 236, 264, 269, 275, 290, 292–293, 304, 326, 347, 350–352, 358. *See also* agony, anguish, harm, sadness, sorrow, suffering, tears.
pairs of opposites 49, 52, 58–59, 68, 92, 120, 142, 199–200, 204, 232, 236, 335, 351. *See also* balance, duality, harmony, equilibrium, paradox, scales.
parable 14, 53, 75
paradox 23, 25, 39, 70, 142, 177, 245, 270
past 20, 39, 45, 56, 69, 89, 113, 123, 207–208, 217, 221, 275, 288–289, 312, 350, 351. *See also* future, present.
path, spiritual 7–9, 11–13, 15–16, 20, 25, 39, 56, 70, 74, 78–79, 89, 91, 96, 100, 102, 119, 133, 137–139, 146, 148–149, 153–154, 156, 158, 162, 164–165, 167, 177, 181–182, 189–191, 200- 201, 230, 233–234, 247–249, 251, 253–254, 256–257, 260, 265, 271–272, 274, 277–282, 284, 286, 209–292, 294, 297, 312–314, 322, 336, 350, 352; alone path 267; inner path 81; sevenfold path 91; shadow path 290; straight path 89; upward path 17, 124. *See also* goal, journey, path of, pilgrim, pilgrimage, quest, road, search, seeking, traveler, wayfarer.
path of balance 126, 142, 165–166, 240, 283, 330
path of devotion 200
path of discipleship 114, 135, 169, 188, 234, 245, 251
path of ignorance 200
path of illusion 7, 56
path of knowledge 81
path of nonresistance 92
path of perfection 162, 278
path of psychism 56, 265
path of return 8, 11, 50, 59–60, 67, 100, 147, 169, 175, 256–257, 312, 359; return path 8, 35, 39, 50, 146; path of the soul's return 107. *See also* returning, Song of Return, way of return.
path of sacrifice 245
path of seeking 81
path of sorrow and suffering 60

path of turning 81
path of unknowing 81
path of wisdom 151, 169, 187, 200, 225, 282
path to God 73, 82, 137, 147, 190, 213, 222, 245, 259, 274, 280–281, 312, 335
patience 83, 109, 110, 252
pattern 59, 98, 150, 206, 209
peace 12, 16, 27, 46–47, 66, 95, 102, 113, 120, 124–126, 131, 142, 161, 163, 173, 177, 197, 215,240– 241, 246, 256, 267, 310, 324, 338, 352, 362, 364; peace of God 8, 43, 102, 240. *See also* Prince of Peace, quietness, stillness.
penalties 15. *See also* justice, law, punishment.
perfume 227–230, 32; perfume seller 355
perpetual youth 20
personality 37, 48, 57, 63, 70, 142, 153, 162, 167, 181, 199, 227, 234, 253, 261, 263, 269–270, 312, 316, 356. *See also* ego, individuality, self.
Pilate, Pontius 22
pilgrim 8, 13, 24, 69. *See also* aspirant, pilgrimage, seeker, traveler, wayfarer.
pilgrimage 12, 49, 61, 70, 92, 138, 203, 219, 300. *See also* journey, path, pilgrim.
planes 91, 93, 142, 181, 204–205, 209, 211, 213, 264, 306, 320, 329–330, 333, 336; higher planes 115–116, 167, 271, 286; inner planes 77–79, 100, 109–110, 121, 167; physical plane 100, 109, 116, 154, 167, 205, 221, 318, 329; ; spiritual plane 205, 271, 309, 354. *See also* astral plane, mental plane, spiritual plane.
planet 29–30, 34, 38, 41, 52, 95, 210, 227, 237, 281, 306, 340; planet Earth 92, 115. *See also* earth.
plant 44, 206–207, 227–228, 230, 342, 352. *See also* root, flower, fruit, rose, seed, trees, weeds.
play 65, 86, 97, 125, 224; divine play of God
pleasure 11, 27, 90, 151, 204, 207, 269, 276, 292–293, 240, 290, 297, 331, 342, 350, 351–352; earthly pleasures 11. *See also* happiness.
poet 127
poison 121, 148, 321. *See also* harm.
positive (energy) 92–93, 175, 182, 204–207, 212, 215, 228, 271–273, 336, 351
power 10, 12, 35, 37, 50, 56, 59, 61, 73, 75, 93, 103, 106, 111, 122, 126–127, 131, 139, 144, 149, 165, 170, 181, 195–197, 203–205, 209, 211, 216, 219–221, 232, 256, 270, 278, 285, 290–291, 299–300, 310, 314, 320, 327, 340, 353–354, 3 362; creative power 26, 51, 117, 238; power of creative thought 34, 108, 190, 207, 211, 214, 302, 353; power of God 127, 149, 197, 204, 330, 360; power of love 121, 192,

340; power of thought 49, 121, 297. *See also* electricity, force, life-giving power; magnetism, strength.
prayer 3, 7, 30, 35, 43, 46–47, 84, 88, 121, 158, 167, 198, 225, 268, 330
prejudice 116, 308
presence 8, 48, 75, 149, 152, 158, 210, 246, 272, 317, 358, 364; presence of God 13, 149, 268, 277, 319, 326, 364; presence of Jesus 152, 181
present (time) 120–121, 123, 196, 217, 280, 306, 310. *See also under eternity*, eternal now; future; past.
priests 314–315; priestly interventions 15
Prince of Darkness 72. *See also* Satan.
Prince of Peace 102, 256. *See also* Christ.
prison 5, 106, 151, 179, 347. *See also* bondage, imprisonment.
problem 36, 55, 70, 73, 92, 146, 148, 195, 202, 274, 320, 335. *See also* barrier, difficulty, obstacle, trial, tribulation.
progress 11, 39, 56, 91, 109–110, 114, 137, 149, 153–154, 165, 221, 251, 253–254, 256, 265, 312, 352. *See also* evolution, development, growth, stage.
promise 7, 25, 34, 50, 83, 102, 165, 329
prophet 75, 105, 351; false prophets 7. *See also* clairvoyance, guide, messenger, mystic, seer.
protection 41, 43, 75, 82, 110, 251, 273, 285, 311, 342; protective thoughts 213
Protestant faith 26
psychism 56, 265, 317; psychic intoxication 348. *See also* clairvoyance, medium; occultism, séances, spiritualism.
punishment 27, 90, 106, 232. *See also* justice, law, penalties.
pupil 48, 79, 182, 251, 288–289, 335. *See also* disciple.
purification 135, 183, 187, 189, 249, 327; purification of air 291; purification of earth 290; purification of ether 291 purification of fire 219–220, 291, 356; purification of water 290. *See also* purity.
purity 67, 93, 168, 188–189, 219, 234, 305, 327, 362. *See also under heart*, pure in heart; purification, sinlessness, virgin.
purpose 13, 38, 41–43, 70–71, 77, 80, 86, 88, 94–95, 99, 103, 151, 158, 183–184, 202, 206, 209–210, 212, 228, 256–257, 263, 275, 294, 309, 331, 334, 341, 352; purpose of creation 185, 204, 209, 305, 331, 255; purpose of evolution 202, 216, 227, 340; singleness of purpose 9, 170, 193. *See also* aspiration, destiny, goal, motive, quest, search.
puzzle, jigsaw 22, 338. *See also* maze, mystery, paradox.

## Q

quest 72; questing spirit 85. *See also* aspiration, journey, path, search, seeking, traveler, wayfarer.
quickening 75. *See also* life force.
quietness 101, 189. *See also* peace, silence, stillness.

## R

race 31, 38, 51, 84, 106, 121, 208, 220, 306
radiance 177, 178, 184–186. *See also* illumination, light.
reality 9, 23, 29, 43, 50, 61, 63, 69, 72, 97, 127, 139, 151, 153, 172, 177, 193, 201, 216–218, 249–250, 258–259, 291, 294, 300, 308, 313–314, 317, 322, 358. *See also* truth.
realization 49–50, 58, 89, 136, 139, 147, 173, 176, 193–194, 196, 203, 217, 219, 223, 254, 277, 319, 359. *See also* awakening, consciousness, discovery, knowledge.
reaping 45, 52, 106–107, 109, 127, 352. *See also* harvest, sowing.
rebirth 11, 51. *See also* birth.
redeemer 183. *See also* Christ, Jesus, redemption.
redemption 84, 183–184, 195, 207, 227, 347. *See also* redeemer, salvation, turning.
reflection 13, 34, 58, 139, 146, 162, 172, 176, 178, 183, 188–190, 199–200, 203, 212, 224, 241, 248, 258, 267, 269, 271–272, 279, 300, 304, 316. *See also* mirror, stillness.
regret 41, 260. *See also* repentance.
reincarnation 56, 312; reincarnation of ideas 294; reincarnated thought 296
reliability 70, 110 316. *See also* dependability, responsibility, steadfastness, strength, trust.
religion 17, 26, 51, 88, 105, 117, 127, 131, 139, 158–160, 179, 181, 187, 196–197, 200, 225, 233–234, 256, 306, 311, 314, 322, 351; religious persecution 257 religious practices 158, 169; religious thought 15. *See also* belief, Buddhist, Christianity, church, mosque, priests, scriptures, shrine, temple, worship.
remembrance 7, 29, 157, 163–254, 278, 285, 287, 302, 309, 313, 350. *See also* memory.
renunciation 11, 50, 93, 135, 270, 361, 363. *See also* sacrifice.
repentance 89, 235. *See also* regret.
resignation 46. *See also* surrender.
responsibility 50, 139, 273, 288–289. *See also* duty, reliability, service, task.
resurrection 51, 60, 84, 178, 183–184; resurrection body 51, 53, 185– 186. *See also* death, Christ, crucifixion, Easter, immortality, Jesus.
returning 3, 7, 10–11, 29, 49, 61, 65, 67, 97, 107, 120, 136, 144, 175, 198, 200, 219, 227–228, 249, 254, 257, 312, 322, 347. *See also* journey,

path of return, Song of Return, turning, way of return.
revelation 25, 142, 160, 163, 177, 184, 206, 217, 236, 279, 338. *See also* unveiling, vision.
revenge 121
reward 11–12, 45, 52, 83, 119, 124, 232, 241, 260, 281, 282, 362
rhythm 65, 136
righteousness 10, 56, 105, 126, 265. *See also* goodness, morality, virtue.
rites 15, 183. *See also* sacraments.
river 67, 136
road 7, 18, 24, 83, 143, 165, 201, 248; road-maker 280–281; road-making 280; road that has been traveled 83. *See also* path.
rock 5, 30, 91, 103, 191, 240. See also stones.
root 6, 162
rose 229, 355, 363
Roland-Skemp, Thomas 39
rules 90, 110. *See also* law.

## S

sacraments 15; sacramental marriage 356
sacrifice 11–12, 34, 84, 135, 142, 149, 157, 192, 215, 219–220, 245. *See also* renunciation, selflessness.
sadness 90, 123. *See also* depression, sorrow, tears.
safety 7, 9, 27, 43, 56, 75, 78, 93, 110, 250–251, 265, 274, 277, 317, 336. *See also* guidance.
sage 19, 131, 135, 146–147, 193, 198, 218, 234, 286, 293. *See also* guide, guru, master, mystic, Sufi, wisdom.
saints 131, 135, 189, 225, 343. *See also* holy ones master, mystic.
salvation 59, 118, 160, 220. *See also* redemption, savior.
sanctuary 249, 327
Satan 79, 215. *See also* devil, Prince of Darkness.
satisfaction 22, 37, 173, 193, 204, 232, 241, 253, 272–273, 285, 300, 310, 314,350, 362–363. *See also* achievement, attainment, completion, fulfillment, happiness, pleasure, success.
savior 183, 351. *See also* Christ, Jesus, salvation.
scales 50, 91, 165, 299; scale of heaven 299; scalc of earth 299; scales of time 217. *See also* balance, pairs of opposites.
scriptures 22, 78, 124, 136, 202, 285, 359. *See also* Bhagavad Gita, Bible, religion.
sculptor 127, 331
sea 32, 67, 85, 136, 220, 240, 250. *See also* ocean, water.
séances 54, 78. *See also* medium, psychism, occultism, spirit messages.
search 9, 13, 16, 19, 25, 48, 51, 136, 139, 160, 308, 347, 250; search for God 13–15, 22, 100, 137, 193. *See also* journey, quest, seeker, seeking.

seed 30, 44, 122, 127, 150, 152, 203, 206–207, 227–228, 230, 321, 342, 354, 363. *See also* sowing.
seeker 7, 13–14, 17, 19–20, 43, 48, 53, 56, 75, 81, 139, 147, 156, 169, 190, 192–193, 314, 363. *See also* aspirant, disciple, journey, path, pilgrim, seeking, traveler, wayfarer.
seeking 9, 16, 19, 23, 42–43, 81, 86, 89, 135, 139, 142, 173, 182, 193, 246, 248–249, 266, 272, 300, 310, 312–314, 325, 347, 350–351, 361, 363. *See also* journey, path, quest, search, seeker, wayfarer.
seer 19, 135, 151, 156, 187, 203, 217–218, 221, 278, 279, 286. *See also* clairvoyance, guide, messenger, mystic, prophet, vision.
self 9, 13–14, 26, 28–29, 34, 37, 45, 50, 70, 73, 84–85, 111, 127, 135–136, 167, 169, 173, 188, 192, 200, 203, 211–212, 219, 225–226, 235, 237, 317, 319; false self 14, 67, 136, 220; higher self 318; inner self 48; real self 34, 57, 127, 142, 147, 173, 208, 214, 219–220; true self 37, 67. *See also* ego, personality.
self-consciousness 49
self-control 55, 70, 110, 162; self-mastery 55, 110, 144. *See also* control, mastery.
self-deception 7; self-delusion 164
self-development 84, 100, 110, 291. *See also* development, progress.
self-interest 111
selfishness 17, 111, 118, 238, 245, 281
self-forgetfulness 164, 193, 235
self-knowledge 147, 160
selflessness 71, 111, 122, 167, 241; self-abnegation 192; unselfishness 12, 280. *See also* renunciation, sacrifice.
self-love 85
self-reliance 55
self-surrender 135, 192, 225. *See also* surrender.
self-will 45. *See also* will, personal.
separateness 67, 84–86, 99, 106, 123, 135–136, 160, 188, 199, 204, 213, 219, 223–225, 228, 234–235, 237, 257, 284, 299–300, 307, 310, 322, 333–334, 338, 340, 345, 351. *See also* ego.
servant 103, 232; servers 115. *See also* service, worker.
service 45, 56, 84, 103, 114–115, 125, 153–154, 167, 260, 346, 361. *See also* duty, responsibility, servant, task.
sex 204–205, 335
shadow 8, 11, 28, 63, 69, 89, 92, 135, 142, 172–173, 188, 199, 215, 218, 236, 258–259, 269, 317, 364; shadow path 290; shadow side 78–79, 93, 103, 313. *See also* darkness, illusion, unreality.
Shakespeare, William 97
Sharaf al-Din Maneri 135, 147, 167, 175–176, 193, 233–234
shell 27, 38–39, 44, 127, 180, 223, 226, 272

shining ones 8, 11. *See also* master, mystic, illumination.
Shiva 44
shrine 13, 237, 325
sight, spiritual 157, 259, 266, 286. *See also* clairvoyance, vision.
silence 24, 48, 96, 127, 138–139, 142, 189, 197, 214, 247, 249–250, 269, 274, 291–292, 323, 332, 339, 360, 363–364. *See also* quietness, stillness.
sin 16, 24, 32, 60, 90, 96, 142, 144, 188, 216, 232, 234–235, 288–291, 351; forgiveness of sin 59, 289, 350; sinlessness 67. *See also* badness, cruelty, evil, sinner, wickedness.
sincerity 32, 43, 46, 75, 81, 88, 139, 167, 259, 288, 327
sinner 343. *See also* sin.
slave 120, 212, 217, 232, 275, 359; slave of virtue 232. *See also* bondage.
sleep 21, 27, 76, 109, 118, 151, 360, 363. *See also* unconsciousness.
son 25; sons of God 262, 299. *See also* Son of Man.
Song of Return 5
Son of Man 181, 360. *See also* Christ, Jesus.
sorrow 27, 33, 35, 37, 39, 43, 52, 59–60, 89, 93, 103, 139, 151, 177, 179, 181, 186, 188, 236, 247, 260, 263, 267, 269, 275, 291, 304, 347, 351. *See also* agony, anguish, depression, pain, sadness, suffering, tears.
sound 65, 124, 142, 209, 210, 231, 240, 250, 257, 272, 305, 323, 332, 339, 343, 364. *See also* attunement, keynote, listening, melody, music, note, overtone, tone, tuning, undertone, vibration, voice.
source 27, 67, 79, 86, 135–136, 207, 219, 223–224, 296, 309, 347
sowing 45, 52, 106–197, 127, 230, 247, 292, 321, 352, 363. *See also* seed, reaping.
space 31, 65, 86, 90, 195, 342
spirit 5–6, 19–21, 28–29, 36, 38–42, 52, 60, 72, 77, 80–81, 85, 92, 109, 119, 130, 135, 149, 157–160, 175, 197, 199, 223, 227–228, 234, 263, 278, 281, 288, 294, 297, 299, 302, 317, 333, 346–347, 350, 354, 356; fruit of the spirit 80; One Spirit 29, 160, 303; solidified spirit 29, 68; spirit of Christ 152, 185, 322, 341. *See also* Spirit of Guidance.
spirit messages 54. *See also* mediums, séances.
Spirit of Guidance 160, 162, 185. *See also* guidance, master.
spiritualism 54; spiritualistic circles 78. *See also* psychism, occultism.
stage (of the journey) 49, 58, 77, 81, 84, 97, 143, 147, 165, 167, 170, 176, 188–189, 192, 198–200, 211, 215, 249, 251, 253–254, 274, 277–281, 288, 299, 306, 350–351; stage of evolution 120, 160, 280; stage of purification 189; probationary stage 251.

*See also* development, path, progress.
star 16, 30, 310
steadfastness 50, 70, 142, 240, 278, 351; steadiness 8, 103, 121, 126, 162, 206. *See also* dependability, faith, reliability, strength, trust.
steel 113, 152, 182, 277
Stevenson, Robert Louis 28
stillness 16–17, 37, 48, 101, 144, 189, 262, 267, 323. *See also* mirror, peace, quietness, silence.
stone 15, 30, 32, 342; mystical interpretation of the stone 185. *See also* rock.
strength 46–47, 54, 60, 69, 78, 83, 88, 101, 118, 137, 169, 189, 197, 213, 215, 232, 260, 281, 330, 363. *See also* courage, power, reliability, steadfastness.
success 12, 21, 28, 38, 94, 103, 164, 169, 282, 290, 306. *See also* achievement, attainment, completion, fulfillment, victory.
suffering 15, 27, 32, 34–35, 46, 51, 59–61, 90, 106, 108, 110, 112, 115, 120–121, 179, 219, 223, 232, 241, 254, 256, 262, 267, 280–281, 285, 304, 307, 348, 356. *See also* agony, anguish, depression, pain, sadness, sorrow, tears.
Sufi 49, 147, 193. *See also* murshid, individual Sufis by name.
sun 30, 36, 63, 69, 117, 162, 171, 175, 188, 198, 207, 219–220, 227–228, 266, 278, 321, 327, 342, 354
supernatural 78
surrender 50, 85, 135, 177, 192, 219, 225, 251, 346, 356. *See also* resignation, self-surrender.
symbol 13, 25, 32, 72, 106, 183, 187, 219, 250, 299, 316, 356. *See also* parable.
sympathy 35, 103, 121, 179, 188, 245, 269, 272

## T

task 13, 19, 50, 59, 70, 88, 103, 109–110, 118, 121, 138, 162, 183–184, 190, 207, 227, 290, 296, 299, 305, 307, 335, 347. *See also* action, duty, responsibility, worker.
teacher 48, 78–79, 96, 115, 124, 147, 157, 182, 213, 234–235, 251, 269, 271, 274, 289 *See also* guide, guru, master, murshid, sage, Sufi.
tears 12, 291
temperament 222, 296
temple 15–17, 32, 72, 117, 327
temptations 11
Tennyson, Alfred 32
tests 11–13, 75, 78–79, 83, 91, 110, 165, 215, 249–250, 289, 291; testing time of nations 114. *See also* trial, problem.
thanksgiving 12, 127
thought 9, 11, 15, 17, 35–36, 45, 51, 55, 70, 94, 96, 98, 106, 108, 110, 113, 121, 142, 144, 150, 164, 167, 170, 175, 181, 185–187, 189, 201–203, 206–208, 211–213, 223,

225, 231, 235, 237–238, 253, 274–275, 278, 282–285, 288, 290, 294–297, 300, 306–307, 316, 321, 327, 329–330, 351, 353, 358–359; control of thought 34, 206, 211, 213, 274; creative thought 29, 34, 46, 49, 93, 108, 138, 190, 207, 211, 213–214, 238, 302, 353; embodied thought 34; evil thoughts 108, 111, 118, 120–121, 200, 320, 353; pure thought 51; sentimental thought 121; thoughts of God 34, 56, 156, 171, 240, 253, 265, 274, 285, 302, 320, 326, 353, 364; thought-power 49, 108, 121; wrong thinking 70, 118. *See also* idea, mental plane, mind, thought forms.

thought forms 36, 54–55, 65, 120–121, 299, 304, 320. *See also* thought.

throne 17, 118, 234, 361; throne of God 24, 32, 60, 81, 191, 269, 338. *See also* king, kingdom.

tone 65, 305. *See also* harmony, keynote, note, overtone, sound, tuning, undertone

training 90, 109, 137, 289, 310, 335. *See also* guidance, instruction, lesson.

transmutation 27, 68, 170–171, 178, 185, 195, 197, 288–289. *See also* alchemy.

traveler 7–9, 13–14, 48, 50, 81, 102, 137–138, 188, 200, 230, 234, 245, 249, 275, 279, 282. *See also* journey, path, pilgrim, search, seeker, wayfarer.

treasure 155, 241, 253, 284, 361–363; divine treasury 167

trees 8, 21, 30, 124, 207, 229, 310. *See also* forests.

trial 47, 88. *See also* barrier, difficulty, obstacle, problem, tests, tribulation.

tribulation 333, 59, 114, 124, 240–241, 362. *See also* barrier, difficulty, obstacle, problem, trial.

trust 91, 103, 109–110, 139, 166, 169, 177, 187, 234, 251, 271, 330, 335. *See also* belief, confidence, faith, reliability, steadfastness.

truth, inner 13, 26, 146

truth, living 73–74, 358

Truth, One 105, 160, 196, 322. *See also* reality.

tuning 37, 65, 109, 131, 151, 208–210, 212, 240, 272, 284, 305, 315, 338; tuning the heart 151, 364. *See also* attunement, keynote, note, sound, tone.

turning 8–9, 12, 56, 67, 69, 81, 89, 91, 147, 164–165, 169–170, 175–176, 182, 212, 221, 234, 236, 245, 253, 265, 267, 269, 273, 348; turning towards God 50, 190, 211, 267, 273, 270. *See also* redemption.

## U

unconsciousness 57, 73, 80, 118, 126, 150, 158, 190, 213, 235, 245–246, 277, 292, 335. *See also* sleep.

Underhill, Evelyn 19
undertone 65
uniformity 95, 324
union 49, 92, 199, 204–205, 228, 271; mystic union 225, 278; union with God 192, 225, 237, 322, 324, 356; uniting the pair of opposites 49. *See also* unity.
unity 40, 49, 95, 115, 173, 184, 194, 197, 199, 200, 206, 223–224, 236, 256, 299, 320, 322, 324; mystery of unity in separation 223; secret of unity 199. *See also* at-one-ment, union.
Universal Soul 334
universe 5, 34, 41, 58, 74, 139, 148, 172, 179, 185, 193, 195, 202–204, 214, 228, 239, 305, 310, 335, 340, 351, 354–355
unmanifest 29, 195, 231
unreality 50, 78, 123, 139, 142, 217, 258, 322. *See also* illusion, mirage, shadow.
unseen, the 17, 25, 78, 108, 126, 145, 148, 329
unveiling 193, 217, 252. *See also* revelation, vision.

## V

vapor 68, 184, 195, 291, 332
Van Dyke, Henry 32
vehicle 37–38, 86, 263, 333. *See also* form, instrument.
veil 56, 64, 75, 141, 147, 179, 193, 209, 265–266, 300, 337, 341; veiling 63, 152, 210, 361. *See also* cover, clouds, mask, unveiling.
vibration 65, 76, 91, 131, 151, 156, 165, 171, 182–183, 189, 195, 207–210, 212, 220, 227, 239, 250, 257, 262, 305, 312, 329, 333, 339, 342, 357. *See also* note, sound.
victory 91, 171, 197. *See also* achievement, conquering, mastery, success.
virgin 168, 356. *See also* purity.
virtue 8, 90, 93, 164, 209, 232, 234–235, 346, 354. *See also* goodness, morality, righteousness.
Vishnu 44
vision 12, 14, 19, 36, 43, 50, 56, 67, 76, 97, 147, 149, 156–157, 162–164, 173, 186, 188–189, 221, 225, 240, 245, 249, 270, 274, 304, 322, 348; vision of God 21, 139, 167, 188, 193, 235, 259, 269–270, 326, 364; inner vision 153, 156, 259, 277, 286; vision of truth 13, 234, 314. *See also* clairvoyance; insight; prophet; revelation; seer; sight, spiritual; unveiling.
vitality 55, 108; vitalization 122. *See also* life force.
voices, angel 24
voice, of God 17, 47–48, 65, 122, 127, 151, 240, 242, 247, 269, 274, 318, 339, 360–362; voice of the Beloved 292. *See also* listening, message.

## W

war 117–118, 306; war clouds 124
washing the feet 187
water 29–30, 40, 67, 144, 184,

189, 230–231, 250, 258, 278, 289, 329, 332, 334, 360, 362; living water 285; purification of water 290–291; washing the feet; waters of life 124, 285, 362; waters of oblivion 317. *See also* ocean, river, sea.
wax 99
way of achievement 165
way of return 7, 9, 25, 59, 70, 124. *See also* path of return.
way of service 153
way of the heart 70
way to heaven 50
way to peace 102
wayfarers 230. *See also* journey, pilgrim, seeker.
wedding robe 25
weeds 44, 150, 207
Wells, H.G. 28
West, the 44, 312; Western mind 171
whirlwind 15, 286–287, 360
wickedness 118, 150. *See also* badness, cruelty, evil.
wilderness of self 37
will of God 45–47, 71, 83, 115, 127, 135, 354; Divine Will 195
will, personal 45, 251. *See also* self-will.
wind 31, 54, 227, 278, 286, 302, 329; winds of fate 91; winds of illusion 289. *See also* air, whirlwind.
wine 127, 278, 348; wine of Christ 278, 347–348, 362; wine of wisdom 127. *See also* intoxication.
wings 27, 38–39
wireless telephony 315
wisdom 10, 13–14, 59, 127, 131, 151, 166, 169, 175–176, 183, 187, 190, 200–201, 225, 240, 256, 263, 282–283, 297–298, 304, 359, 362. *See also* intelligence, knowledge, realization.
womb 51, 178, 200, 208, 228
women 21, 63, 97, 115, 118, 121, 204–205, 280, 335. *See also* female, mother.
words, holy 158
workers 71, 110, 115, 167, 281, 320. *See also* servant, task.
workshop of God 111
world of form 38, 167, 329
world of illusion 55, 149, 172, 236, 278, 312
world travail 114
world government 116
worship 105, 118, 142, 196, 234, 351; worshiper 5. See also belief, devotion, faith, religion.

## Y

Yoga 171; yogi 285. *See also* mystic.

## Z

zenith 228, 330

*For more information on*
*the Sufi path of Hazrat Inayat Khan please visit*
www.sufiorder.org